Valuation of Physician Practices and Clinics

Bruce G. Krider
Senior Partner
American Health Care Appraisal
La Jolla, California

AN ASPEN PUBLICATION®
Aspen Publishers, Inc.
Gaithersburg, Maryland
1997

Library of Congress Cataloging-in-Publication Data

Krider, Bruce G.
Valuation of physician practices and clinics / Bruce G. Krider.
p. cm.
Includes bibliographical references and index.
ISBN 0-8342-0962-4 (hardcover)
1. Medicine—Practice—Valuation. 2. Clinics—Valuation.
I. Title.
[DNLM: 1. Practice Management, Medical—economics—United States.
2. Ambulatory Care Facilities—economics—United States. 3. Costs
and Cost Analysis. 4. Ownership—economics—United States. W 80
K92v 1997]
R728.K75 1997
362.1'72'0681—dc21
DNLM/DLC
for Library of Congress 97-23180
CIP

Orders: (800) 638-8437
Customer Service: (800) 234-1660

Editorial Resources: Brian MacDonald
Library of Congress Catalog Card Number: 97-23180
ISBN: 0-8342-0962-4

Printed in the United States of America

1 2 3 4 5

This book is dedicated to my wife, Laura L. Dolata, RN, BSN, CCRN, and soon-to-be MSN (Nurse Practitioner—University of San Diego), who has endured being married to a hospital/health care consultant, graduate school professor, and health care entrepreneur (simultaneously) for 10 years. . . something no one deserves! Health care professionals today need supportive understanding mates, and Laura, while advancing her own career, has been there for me. Much of the time she would otherwise have had from me is in this book.

Table of Contents

Preface

In 1987, I left a 13-year career in hospital administration and a CEO position at the wrong end of some board politics. That exodus launched my consulting career.

I began consulting in a special area of Medicare reimbursement in which I had some special expertise and qualifications. After a short time, I reasoned that if I was going to really be a good consultant, I needed to be able to be clearer on the value of business recommendations that I was making. So I decided to learn about "valuation" science and apply it to what I knew in health care management consulting and finance. It turned out to be a life- and career-changing decision that led me into a new career—"health care valuation."

When I went to graduate school at The George Washington University in Washington, D.C., for a master's in hospital administration in the mid-1970s, I learned about *how to manage hospitals* like everyone else in such programs. Unfortunately, many of the crucial business techniques, methodologies required today, were notably absent. Things that are a part of the health care landscape were there in 1975. We had classes in sophisticated statistical analytical methods given by faculty who worked principally at NASA in Washington, D.C., but that did not help me later on the job. As a result of my work experience and training in business valuation over the past seven years, I developed "what they didn't teach in graduate school."

The objective of this manual is to provide a basic level of understanding for appraising physician practices and clinics today. Its not meant to be a comprehensive treatment but rather to go over the practical nuts and bolts and tie those in with tips on not only how to approach prospective clinic acquisitions but also considerations from the physician side on what to consider in offers. I also discuss what can be done to prepare a practice for sale.

Acquisitions of physician practices, large group practices, or other health care facilities consume precious and limited financial resources. The "wheeling and dealing" approach to buying practices needs to go in the closet. *Ridiculously* large sums are being *needlessly* spent because executives are not taking a little time to go through the process of valuation correctly, jeopardizing their tax status, their organizations' financial future, and their personal and professional lives. Perhaps the most disturbing fact is that deals are still negotiated using crude rules of thumb instead of valuation techniques and due diligence.

This period is a unique one in the history of health care. The kinds of decisions that you make *now* are crucial to the survival of your institutions in the post-transaction period. In the near future, you will be called on to make more tough decisions regarding the use of scarce resources. This manual is dedicated to health care administrators and physicians in the hope that it will help provide guidance during this current heyday of health care provider organization and physician practice sales and acquisitions.

Acknowledgments

The author acknowledges the contributions of FPA Medical Management to this book and especially Ms. Lisa Bingham, FPA Senior Corporate Analyst, who provided special insight into the approaches and considerations used by physician practice management companies.

Margaret Singleton, MAI, SRPA, ASA, of G.R. Bill Co., San Diego, CA, has provided great advice and counsel as a mentor over the past seven years. Paul Rice, ASA of The Rice Group, La Habra, CA, and Melvin Fineberg, ASA of Fineberg Consulting Service, Rancho Cucamonga, CA, have served as advisors to the author.

Introduction

The purpose of this book is to provide you with a basic level of background in the area of appraisal and valuation in health care, especially regarding physician practices. I do not intend to make you a professional appraiser. Rather, I hope to help you navigate through these issues in a way that will result in your being able to perform a basic appraisal to come up with a range of ballpark values when considering buying or selling a practice. I provide you with a wide variety of approaches, tools, formulas, and other practical advice relating to buying and selling physician practices. This manual should also be particularly helpful in performing "what if" planning scenarios.

I also hope to provide you with a level of understanding of the appraisal industry so that you are better able to work with professional health care appraisers. It is, however, the best single resource out there because it incorporates issues on health care legislation, business valuation, negotiations, preparing a practice for sale, and various techniques that you can use to value a practice or clinic.

Approaching practice valuations correctly involves concepts in business valuation and experience in identifying areas that should be discounted or ignored, such as unusual or one-time expenses or income. It also takes a trained experienced appraiser to recognize certain problems and red flags that can have a significant effect on the value of the practice.

Unrelated to hospital–physician transactions, for example, valuations of practices being prepared for marital dissolution cases frequently require additional scrutiny because, somewhat like tax returns, practices are "presented" with an eye toward minimizing the negative impact of taxes or divorce settlements.

ACQUISITION OF PHYSICIAN PRACTICES BY HOSPITALS

Beginning in the mid- to later 1980s, hospitals began acquiring physician practices. The real fray did not start until the early 1990s, but by 1993 it seemed like a national pastime. The threats of health care reform and managed care together with marketing pressures that had existed all drove home the point that hospitals needed to develop organizations that had solid market penetration. Physician practices were one way to accomplish it. The country had not seen anything quite like it since the 1880 California Gold Rush.

Some hospitals acquired every and any practice around without regard for physician case management performance or any other criteria that would distinguish one practice from another, paying ridiculous sums for them. They thought that they would grab what they could and worry about sorting out the details later. It got that bad. That was more common a couple of years ago than it is now, but it still goes on in some areas.

Now that some of the dust has settled (although the stampede is not over), a little more caution is going into the selection of practices for sale. A little more concern is also being exercised in terms of what hospitals pay for practices for primarily two reasons. First, many hospitals have nearly exhausted their liquidity and credit by acquiring scores of practices, leaving less and less to throw at additional ones.

Second, the Office of the Inspector General, Health Care Financing Administration, and the Internal Revenue Service are watching the scene with respect to Medicare fraud and abuse violations of paying in excess of fair market value. They have announced their concern with payment for goodwill and are barring payment in excess of fair market value for practices by hospitals.

Hospital Management Response

In trying to deal with the issue of fair market values, hospitals have responded in a variety of ways. Unfortunately, most could have used a more sophisticated approach. They negotiated more or less what they "thought practices were going for." They may have read a few articles or attended a workshop on the subject.

Some had set their own formulas based on what they thought, and still others ignored the whole situation and paid what it took to pull in certain practices, worrying about what the hospital down the street would pay in a bidding war. A few executives enlisted the services of health care valuation experts to provide value data on the practices and on which to base their fair market offers.

Throughout the course of this discussion, you will begin to gain the appreciation that a competent appraisal is a well-thought-out and developed indication of value, documented and supported by the marketplace. It is the kind of report you owe yourself when you are seriously anticipating spending a large chunk of capital.

CHAPTER 1

Doing the Report: Where Do I Start Looking for Data and How Much Is Enough?

WHAT DO I NEED?

Exhibit 1–1 is the basic request for practice documentation. This information gives the necessary financial information needed to do the appraisal.

Financial Statements

The financial statements prepared by the practice's accounting firm are your basic tools. Most practice statements are cash basis instead of accrual basis, and they *are usually not audited* but rather only "prepared," based on the information management has provided. So, do not be surprised if you see this. Practices are small businesses and not what hospital officials or those of larger health care provider organizations are used to in terms of the sophistication and formality of, perhaps, a major health care provider you are employed by.

❖ Hint

Ask for five years' but do not settle for less than three years' worth of financial statements (unless, of course, the clinic has not been operating that long). It is easier to spot trends and get a better sense of where the practice is going with five years of data. Three years' data are really a bare minimum. Some sellers may only want to provide you with the latest year's data, but you will not be able to provide more than a qualified (meaning a limited) appraisal. You need to view the activity within the context of the historical performance. With only one year's data, you would not know whether the practice was on the way up or on the way down. You cannot trend anything with one year's data.

Tax Returns

Both the practice returns and the personal returns of the physicians for the past five years are requested. Why? You want to be clear on what the practitioner is taking home, and you want to be able to compare the two reports. Also, corporate tax returns are compared with corporate financial statements to help clarify questions that invariably come up.

Questions come up as you review financial statements, and it is usually very helpful to have the personal income tax return to review in concert with the practice return. Many times, you are able to give the physician credit in the appraisal for greater income. (Tax returns are designed to minimize tax. Your job as an appraiser is to make sure that all appropriate forms of practice revenue are identified and included as such in the appraisal report.)

Getting all the tax returns means to get *returns with all the schedules, not just the two front pages of returns.* You will need the schedules to review the breakdown of the expenses to see if they are reasonable and to be able to better reconstruct the income and expense sheets when preparing to project revenue. The front-page tax return categories are far too broad for your analyses, so you need schedules to get to the detail in analyzing practice expenses.

So you have three things in terms of financial reports: the financial statements from the practice accountant, the tax returns from the practice, and the tax returns from the individual physician.

Dealing with Resistance in Requesting Tax Returns

There is sometimes resistance to getting physician's personal income tax returns. Practice management consultants have said, "You don't need those!" As appraisers, it is not uncommon at all to have *others tell you what they think you*

Exhibit 1–1 Documents Needed for Medical Business

- Annual compiled financial statements (balance sheets, income and expense statements) for the past three to five fiscal years. Monthly financial statements are also requested covering the period from the last annual financial statement through the last completed month.
- U.S. *corporate* income tax returns (with all schedules) for the corporation for the past three to five years.
- U.S. *individual* income tax returns (with all schedules) for the seller for the past three to five years.
- A copy of all and any leases or agreements to which the professional practice is a party.
- The clinic fee schedule in effect and for the past three to five years, as available.
- Depreciation schedules for furniture and equipment owned by the practice. (If not available, schedule on corporate tax returns will be used.)
- Minutes of shareholders and board meetings for the past three to five years, if available.
- Schedules of current gross fees charged attributable to various payers.
- Print-out of patients by ZIP code (usually available on practice computerized billing program).
- Accounts receivable aging report for three years (with, if possible, gross billings, contractual allowances, gross receipts).
- Patient volume data by year.
- Name and address of practice accountants.
- Current checkbook balances and documentation of other current asset accounts.
- Compensation in the form of salary and fringe benefits for physician owner(s).
- Complete information on malpractice or any other legal proceedings in which the practice through its owners has been or may be a party.
- If not adequately described on tax return schedules, a complete inventory of all equipment will be required.
- Current inventory of supplies and their purchase price, if available.
- Annual referrals by source.
- Managed care agreements or other contracts with terms and discount rates, whether these agreements are with the physician or with the clinic (assumable).

need. Merely remind them that it is an accepted practice, and that for you to perform the appropriate type of review, it is something that is typically included in the due diligence part of the appraisal research. (Further, the practitioners are usually better off for you having had the opportunity to review the personal taxes because you often are able to clarify and give them appropriate credit for forms of income not otherwise identified were you just able to get financial statements.)

Leases and Agreements

Leases and agreements can obligate the practice financially, and they can represent a source of value that you should take into account. As an appraiser, you need to identify these and take them into account for several reasons.

Leasehold Improvements

First, if the physician has provided for any improvements in a leased office space, he or she may be entitled to any remaining life on these leasehold improvements. The remaining life of the leasehold improvements is tied to the life of the lease and optional extensions. The maximum life of the improvements is the life of the lease and its optional extensions.

Let's consider the following *simplified* example in Table 1–1 for illustration purposes. This is a table showing the values of leasehold improvements (draperies) in a large multispecialty facility that is being leased by the group. The cost new and the useful lives were all the same, but the age/remaining useful lives change.

Leases are by suite, so those terms are not necessarily the same. Notice that, in no circumstance, is there value beyond the life of the lease.

The point of the table is that the remaining length of the lease and its optional extensions represent the maximum remaining life of the leasehold improvements. If, as in suite E, you had draperies that had a remaining life of three years and a corresponding depreciated book value of $2,571 but there were only two years left on a lease with no extensions, you view the assets as in their last two years of life because, for purposes of the lease and remaining use to a buyer, they are the last two years. You cannot sell the benefit of three years' use when there are really only two. If you have an asset that would normally have a life of 12 years but your lease with all extensions totaled 10 years, the asset should be (straight line) depreciated over 10 years.

❖ Hint

If you are the seller and you have made leasehold improvements that have some remaining useful life that would extend past the date of the lease termination date, you might decide to approach the landlord and ask for the *option to extend the lease another term* of, say, three to five years with the ability to sublease

Table 1–1 Example: Values of Leasehold Improvements

Item	*Age*	*Useful Life*	*Balance Useful Life*	*Cost New*	*Remain Deprec. Value*	*Remain Lease Life*	*Practice Appraisal Value*
Draperies Suite A	3	7	4	$6,000	$3,428	5	$3,428
Draperies Suite B	5	7	2	$6,000	$1,714	5	$1,714
Draperies Suite C	1	7	6	$6,000	$5,142	3	$2,571
Draperies Suite D	1	7	6	$6,000	$5,142	1	$857
Draperies Suite E	4	7	3	$6,000	$2,571	2	$1,714

the space. That way you would be able to get credit for the actual remaining life of the improvements (if their useful lives fell within that period). It could be a little or a very significant amount.

Below-Market Lease Rates

Second, if the physician has a particularly good lease with significant below-market rent and it can be subleased, there is value in the negotiated lease that can be included in the appraisal. You identify the current market rates and the rates being paid by the practice and identify the difference over the term of the lease, which is the value. Technically, you would do some present-value calculations of the difference between the clinic rent and fair market rent by month over the remaining lease life for an actual value. There is a little more to it than that to be technically correct, but unless you are going into the profession, this is a good stopping point on fair market value of leases.

It is also possible that the reverse can be the case. That is, if the physician is paying more than current market rates, there can be a negative value that can bring down the value of the practice.

Other Agreements

Any other agreements that obligate the practice to pay something can be viewed as having an effect on value as well.

❖ **Hint**

Keep in mind, if you are not purchasing the stock but only selected assets, you are not necessarily locked into anything unless you agree to it in the negotiation of the purchase. The office lease is a difficult one to avoid because it is not likely that you will want to abruptly move the office to a new location because of the patient attrition that would result. Other agreements and leases are more negotiable.

Equipment leases would typically be leases that the physician-seller would like to have the buyer assume, especially if the physician is going to stay on and work. In that scenario, the physician does not need them and would not want them unless he or she anticipates setting up practice in another location at some point in the future. This often requires advance approval of the leasing company, so be sure to address this early.

Most practices have major and minor equipment and furnishings that they have had for 10, 15, or 20 or more years. This equipment has been reasonably maintained and is not worth all that much on the used medical equipment market but would still continue to be perfectly acceptable to use in a practice if needed in the future.

❖ **Hint**

From a buyer's standpoint, you will want to buy the equipment if you can. It is already on site. You will not likely find anything less expensive. Beyond that, if the physician has been using the same things all along and you just bought the practice, you will not likely be faced with a request to replace items.

❖ **Hint**

One good thing about negotiating which assets to buy or which liabilities to assume and their terms is that it gives the buyer and seller a little more room to negotiate while the "give and take" of negotiations ensues. If the seller "gave" on some earlier issues, he or she might be inclined to try to have the buyer assume some liabilities in the form of contractual obligations that the seller had and wanted to be free of.

Clinic Fee Schedule

It is important to see what the practice is charging and being reimbursed over time to see how the fees compare with the standard. Obviously, if the fee schedule is on the low side, a buyer might feel better about the purchase beyond what is apparent from the income statement because he or she knows that there is room for a change in the fee structure that will improve the profitability.

Also, in the forecast of income and expense, one can make some reasonable assumptions about increases in revenue and include those in the projections for the discounted cash flow (DCF) technique later.

Depreciation Schedules

Once again, it is helpful to have as much information as possible about the practice. An inventory of equipment, furnishings, and fixtures with their original cost is quite helpful. If there is not a current asset appraisal, you will need to have one done in order to provide a current value for the assets.

Often, there is not a schedule of the inventory available. Sometimes, the only things around are the schedules in the tax returns of the practice that are provided to quickly depreciate the equipment, furnishings, and fixtures to offset income tax. The depreciation life will always be as abbreviated as possible for the obvious reason stated, and the remaining value will therefore not be very reflective of the fair market value of the equipment in the practice. Book value, whether in financial statements or income tax return depreciation schedules, has little correlation with the market value of equipment.

The most valuable information in the depreciation schedules are the manufacturer, model numbers and type, and cost information. With this information in hand, you can either begin making telephone calls and rely on your ability to do a good job finding market prices or turn the information over to an equipment appraiser with whom you have negotiated a good fee structure to give you the adjusted fair market values of the items in the practice. My advice on this is that, unless you plan to become very proficient and spend a great deal of time appraising equipment, it will simply not be worth your while to spend the time it will take to find market values for equipment. (Equipment appraisers have a great deal of data at their fingertips, so they can do these cost-effectively.)

Minutes of Shareholders and Board Meetings

Among the most significant information you will find in corporation and board minutes of practices, especially multiphysician practices, relates to income distribution plans, benefits, and other forms of remuneration that will be good to determine as you try to identify income attributable to the sellers. Keep in mind that you need to have this type of information for performing excess earnings methods of valuation.

Sometimes, information relating to buy–sell agreements in which an option has been exercised, for example, to buy out a partner, can offer value information. After all, if the buy-out transaction was recent and was based on the value of the actual partnership or corporation, you may have something to use. (The thing to keep in mind when looking at partial interests, if the valuation was done by a professional valuation expert, is that a partial interest does not equal its percentage in value.) A minority interest has no control so its value is somewhat less than the percentage of the whole would indicate.

Payer Gross Fees

There is also the need for information on what kind of payer mix the practice has. Obviously, a 100 percent Medicaid patient mix is not real good right now. (Alternatively, if sometime in the future we all are under a universal payment system with all payments being equal, then it would not much matter.)

From information on which payers the practice has relationships with and how much is coming from each one, you can make comparisons with the norm for the area and make some judgments regarding whether the patient–payer mix is favorable or unfavorable. This issue, too, needs to go into the formation of an opinion of value. Payments from the collective mix of payers will certainly manifest themselves in the financial statements and have an impact on the accounts receivable account.

Patients By ZIP Code

A print-out of patients by ZIP code is not a necessary item to have, but it makes the analysis of the practice easier and better if the information is readily available. Such data often is available from most physician billing and patient information systems in use today. If you are a hospital, the market information provided by this type of data would be important to you. Although you might be able to call up physician and patient by ZIP code information from medical records and get a good idea of where patients are coming from via the practice in question, you would not know the volume of patients (information that you will want if you are negotiating with managed care companies).

Accounts Receivable

As with the patient ZIP code information, many patient billing software systems can pull up reports on accounts receivable in several ways. You will need to analyze the accounts receivable of a practice to determine what its collection rate has been, by payer, if possible, over time. Only when you know this will you be able to place a value on what the seller is stating as the current accounts receivable.

❖ Hint

The question frequently comes up, "Accounts receivable and cash in the bank change on a daily basis. What good does it do to count up all the numbers when the day after the appraisal, it could be totally different?"

There are a few answers to that. First, *all you can do is count what is there* (check the checking account book balances) when you are there. (Make sure there are no big cash deposits for the day waiting to be taken to the bank that you do not know about.) Place the current information in your updated balance sheet. You obviously cannot provide a running balance on all the current assets.

Second, *that is precisely why there is a date on the appraisal.* You are only providing an appraisal for that point in time. The next day is technically not covered. The place could blow up or one of the physician partners could take off for Rio with all the cash assets.

Third, I always tell clients that *they will need to reconcile those balances* just before closing on the sale to be accurate. (Have the accountants between the buyer and seller get together and provide those numbers.)

Table 1–2 is an example of an analysis of accounts receivable by two physicians.

Patient Volume Data by Year

Again, many if not most billing and patient information software programs used by practices today can provide you with a near-instant print-out of such information. To the extent that this can be provided for five years, you will have a better idea of which way the practice is going. In many instances, this breakdown should also be available by payer. Graphing such activity is often very helpful in viewing the change in direction of a practice. Changes may be due to external factors such as the change in the composition of the neighborhood or the change in the types of health care coverage available locally.

You can get fancy with this type of information and even evaluate it from a ZIP code by payer mix by volume standpoint to see what the specific changes have really been. If I were personally purchasing a practice, I would want that type of information. This depth of analysis is difficult to do, however, if the total practice appraisal is priced at less than $5,000.

Name and Address of Accountants

Answers to questions you may not otherwise be able to get an answer for often can come from the accountants. My experience with this has always been very good, and the accountants tend to be quite helpful. Your adjusted balance sheets will be different from what the accountants have done because you are changing them from a cash basis to an accrual basis. Yours will include updated tangible asset fair market values, instead of book values. But you should make sure that you have started the process of changing over the financial statements with a complete understanding of the accountant's prepared statements.

Also, there are often things that do not appear on the financial statements that can be learned by talking to the accountants. Some may have an important bearing on the value and even the ultimate interest in purchasing the practice.

Current Checkbook Balances

To provide an up-to-date adjusted balance sheet, you will need to use a number as of a given date for "Cash." I always advise clients (buyers or sellers) that the appropriate way to handle cash and other liquid accounts is to perform a review of them just before (immediately) closing if they are to be included in the asset purchase. There is always a delay between the closing and the appraisal date.

Owner Compensation (Salary and Fringes)

Although you should be able to find this information in other source documents, it is good to get the owner's rendition. Experience is that there are perks that are not found or there are overstated expenses that should be normalized. For example, you often find that there are two organizations: One is the practice, and the other is a real estate company/landowner that overcharges the practice for several reasons. It puts money in the hands of the physician real estate company but takes it out of the practice, increasing business costs and resulting in lower taxes.

In this type of case, you would make a note in the projected income tables that you have adjusted the rent to market rent and have increased the physicians' income by that additional amount in the practice that is ostensibly available for physician salaries.

Malpractice and Other Legal Proceedings

If you are a hospital interested in buying a practice or its tangible assets and employing a physician and you determine that there is a nonfrivolous case pending, that is information that you should have. Litigation poses a risk and lowers value.

Table 1–2 Weighted Aging Analysis of Accounts Receivable

				PHYSICIAN A *Percentage Breakdown by Days*					
Days in AR	*0–29*	*30–59*	*60–89*	*90–119*	*120–149*	*150–179*	*180+*	*Total*	*Collection Rates*
Wt. Factor	1	0.9	0.8	0.7	0.6	0.5	0.4		
Patient Pay	15.01%	7.09%	2.90%	2.68%	10.75%	4.13%	57.44%	100.00%	
Actual Amount	$1,274	$602	$246	$227	$912	$350	$4,874	$8,485	
Likely Receive	$1,274	$542	$197	$159	$547	$175	$1,950	$4,843	57.08%
Wt. Factor	1	0.95	0.9	0.85	0.8	0.75	0.7		
3rd Party	54.55%	19.28%	7.39%	4.35%	5.19%	0.55%	8.69%	100.00%	
Actual Amount	$6,934	$2,451	$939	$553	$659	$70	$1,105	$12,711	
Likely Receive	$6,934	$2,328	$845	$470	$527	$53	$774	$11,931	93.86%
Pvt Pay & 3rd Party Totals									
Actual Amount	$8,208	$3,053	$1,185	$780	$1,571	$420	$5,979	$21,196	
Likely Receiv.	$8,208	$2,870	$1,042	$629	$1,074	$228	$2,723	$16,774	79.14%
				PHYSICIAN B *Percentage Breakdown by Days*					
Days in AR	*0–29*	*30–59*	*60–89*	*90–119*	*120–149*	*150–179*	*180+*	*Total*	
Wt. Factor	1	0.95	0.9	0.85	0.8	0.75			
Patient Pay	30.82%	28.26%	14.71%	7.42%	8.40%	2.46%	7.93%	100.00%	
Actual Amount	$4,578	$4,197	$2,185	$1,103	$1,248	$365	$1,178	$14,854	
Likely Receive	$4,578	$3,987	$1,967	$938	$998	$274	$0	$12,741	85.78%
Wt. Factor	1.00	0.95	0.90	0.80	0.70	0.60	0.55		
3rd Party	26.88%	25.60%	12.50%	7.23%	8.33%	2.46%	16.98%	100.00%	
Actual Amount	$5,745	$5,471	$2,672	$1,545	$1,780	$526	$3,629	$21,368	
Likely Receive	$5,745	$5,197	$2,405	$1,236	$1,246	$316	$1,996	$18,141	84.90%
Pvt Pay & 3rd Party Totals									
Actual Amount	$10,323	$9,668	$4,857	$2,648	$3,028	$891	$4,807	$36,222	
Likely Receiv.	$10,323	$9,185	$4,371	$2,174	$2,244	$589	$1,996	$30,882	85.26%
TWO PHYSICIAN TOTALS–AGED A/R									
Actual Amount	$18,531	$12,721	$6,042	$3,428	$4,599	$1,311	$10,786	$57,418	
Likely Receiv.	$18,531	$12,055	$5,413	$2,803	$3,319	$817	$4,719	$47,656	83.00%
	The Bottom Line of Likely Collectible Accounts Receivable								**$47,656**

Current Inventory of Supplies

> ❖ **Hint**
>
> It is not practical for an appraiser to go through and inventory all the supplies in the office. It would take too long, raise the cost of the appraisal, and is basically not necessary.

There are one or two other ways that you can approach this issue. To start with, it has been determined by experience that most practices keep on hand about a one month to one and a half month's level of medical supplies. You should also quiz the office manager regarding what kind of time supply is kept on hand. Chances are, he or she will say "about a month." If that is the case, take from the most recently completed financial statement for the past 12 months the "medical supplies" figures and divide it by 12. Use that for the amount of supplies inventory in the balance sheet for supplies.

That may sound crude, but experience is that it is reasonably close. If the office manager says, "three months on-hand," he or she should have something to back it up.

Annual Referrals by Source

Another type of data that is helpful, especially for specialists, is some indication of referral sources. Try to establish how this is changing and, if so, how it has changed over the past several years. What are the likely impacts of these changes? Is the patient referral base for the specialist eroding? Is it growing?

Unlike the patient ZIP code and account information, this information is probably not going to be available on some software program. It may be that the office manager or the physicians via an interview will have to provide you with this.

Managed Care Contracts

One of the reasons hospitals and others are buying practices is to gear up for managed care by controlling blocks of patient populations. My view is that if physicians are not enrolled in sufficient managed care contracts, the worth of their practices will diminish. Unless this is an exclusive Beverly Hills "private pay" practice, it must be able to service as many types of patients (covered by as many insurers) as possible in order to survive.

The significance of this issue further depends on what is being purchased, if the physician is staying, and in what capacity (as a hospital employee or as a participating physician). Also, can the purchaser retain the managed care contract? If not and a huge patient base is lost on sale of the practice or practice assets, that has an effect on value.

One of the main ways to retain the managed care contracts is to purchase the tangible assets and manage the practice but allow the physician to retain ownership of the "business" or the practice.

CHAPTER 2

Going Through a Few Basics

YOU HAVE WHAT I WANT!

The Reason Anything Changes Hands

The reason anything changes hands is because parties identify greater value in what you have at the moment than what they have. In the changing health care marketplace, many physicians see more value in employment or affiliating with a medical organization of some type than they do in owning the tangible assets and the goodwill in a practice.

In fact, in any deal, "mutual advantage" must be perceived. So it is in the sale of businesses or professional practices. The buyer and the seller must both believe that there is a potential advantage for them in transacting the sale/acquisition of a practice or there is no deal. If you are a hospital executive, you have at least one and perhaps more potential advantages in mind. Most administrators are interested in firming up their physician referral base. In my experience, the revenue from the practice is important, but it tends to be a distant second place to locking up a patient base.

From the physician standpoint, nationally physicians are seeking refuge from the uncertainties of life under health care reform. They reason that selling either assets, or better yet assets and goodwill, and taking a handsome paycheck sounds pretty good. Certainly, the hours are better, the liabilities are less, and coverage is easier if need be.

Other physicians are just "getting out." One general practitioner I know sold his practice for what he could realize and went away to sell Amway products.

In this regard, the hospital–physician practice acquisition scenario is somewhat of an anomaly. The *main* reason for buying practices, although in keeping with a mission of strengthening the health care provider role, is *not* a standard business motivation with the hope of making the business generate a direct income stream. Instead, it is because network development, market positioning, and referrals for inpatient services are important for hospital survival. Nonprofit hospital objectives might be what most business executives would consider a secondary benefit to the direct income or revenue. It is to maintain or gain a market share. It is true that when health maintenance organizations (HMOs) or other managed care companies come calling, hospitals will certainly be best served if they have the leverage of a large patient population.

Still, the Price You Pay Must Be Justified by the Practice Income

The current regulatory agency interpretation of the regulations still requires that hospitals value the practices "in ways that physician purchasers would" (via primarily an income-based approach). The reason is . . . that the federal government does not want to see any "value-added considerations" a hospital would have (i.e., referrals) being included in the price.

Such being the case, it is important that both the hospital-buyer and physician-seller understand that as with any business *the asking price for a practice needs to be justified by the income the practice generates.* The Office of the Inspector General (OIG) says that you must use the same logic a prudent investor uses in analyzing and buying a business—presumably according to the value of a future stream of income. Of course, this does not include the income generated from patients whom the physician puts in the hospital but practice income (the income available to the physician-owner) only. Although you may anticipate patient admissions and indirect financial benefit, for purposes of the practice acquisition you would be well advised to leave those thoughts for another time. They do not legally belong in the negotiation of a practice acquisition.

The real irony here is that physicians tend to be among the least prudent investors (sorry, but business is still not taught in medical school) so that when the government says to behave in a way consistent with the way that physicians conduct business affairs, more than a few find that a little ironic.

Value

It is important to start any discussion of business valuations with a discussion of "value." Why? Because for you to communicate the value of a practice to would-be buyers, you need to understand the basis for value. Although health care is somewhat different, you need to understand underlying principles of valuation. So, let's start.

Rewards of Ownership

Value and price are a function of the anticipated rewards of ownership. For a hospital or a group practice, the benefits of acquiring a practice are viewed in two contexts. First and foremost, they are concerned with getting the patient base. Especially under managed care, the motivation will be to get as thorough a market penetration as possible, and the most readily available way to do that is to buy practices or buy practice assets. The second reward (more true of larger multiphysician clinics than a single- or two-physician practice) is the issue of clinic income. More on this later.

Value: A Function of Three Things

The price asked for a practice or clinic must be a function of and justified by several key components:

1. Potential return; the net earnings
2. Cost of capital to acquire the clinic
3. A risk factor to provide the investor with a higher return for riskier investments

Potential Return

Contrary to some, who prefer merely to set an arbitrary asking price for a practice, price cannot be determined in a vacuum. As indicated earlier and alluded to later as well, the valuation of the clinic will primarily be based on the income it generates and is anticipated to generate. That is what businesses are for, to make money, so it naturally follows that the primary focus will be on the finances. The price assumes financial returns. In other words, the price must be justified by projected returns. Later, the method is discussed by which you tie the price and the value.

Cost of Capital

A big part of the transaction that will allow the sale of the clinic is the cost of the capital. How much capital will it take to finance the acquisition, and what is the cost of the capital to the investor? This financial cost should be included in the required return when developing a present value of discounted cash flow method.

A buyer cannot pay so much for the clinic (including principal and interest—as well as provide an adequate income) so that the future clinic income will not more than make up for it. In other words, *the income from the clinic must "pay the freight"* of what the investor has to have for income from the practice plus the cost of principal and interest on the financing. In the words of Ross Perot, "You got to take in more than you pay out!" No pie chart should be needed to demonstrate that one.

Risk Factor

So, what is all this talk about risk, and why should we lower the price for our clinic because of it? Standard in business and investment is the cost associated with risk. That is why riskier stocks pay more than no-risk Treasury bonds. It does not need to get more complicated than that. *Uncertainty about the rate of financial return creates uncertainty about price. Rate of return is the key to price.* If your clinic has not demonstrated a reason to be concerned about risk and has a stable and growing annual income, risk will not likely play a detrimental role in discounting the value of your clinic. If the federal government has been thinking about changing regulations that would have a negative effect on your particular type of clinic, that counts as a risk factor until it can be eliminated.

Again, "the risks the price contemplates" need to be countered to justify the price. How are you going to address the issue as a seller? As a buyer? The income from the clinic is not a "sure thing," so there is *some* risk. If the clinic has been around since the French and Indian War and the income stream is strong, the risk discount factor should be minimal.

Please excuse the time I am spending on these points regarding the underpinnings of *risk and corresponding value*, but it is important to drive them home because you need to be familiar with the value concepts and exactly how they figure into the price. After all, it's better to go into negotiations prepared. Armed with this knowledge, you will make your best case for selling/buying the practice at a price that is fair to you.

The Price Must Seem Reasonable to Both Sides

Without the ability of both sides to identify reasonableness in the price, the transaction will not happen. The objective in negotiations is to reach the "mutual ground" point at which both buyer and seller are satisfied enough with the deal to go ahead. If the deal is going to happen, there is a general overlap of numbers. If the buyer's current best offer is below your "Go to Hell" point, there is not the overlap of mutually accepted pricing, and each will go away a little more frustrated.

The solution to this problem can often be put together in the form of combinations of terms that are discussed elsewhere in this book.

What Fair Market Value Isn't

A. The best deal you can cut
B. What you think fair market value probably is close to
C. What the other side wants you to think it is

What Fair Market Value Is

Fair market value (FMV) is what a given asset typically sells for in the marketplace, based on its characteristics as valued by the market. FMV is a matter of record if adequate research of transactions is available.

The official IRS definition as excerpted from Revenue Ruling 59-60 is

> The price at which the property would change hands between a willing buyer and a willing seller, neither being under any compulsion to buy or sell and both having reasonable knowledge of relevant facts. (Treas. Reg. 20.2031-1(b); Rev. Rul. 59-60, 1959-1 C.B. 237)

What Does Goodwill Really Include?

It seems as if everyone has a definition for goodwill. I tend to define it in terms of the value of a flowing income stream of business and profits versus a new startup business. Goodwill recognizes the effort to bring a business to the point in profitability that it has achieved. Some hospitals look at the worth of goodwill of a physician practice as the cost to set up a practice and get it breaking even. Others, more sophomorically, look at goodwill as the number of "active patients" or charts. In either case, there is value associated with the stage of development of a business—the recognition that it took resources and time to move the business that they are considering buying to the point of maturity.

Some health care executives say that they do not pay for goodwill because "as soon as the physician leaves, so does the goodwill! So why pay anything?" they ask. They make an assumption that the physician will be leaving or could leave at any time. If that is a major concern, just include them in an independent practice association or get a provision in the agreement that ties them to your organization.

It is true that practices erode or lose patients when physicians leave and that you have to work hard to minimize that, but the contention that "there is no goodwill when physicians leave" (unless the practice has already been closed for a period) is overstating the case.

Patients will continue to stream into the practice, especially if the departing physician has written them, encouraging them to do so. They may diminish, but there is still a flow of patients generating an income stream and that is worth money. Those of us who have built businesses readily understand the value of a viable business with an established customer base.

Going Concern Value

You may hear the term *going concern value* from time to time. I tend to equate it with "goodwill," but if I were to get into a cocktail party discussion and were asked to distinguish it from "goodwill," I would probably say that the going concern value of a company is the recognition of the established business volume and income stream. Further, "goodwill" can mean more than that. It can also recognize, as some have suggested, the value of a business to the extent that it is producing more than the average similar business. This later version is the interpretation that the excess earnings method of income or goodwill valuation ties to higher-than-average income for the business.

I disagree philosophically because I do not believe you have to produce more than the average similar business to establish value. I think that significant value is established if you have built a going business.

To take the example to the absurd (to better make my point), if IBM and Xerox were in identical businesses and both were making about the same net to bottom line and they were about average for their respective industries, there would be no value to their established businesses according to these excess earnings value proponents.

Medicare and Goodwill

The following are excerpts from the Medicare Provider Reimbursement Manual, Chapter 1, Sections 100-136.16:

> Medicare Principles re: Goodwill
>
> a) Goodwill is based on prospective profits rather than past profits.
>
> b) Generally, a five-year past period is used to forecast future trends.

c) Calculations should rely on operating profits.

d) Operating results should be adjusted for abnormalities before being used in the forecast of future trends.

e) A forecast should consider adverse possibilities or probabilities which may reduce profits.

f) A forecast should try to adjust for dollars of constant value.

Leasehold Improvements and Leases

Generally speaking, as a seller, if you have made leasehold improvements, (i.e., cabinets that you may have added that are used by the practice), they would carry a value and you can expect to be paid for their remaining useful life or to the end of the lease (whichever comes first). When the leasehold improvements become the property of the landlord at the end of the lease, you cannot sell them to someone else.

Leases may have value as well if (1) there is time left on the existing lease, (2) you can sublet the space, and (3) the rate at which the lease is written is below market value.

Technically, you need a rent survey to compare rents and terms of rents for comparable properties to see if there is value there. The price for a survey could be more than the additional value of the below-market rent, though, so tread carefully. Alternatively, there can be quite a bit of difference in value, however, especially if there are a few years left on the lease and you can sublease.

❖ Hint

A few telephone calls to area commercial office brokers who are located near the practice would be worthwhile. Merely ask them what medical office rents are currently going for. Describe the type of office facility that you want to know about (the subject practice is in) and see what several brokers tell you. Do not settle for just one. Try for at least three, if possible, and more if they are around.

This exercise in *phonemanship* will tell you a great deal, and you will know at that point generally what the market expects for rent in the subject facility. Then if you are the seller and you have a below-market rent, do the multiplication on the time left and do a present-value calculation on the amount (discussed elsewhere in the book). Add this amount to the array of values (i.e., equipment, furnishings, fixtures, supplies, goodwill, etc.).

APPRAISAL PRINCIPLES VERSUS ACCOUNTING PRINCIPLES

Many individuals confuse accounting concepts with appraisal theory: they are not twins! Appraisal shares some common ground with accounting, but the two *are* different. To use a simple example, some analysts attempt to use depreciation as an indication of value in their negotiations with physicians. The (accounting) depreciated value of an asset has some correlation with market value, but it is not the same. Market values are based on demand in the marketplace. Alternatively, depreciation is based on straight-line, double-declining balance, sum-of-the-years, or some other depreciation method.

Example of Book Value and Impact of Marketplace Obsolescence

Let's say you sell a computed tomography (CT) imaging clinic partnership for the straight-line book depreciated value for two-year-old equipment. You may well have sold the equipment for far less than what you could have realized valuing it as "fair market value—in use." To the fair market value of the equipment you must add taxes, freight, and set-up costs, which can be very substantial indeed.

Value of Income Producing Equipment versus Equipment in a Crate

Accounting does not take into consideration the value-added aspects of tangible assets producing income. Equipment actively engaged in the process of generating an income stream has a value tied closer to an economic benefit than to other approaches. This is particularly true in the case in which the equipment is a or *the* central aspect of the business. As evidence of that, it is not uncommon to pay an *in-use value* of 40 or 45 percent of the original value for something that has far outlived its "useful life" according to the books but that has been well maintained and is not functionally or technically obsolete. It sounds somewhat outrageous on the face of it, but do not be surprised to see this. Again, it is a financially contributing asset and deserves the recognition as such.

Hospitals are usually more oriented to underpaying than overpaying in this type of situation, but in terms of allocating portions of the purchase price, it is important to both the seller and buyer what portion of the purchase price is allocated to goodwill versus tangible assets. Clearly, if you have a seller who would be happy to sell you equipment at its depreciated book value (and it has been maintained well and is generating revenue), take it.

APPRAISALS VERSUS VALUATIONS: WHAT IS THE DIFFERENCE?

It might be appropriate to clarify the difference between the two terms *appraisal* and *valuation*. If you are not in the business, it can be confusing. Appraisals tend to relate to real property, real estate, and equipment. Valuations relate to the value of a going concern, a "business," whatever the organization type. Although the literature discusses appraisals of practices, you will find others, including me, using the term *valuation* when it comes to any kind of business entity.

CHAPTER 3

General Categories of Appraisal Approaches and Methods

There are several general categories of appraisal approaches that should be briefly mentioned before we move to the methods most applicable to physician practices and clinics. The following is a brief listing.

ASSET-BASED

Asset values focus on the balance sheet, so the analysis is limited in terms of recognizing issues such as the present state of the practice or the nature of increasing or declining patient base. Asset values tend to be more popular between existing partners or owners or in sales of stock to large group clinic employees. An asset-based approach ignores the value of the business established and relies exclusively on the value of the assets.

Book Value

The simplest way to approach valuation is the book value method: subtract the liabilities from the assets. The difference should be the equity of the owner.

There are a host of problems with book value, however; the biggest is that assets are based on historical cost that can be *extremely* misleading, especially in health care because of the rapid turnover in technology. It may be helpful, however, to include it in a field of values to develop perspective. With the exception of liquidation values of assets, the book value will be the lowest.

Adjusted Book Value

Adjusted book value is the next step up from book value. Adjustments are made to a variety of assets based on their current market value or current adjusted values. The quality of this process will have everything to do with the quality of the numbers. The main merit of this value is that it is better than book value by bringing the asset values current. In some health care valuation approaches, the adjusted book value is used in concert with an income stream approach to arrive at a conclusion of value.

Liquidation

Liquidation is an approach to value that determines the net amount that the owner would realize if all the assets were sold and the liabilities paid. It is generally defined to mean the net proceeds that could be realized if the assets of the business were sold off piecemeal and the business terminated. Liquidation value tends to set a floor to the price range. This approach also presumes that there is a sense of urgency and that liquidation is necessary in the immediate future.

Orderly Liquidation

Orderly liquidation is very similar to the liquidation value but presumes that the assets do not have to be liquidated immediately. The idea is that there is more time and hence more potential for return on the assets. The additional amount available above what can be realized over basic liquidation value will vary according to the market and the specific equipment, but the range may be 15 to 45 percent greater.

"Assets Plus" Rules of Thumb

"Assets plus" rules of thumb are rampant and can provide you with a ballpark number to begin looking at value, but they should not be used by themselves to come to a conclusion of value. They are most helpful because they are simple and quick. The degree to which the practice that you may want to buy varies from the number that comes up can be substantial though.

In general business, the assets plus formula goes something like this. Market value of furniture, fixtures, and leasehold, the cost value of inventory, plus one year's adjusted net income before taxes, including depreciation and the owner's salary, fringes, and perks *or* "all assets, plus one year's net, plus the owner's salary and perks."

Historically, in physician practices, purchasers have paid for tangible assets and a percentage of the annual gross patient revenue; however, the percentage varies significantly with the specialty.

Over the past several years, for example, average family practice goodwill payments have averaged close to 30 percent of the annual gross income.

❖ Hint

In my experience, hospitals tend to pay more than what is fair market value for several reasons. Physicians tend to ask for much more than the practices are worth, and the hospitals, fearful of losing a prime practice, do not counter with an offer that is likely to lead to a value based on reality. It is, I believe, happening less often as hospitals are approached by more physicians interested in selling. I suggest you may want to agree to mutually select an independent appraiser whose value you will agree to agree on.

If, for changes in the marketplace, you believe that the *future* financial performance of the practice will be diminished, make sure that the appraisal firm is fully aware of the changes. The danger is that if they did not recognize the changing health care marketplace and leaned heavily on *historical* financial performance when performing projected income streams, the value of the practice would be exaggerated. "General" appraisers may tend to do this. If you use a generalist appraiser, one of those individuals who appraises everything from gas stations to flower shops, you will have to do some baby-sitting because he or she may not have the sophistication in health care to look for the right things or ask the right questions.

INCOME APPROACHES

Earnings approaches focus on the *historical* profit and loss statement that, like the asset approach, tends to limit the attention paid to the present state of the business.

These approaches are most appropriate in organizations in which equipment plays a minor role and in which labor is the major component. Professional practices are among the prime examples of businesses in which these methods could be applied.

Capitalization of Earnings

Let me preface the description of the capitalization of earnings technique by saying that it is usually only applicable to larger group practices or clinics that actually have a bottom line. Most physician practices do not have any corporate income because the physicians take the income in the form of salary or other compensation. Capitalization of earnings is done on bottom line corporate income—*after* owner compensation. So obviously, if there is not income to capitalize beyond the income available for physician compensation, for valuation purposes, this income approach would not make sense. I include the approach in Exhibit 3–1 because you clearly may have an opportunity to acquire a large group practice that does have a bottom line to capitalize. Use this as a rough measure.

Different investors take different positions regarding what they count as income for purposes of computing valuation. Some use net profit (before taxes). Others capitalize earnings (before taxes, interest, and depreciation). Still others take slightly different approaches. The preferred type of capitalized earnings is the DCF model.

Discounted Cash Flow Model

The DCF model takes into consideration many factors in building a spreadsheet income model. It should include assumptions based on research regarding the health care market, the cost of capital, the risks of the particular health care business being considered, and the rate of return necessary to you the investor to make the whole thing worth your while. (*Again, I realize that many acquisitions are based on the development of a referral base versus the level of income from a given practice or clinic, but even Medicare says that you will base your purchase price on what a prudent investor would.*)

To develop a five-year income stream to capitalize, I suggest that you perform a DCF analysis of the clinic or group practice to determine the nature of the income that can be realistically anticipated. You should also include a terminal value (sometimes referred to as "reversion"). During the process, you need to identify a rate of return that begins with a risk-free rate to begin building the rate (i.e., 30-year Treasury bonds), which adds the cost to you of your capital plus what kind of return you want and which also considers risk.

Exhibit 3–1 Basic and Quick Goodwill Formulas

Approaches taken by investors differ. Some use refinements or factor out considerations others would not. As an example, some buyers use EBIT (earnings before interest and taxes). Others use EBITDA (earnings before interest, taxes, depreciation and amortization).

Similarly, below we have several formulas which vary in several respects based on differing tastes. Both take **known income streams, known equipment fair market values** and apply rates of return and capitalization rates.

Model 1 subtracts net tangible asset value from the value of the business as calculated by capitalizing the projected earnings.

MODEL #1 Capitalization of Earnings Method of Determining Goodwill

INSTRUCTIONS: Enter the financial data below where indicated [Enter]

			COMMENTS:
[Enter]	Expected Earnings*	$400,000	(This should be based on projections based on your best data)
[Enter]	NTAV	$45,000	(This should be from the Balance Sheet which you have adjusted)
[Enter]	Rate of Return**	0.2	(This should be based on what the rate of return you require with risk and cost of capital using a "build-up" method)
	Capitalized Earnings***	$2,000,000	"Value of the Business"
	less NTAV	$45,000	"Fair Market Value of Net Tangible Assets"
	Equals Goodwill of	$1,955,000	"Goodwill Portion"

IMPORTANT: *The earnings are after owner compensation.

**The most crucial factor is the development of the rate of return or discount rate. Build it carefully. See the Discount Factor Section of this book.

***This does not include a payment for terminal or residual earnings (Present Value of DCF Model).

Model 2 is referred to as an Excess Earnings method because it subtracts the return of practice income attributable to tangible assets (recognizing their value to the production of income) from the overall income.

MODEL #2 Capitalization of Excess Earnings

Expected Earnings		$400,000	This refers to excess earnings as those which are in excess of earnings attributable to equipment or hard assets with a return rate of their own.
NTAV		$45,000	
Times Expected Rate of Return on Assets		0.15	←
NTAV ×	0.15	$6,750	
Excess Earnings		$393,250	
Then			
Capitalize Earnings		$393,250	
	Divided by	0.2 ←	The capitalization rate here needs to be developed based on comparisons with comparable organizations.
Capitalized Exc Earnings		$1,966,250	

Once an income stream is developed (which means you have normalized the various years' net incomes), you must then discount it back to present value. Consider Exhibit 3–2.

I recommend that you use a business calculator such as the Hewlett Packard 12C or a Texas Instruments Executive Business Analyst II (BA-II), to name two common ones, but any calculator with features that can calculate the time value of money is fine. Better yet, use a spreadsheet program with those features such as Excel, Quattro Pro, or Lotus. I refer you to the present-value template on the accompanying diskette.

Income Multipliers—Factor Gross Patient Revenue

There is a database called the "Goodwill Registry" (see Data Sources in the back of the book) that compiles all physician practice sales (reported to it), which number in the

Exhibit 3–2 Present Value = Earnings / $(1 + R)^i$

Where R = required rate of return
i = number of periods
On the basis of your analysis, you would buy the subject clinic according to the total analysis below:

Year 1	Year 2	Year 3	Year 4	Year 5
$300,000	$327,000	$356,430	$388,509	$423,474

For years beyond the five above, *you will assume* an earnings saturation of $423,474.
Through a process of rate building, you have developed a discount factor for the calculation of 20 percent.

Where: Present Value = Earnings / $(1 + R)^i$
R = required rate of return
i = number of periods

	Year 1	Year 2	Year 3	Year 4	Year 5	Year 6	Total Value
	$300,000	$327,000	$356,430	$388,509	$423,474	$2,117,370	
	$(1 + 0.20)^1$	$(1 + 0.20)^2$	$(1 + 0.20)^3$	$(1 + 0.20)^4$	$(1 + 0.20)^5$	$(1 + .20)^5$	
OR	**$250,000**	**$227,083**	**$206,267**	**$187,359**	**$170,184**	**$850,923.51**	**$1,891,816.51**

Calculating Present Value of the *Terminal Value*
At the end of the five-year DCF period, you projected that $423,474 was the saturation income level in this particular practice.

Value of projected earnings starting at the end of the fifth year can be determined as follows (dividing the projected income by the capitalization rate of 0.20):

$423,474 divided by 0.20 equals **$2,117,370 Capitalized Value**
Capitalized Terminal Value of $2,117,370 — Discounted to Present Value = $ 850,924
Add the Above Present Value of the Capitalized Terminal Value to
the Present Value of the First Five-Year Income Stream — $ 1,040,893
and the Grand Total Is: — $ 1,891,817

On the basis of this, you would decide to buy the clinic if you can negotiate a price at $1,891,817, or $1,890,000 (rounded), or less.

thousands at this point. Until recently, it was free to data contributors but now costs approximately $400 per year. In recent years, I have noted that the mean family practice paid was (rounded) 0.30 of gross patient revenue for goodwill.

Now, this is for the entire country, but there is some value due to the large number of transactions. The problem is that family practices in San Diego are likely to go for more than those in Backwater, Montana, so you have to adjust from the norm based on what impact the location has. I have not done it, but perhaps using the RBRVS geographic factor differential/weight may be one tool to help adjust toward geographic differences.

Business brokers may be of some help, but the problem is that the transaction terms are not public, and it is extremely difficult to learn the terms of transactions or the conditions of the businesses or practices. You will have to do some homework and search around for what data there are and then apply your best judgment as to the variables in the practice you are trying to value and the individual financial merit. If you can justify the cost, a good starting point is the Goodwill Registry mentioned earlier and referenced in the Data Sources listing.

Let's say that the gross patient revenue for a practice you want to buy has been analyzed and its historical weighted amount is $400,000. Let's also say, for this example, that the practice in mind was very typical, with nothing to distinguish it from the average practice (that way you can use the average goodwill factor of 0.2975, or 0.30 rounded).

When you multiply 0.3 times the weighted averaged gross income of $400,000, you arrive at a value of $120,000 for goodwill. This is then added to the net tangible asset value of the practice.

One gauge you may have occasion to use is that the income to the physicians should be between 45 and 55 percent of the expense to the practice. It obviously depends on the type of practice, but if a practice brings in $250,000 gross, the physician-owner should be taking home about (in all the forms of income) $125,000 or more. When you look at practice financials, if the physician is not taking out about half, take a closer look to see what is happening with the costs. Alternatively, if he or she is taking out 70 percent, maybe some things are being shortchanged at the cost of good practice.

Capitalization of Excess Earnings

Background

The excess earnings approach is one of the most widely used valuation techniques for small business assignments. This method was originally known as the Treasury Method, which first appeared in a 1920 publication by the U.S. Treasury Department, ARM 34, which stood for Appeals and Review Memorandum Number 34. See the example in Exhibit 3–3. Methodology includes

1. Determine net tangible asset value (using fair market value for tangible assets).
2. Determine a normalized level of earnings (eliminate the unusual income or expense items—so that you can use the revised income to project a more normal income stream).
3. Determine an appropriate percentage rate of return you require (capitalization rate).
4. Multiply the net tangible asset value (NTAV) by the rate of return attributable to tangible assets (usually 10 to 15 percent *only* because medical practices are a labor-intensive industry as opposed to a machinery- and equipment-based business).
5. Determine excess earnings by subtracting tangible asset earnings from the step above from normalized earnings (which is the amount of earnings above a fair return on the net tangible asset value).
6. Determine an appropriate capitalization rate to apply to the excess earnings (usually about 35 to 50 percent because "excess earnings" are by definition harder to achieve). Capitalize the excess earnings at that rate (divide the earnings by the cap rate, i.e., $105,000 / 0.50).
7. Add the values from steps 1 and 6.

Common Errors/Omissions With the Excess Earnings Method

1. Many do not ensure that projections developed are truly normalized.
2. Current market values are often not used for tangible assets vs. "book values" or other numbers.
3. Inappropriate rates are often chosen for allocation of earnings between tangible assets and labor.
4. The salary of the owner is often not deducted in the expenses of the business.

Biggest Problems with the Excess Earnings Method

1. Subjectivity in crucial judgments can be a big problem, especially if the appraiser is not familiar enough with the medical field. Excess earnings should only be used by those familiar with health care.
2. The market is not recognized under excess earnings, so it can overstate the value of goodwill.
3. Excess earnings does not address the value of goodwill or the going concern elements of a practice already in place (even one that does not have excess earnings).

Income Multipliers—Earnings-Based Multipliers

Larger, more stable health care organizations are sometimes valued (ballparked) by a gross revenue multiplier approach. This form of "whole number" multiplying is acceptable for larger practices that actually have a stable and substantial bottom line but not with a practice in which the physician takes all the revenue.

In health care businesses, you find that appropriate multiples of gross income range from 1 to 10 but with the median between 3 and 5 (e.g., a multiplier of three times the amount of annual earnings before taxes, interest, and depreciation for valuing the goodwill component). In these cases, the assets may or may not be included in the price. It is somewhat case-specific. Some investors theorize that if you buy a business, the equipment comes with it because those things are needed to generate the income stream and it was the income stream you bought when you bought the business... Follow that logic? The bigger the business, the truer this is.

Income multipliers tend to be used a great deal by hospital chains in acquiring other hospitals (as opposed to practices). They tend to pay from three to five times the earnings before interest, taxes, and depreciation. *But don't do this with practices.*

Professional practices are dealt with differently for a variety of reasons. A major one is because the professional or professionals involved usually take all the net income home, leaving the corporation with no income. So, from the standpoint of comparing income streams with a large clinic or hospital (with a bottom line), there usually is none in a professional practice. If you multiplied the "zero" on the bottom line by 5, you would still get zero. That is why when you look at income at professional practices, you look at income available to the practitioner. Then you use a gross income multiplier on the weighted historical income.

Technique for Weighting Historical Income for Arriving at an Income to Factor

Under this relatively simple methodology, the historic weighted averaged net income of usually the past three to five years is divided by the capitalization rate to arrive at an indication of business value. Some individuals prefer to use the previous 12 months' earnings, but because that is less likely

Exhibit 3–3 Example of the Excess Earnings Approach

A. Net Tangible Asset Value			$200,000
B. Normalized Earnings, which includes **all earnings available to the practitioner** and			
Practice Net Income		$145,000	
Less Nonrecurring Income		($25,000)	
Less Excessive Expenses (not related to income generation)		$5,000	
Total Normalized Earnings			$125,000
Standard Method for Determining Excess Earnings Portion			
Earnings attributable to tangible assets $200,000 × 0.10 Alloc. Rate			= $ 20,000
Excess Earnings ($125,000 – $20,000)			= $ 105,000
Value of Excess Earnings ($105,000 / 0.50)			= $ 210,000
(Excess earnings tend to be discounted at a high rate because they are riskier to obtain as "excess" earnings compared with normal earnings.)			
Total Value under the Standard Method ($200,000 NTAV + $210,000 Cap. Excess Earnings)			= $410,000
To Help You with the Concept, the Following Example May Be Helpful:			
Capitalization of Excess Earnings			
Expected Earnings			$400,000
Net Tangible Asset Value (NTAV)			$28,000
Times Expected Return on Assets			0.15
Expected Earnings			$400,000
NTAV × 0.15			$4,200
Excess Earnings			$393,250
• Rate for allocating income contribution of assets can vary based on the degree of equipment required in practice.			
Then			
Capitalize Earnings			$393,250
[Enter]	Divided by	Cap Rate	0.2
	Capitalized Exc Earnings		$1,966,250

to be a representative income value, an average weighted five-year income stream is preferred. See Exhibit 3–4.

Add to that the current fair market value of the other practice assets you want to acquire and you have the value of the practice.

❖ Hint

A word of caution here. In single- or small physician practices or practices in which there is no practice bottom line or profit, income available to physicians is not usually the figure that is used with a "multiplier" to come up with a rough value.

In some negotiations, I have heard sellers state that they want "one times their annual operating income," but this is a hybrid variation on the technique in which one uses a multiplier on *gross patient revenue.*

The one times physician available revenue case actually yields more cash to the seller than the more accepted goodwill factor times gross patient revenue. Consider the following: The $210,330 from the above physician income is multiplied by 1 for a goodwill value of the same number, $210,330, or rounded to $210,000.

More typically, a gross income multiplier is arrived at by taking a typical goodwill factor for the type of practice and modifying it by assessing the quality of the practice, its strength in the marketplace, the practice operation, etc. (See my physician practice matrix in Appendix B.)

For purposes of this illustration only, let's say that the adjusted figure for goodwill based on your analysis of the practice is 0.30.

A typical gross patient revenue for this type of physician might be about $380,000 to $400,000 (in which the physi-

Exhibit 3–4 Average Weighted Five-Year Income Stream

As an example, let's review the following example on the income attributable to the physician practice owner from 1989 to 1992.

Begin by weighting the oldest income data lowest (say, with a weight of 1 and the most recent data weighted with a 5).

1988	1989	1990	1991	1992
$150,000	$175,000	$195,000	$205,000	$250,000
Wt 1	Wt 2	Wt 3	Wt 4	Wt 5

1 × 150,000 = $ 150,000
2 × 175,000 = $ 350,000
3 × 195,000 = $ 585,000
4 × 205,000 = $ 820,000
5 × 250,000 = $1,250,000

Wtd Total = $3,155,000
This is then divided by sum of weights (1 + 2 + 3 + 4 + 5) = 15
...which equals a historically weighted net income available to the owner of $210,330.

cian realizes 50 percent of the gross income). *Applying the 0.30 times the gross revenue of $380,000 equals a goodwill value of about $114,000.* The "one times the gross revenue" approach yields about three times what is common for goodwill. If the proposal is one times annual operating income (before owner salary), then you will pay about twice what is common for goodwill.

Discounted Cash Flow or Discounted Future Earnings

DCF attempts to value a business or practice by predicting the most likely future earnings, discounted to the present, using risk-adjusted interest rates for that practice or clinic over that period.

A detailed analysis of past trends in and future expectation of the practice, the industry, and economic conditions is required. Although this approach is one of the most widely used, it is less commonly used in small business valuations because projection of income is frequently too speculative to be useful. If the practice or clinic is a mature one with a fairly stable income stream and volume, a strong argument for the use of DCF can be made. Some potential investors, however, want to do a DCF exercise for their own use.

The approach is to project the income stream up to five years in advance and then discount it based on cost of capital, risk, and return on investment required.

Selecting an Appropriate Discount Rate to Use in Discounted Cash Flow Projections

A problem in selecting the appropriate discount rate is the rate of return that the market requires for comparable investments. If the future earnings projection is the earnings available to equity, then use the cap rate that applies to an equity investment.

There are several ways to develop risk rates to build into the overall discount rate. My firm has developed a six-page matrix that evaluates practice systems and status ranging from everything from marketplace penetration to the physical plant facilities and financial management. We add the risk factor to the cost of capital, the percentage return we think is appropriate, and the current percentage for "risk-free" money (30-year Treasury notes).

The full discussion of this approach is beyond the scope of this book, especially because individual practices are not as likely to use a DCF approach.

Price-to-Earnings Ratio

A price-to-earnings ratio (P/E) is just that. You look to see what the ratio is between the annual earnings and the price for similar types of medical clinics selling. In other words, if practices that are earning $150,000 are selling for 1.5 times their earnings, the practices are worth $225,000 in the marketplace. Usually, P/E approaches would include equipment.

P/E ratios are not used commonly for practices. Publicly traded clinic stock may be easier to locate, but practices tend to be private, closely held businesses. Anything you find in the financial columns would not likely be comparable with this level of business. When you find P/E ratios published in the financial pages of whatever periodical you use, they tend to be for "regular companies." For example, if you were performing a valuation on a diabetes treatment center, you would find P/E ratios ranging from about 15 to

30 for major companies that provide these kinds of service. Unfortunately, there are not many good opportunities for comparable physician practices and clinics that you could use from the financial papers.

DEVELOPMENT OF CAP RATES

General

The term *capitalization rate* is used most commonly to mean a percentage rate (use a decimal, for example, 20 percent would be shown as 0.20 in a formula) by which a constant income stream is divided to indicate a value. For example, if a business made (net to the bottom line, before taxes) $100,000 per year and there was a 10 percent return expected on the investment, the stream of income would be worth $1,000,000 (or $100,000/0.1) to the investor. Cap rates are a matter of fact. They are the rate acceptable to the market for comparable income streams at the time of valuation. If adequate data exists, rates should be developed from an analysis of the sales of comparable practices.

For a general idea of what appropriate current cap rates may be for the area, contact a reputable business broker. Although this is certainly not good enough for appraisal purposes, current research from a broker active in the medical field can provide an initial idea.

After you do an initial review based on general information obtained above, it may then be appropriate to conduct further research on your own or have a formal appraisal done if the practice price appears to meet your overall investment criteria.

Summation of Build-Up Method

The build-up method is based on external risk returns for businesses. It is developed by adding up a sequence of rates applicable to each of a variety of factors critical to the enterprise. A very basic approach would start with a safe (no-risk) interest rate such as a 30-year Treasury bill. You then add other factors that cause the rate applicable to the income stream to be different from the risk-free rate of the Treasury bill. See the example in Exhibit 3–5.

Exhibit 3–5 Simplified Example of Build-Up Method

Long-Term Treasury Bill Rate	7.50%
Risk Return for the Industry	11.00%
Premium for Management Stability	5.00%
Discount Rate for Future Earnings	23.50%

This technique is not particularly useful, and I believe it is crude for physician practices. It is more commonly used in conjunction with Robert Morris Industry Profiles for many types of businesses and other professional practices.

Qualitative Build-Up Method

The qualitative build-up method is based on subjective factors and judgment relating to the practices' internal, external, and competitive performance. For obvious reasons, it should only be undertaken by someone with the requisite background in health care. This method is most useful when no industry statistics are available. The components can be modified to the following example to suit your particular situation. The qualitative model is structured similar to Exhibit 3–6, in which 1 equals strong and 5 equals weak.

Add this factor to the risk-free rate of a 30-year Treasury bill for the total cap rate. Again, this is a subjective approach and one tailored to the values of a given health care investor. In my professional practice valuations, I use a six-page matrix that deals with the above issues and more, blending them into a final cap rate for use in developing an indication of value. (See Physician Practice Evaluation Matrix in Appendix B.) The above technique is more appropriate for large, solid practices that have a bottom line of their own (versus small practices that have no bottom line after owner compensation).

Multiples of Cash Flow

(This is not the same as applying a factor for goodwill on the gross patient revenue, which you read about earlier.) You will not often run into multiples of cash flow in physician practices, but in case someone talks about it, I want you to know a little. This type of approach is used more with hospitals and other larger health care providers. I do not recognize it as a legitimate, sophisticated approach because it is a crude basis for anything but a gross ballpark idea of what something *might* be worth.

Large multihospital organizations have used this, and they are paying way too much for hospitals that they are buying in their zeal to take over the market. But to each their own. The irony is that it is happening on such a wide-scale basis that it is redefining the market values—but based on a "half-baked" approach to valuation.

Anyway, the concept is that you want to "capitalize" a base of earnings. Individuals use different earnings bases to do this. There tend to be four or five earnings bases, which are

1. Pretax earnings (EBT)
2. Pretax cash flow (EBDT)
3. Debt-free pretax earnings (EBIT)

Exhibit 3–6 Qualitative Method Example

1.	Stability of Earnings (beta)	3
2.	Quality Staffing	3
3.	Continuity of Referrals	3
4.	Current Market Penetration	3
5.	Regulatory Issues	3
6.	Location	3
7.	Competition	3
8.	Physical Plant and Equipment	3
9.	Practice Operations/Risk Management	3
10.	Financial Management	3
11.	Current Ratio	3
		33%

4. Debt-free pretax cash flow (EBDIT)
5. Debt-free pretax cash flow—less amortization (EBDITA)

The debt-free approach factors out the effect of varying debt structures on the income and expense statement. The pretax cash flow method removes the impact of depreciation methods. The debt-free pretax cash flow method removes both debt and depreciation methods. The last method also factors out the impact of amortization. Get the idea?

Select a level of earnings you want to work with for multiplying into a value. Which level you select will depend on a wide variety of factors, which would require yet another book. But if you were involved in transactions, say, to buy hospitals or nursing homes, you would first select a common measuring stick by which to compare your potential acquisitions. Further, in your analysis of which level of earnings to focus on or use in your comparative analysis, consider how each of the issues, "D," "I," "T," and "A" in EBDITA may play into the financing or post-transaction period. EBDITA factors out everything to give you the best picture of what "business is being done." Each one of the other methods, going from bottom to top of the list, leaves in another element that could cloud your comparison of the target acquisitions.

From a logic standpoint, you would apply lower multiples as you move from the top method (EBT) down to EBDITA, because the dollars will be smaller as you go from 1 to 5. A major acquirer of hospitals tends to have a range of multiples of 3 to 5 for a multiple on EBDITA, depending on how attractive or strategic the target acquisition is. The overall multiple on EBDITA may be from 1 times EBDITA to 10 times, for something exceptionally attractive.

As a capstone to this topic, let me just say again that I do not recognize this as anything but exceptionally crude. But you may see it out there, and now, if you do, you will have some indication of what they are talking about and how they prefer to capitalize income.

MARKET APPROACH

Although asset and income approaches are internally oriented, marketplace approaches are externally oriented, looking at what similar practices are selling for in the marketplace.

The major flaw with the market approach is that it tends to ignore internal statistics. The counter to this criticism is that "if that is what they are selling for, then that is what the market says they are worth." The internal statistics are irrelevant in a "strict" market approach.

The market or sales approach attempts to identify what the same types of practices are selling for in the same market area. This approach is always hampered because it is difficult to ascertain specifics such as special terms or special features about the practice sale transaction. Both of these can have a very dramatic effect on the value and therefore the price. Whoever said that the "devil is in the details" would probably let us borrow that phraseology and say that the "deal is in the details or terms."

❖ **Hint**

Brokers are often not cooperative in sharing data. A friend of mine had a broker say to him, "Why should I tell you? What's in it for me?" (*If they somehow think that you may be in a position to assist them in listing more practices, however, you may have a better chance of getting cooperation.*) If you tend to be in a position to learn of businesses or practices for sale or those which are about to become for sale, the value of cooperating with you might dawn on the broker. It can be a symbiotic relationship.

Be careful not to use listed asking prices. They are not sales, so they do not reflect the market. They reflect a little wishful thinking and a little of what the sellers have seen in the market, so you can generally assume that these numbers are high. Keeping in mind that most businesses sell 10 to 20 percent below the asking price, you might be able to adjust the asking prices if you know what the disparity has been in the market as a general guide—but the point is that "sales" are what counts.

Sometimes attorneys and CPAs with physician clients can be helpful in obtaining practice data. So, as you can see, it is a "royal pain" to get good data, and usually it is difficult to feel comfortable that you have "all the details."

If, by chance, you find someone willing to share data, in the least, ask him or her for the following:

- Sale price
- Any seller financing and terms (interest rate and term of the carryback)
- What was included in the sale (hard assets, goodwill, accounts receivable, and other liquid assets—worth how much, other intangibles)?
- What approaches to valuation were used?
- What shape was the practice in?
- How many active patients, and which way has that number been going?
- What was the net?
- Were the books reviewed by an appraiser to "normalize" them for reasonably projecting income?

. . . and the list goes on, but you probably will not get that much information. This is just an observation, but brokers sometimes get a little irritated at appraisers and others who are "prospecting" for information. Again, let them know that you will keep their name handy in case you have a need sometime for a broker. That might help.

So, in summary, the market approach has much more value and is the primary approach in real estate appraisal. It is easy to find comparable sales in real estate because of the information systems that have been established for that industry. I am aware that there are several databases that purport to have business sale transaction data, but in some instances, you must be a member and, in other instances, the integrity of the data is less than good.

Most appraisers network with other appraisers for data from transactions of which they have been a part. All appraisers keep files on their previous projects and exchange information, but the problem is to provide *current* fair market values, so outdated information is not much more than an indicator from the past. (See the discussion on the market-based PSA in Appendix B.)

It is appropriate to add two things at this point. The OIG does not recognize the usual economic market model of supply and market demand when it comes to hospitals and physicians transacting. Their position tends to be that values paid by hospitals are not to be used in performing marketplace value analyses and therefore in fair market value because they will not reflect true values. They claim they are stilted (the prices, that is).

This position has actually worked out better for hospitals because it has tempered the purchase prices, which would have probably destroyed a few of them without the federal government saying that there is a limit. More on that later.

Even professional appraisers tend not to give too much credence to what hospitals pay for practices because experience has shown that the moneys paid by hospitals are not justified by the values of the practices. Instead, they look to what other physicians pay to purchase a practice or buy into a partnership.

As discussed elsewhere, one measure of goodwill market-based value can be obtained through the Goodwill Registry offered by The Health Care Group in Plymouth Meeting, PA. (See Data Sources.) The company conducts a national survey and compiles what is paid for what kind of practice and where. It relies on those who receive the publication to send in transaction information. If you are actively engaged in performing physician practice appraisals, you may want to purchase these data.

COST APPROACH

The cost approach attempts to identify a value of a property based on the cost it would require to duplicate or replace it at the current depreciated point. It is based on the belief that the best way to set a value for a business is to determine what it would cost to replace or reproduce the items based on *current* costs. If real estate is discussed, the appraisal term used is *reconstruction—cost—new less accumulated depreciation.* (Inflation and annual depreciation of capital assets usually have the effect of making the replacement value much higher than the book value.)

The cost approach does not consider goodwill and totally ignores the market. It also ignores the fact that certain of the equipment would probably not be reacquired if the business were rebuilt. Inasmuch, the cost approach only reflects cost and is probably more suited to appraisal situations relating to insurance replacement costs. Occasionally, items in the market are worth less than the cost to build them because of economic conditions. It probably is safe to say that unless we are in the midst of a recession or depression, the cost approach represents the "floor" of values.

In physician practices, several types of values for the equipment are often used. One is *fair market value.* This value entails having an equipment appraiser provide individual values for the items in terms of what they would bring on the used medical equipment market (without circumstances requiring immediate liquidation). This is the predominant value approach used by hospitals and other health care providers in acquiring practice assets.

A second approach that may be used is called *in-use value.* This value recognizes the equipment including the depreciated value of the transportation, installation, taxes, and education needed to get the equipment up and running.

In a related definition of in-use value, some view operating equipment in the context of active business assets in the process of generating an income stream. The equipment is viewed as an economic contributing asset, and its value is tied to the income stream instead of to what is going on in the market for the same item.

Although it may seem somewhat esoteric, it is an approach used by some. Under this form of value, the seller can expect more than fair market value for the equipment, even if it is older equipment—as long as it has been reasonably maintained and is helping generate an income stream. In the excess earnings approach, in which the contributing value of the assets shown earlier are considered, you saw 10 and 15 percent being used as asset contribution levels to the income stream of the business or clinic.

❖ Hint

It is reasonable to assign a percentage of income stream to the hard assets at a level that is at least as high as the percentage of interest that you would pay to acquire it, and probably add another 3 to 5 percent.

In other words, using this approach, if a four-physician practice generated $1,000,000 income, those using this perspective on in-use value would say that the equipment was worth $100,000 to $150,000. This allocation of purchase price based on contribution to the income stream is seldom, if ever, used in appraising practices except by generalist appraisers who try to apply industrial techniques to health care. Personally, I think this is more fodder for parlor games and tools for some appraisers to try to make a value fit a situation than useful in valuing practices, but this book is not about my philosophies. I just want you to know some of the more common terms. Let me add briefly that this procedure may be useful as one of several approaches in developing an "array of values" to consider when buying or selling a practice (or any business).

If the equipment is not being purchased as a part of the practice (which is being purchased), in-use value will not be deemed appropriate. The greatest likely value would be fair market value that might be more or less than in-use value, depending on the age, condition, and demand for the equipment.

As noted earlier, if a practice has closed and the equipment is sitting there, liquidation value may be the most appropriate value. If the physician is not in a big hurry/does not have to sell the equipment, orderly liquidation value, bringing him or her slightly more value (about 20 to 50 percent of fair market value) could certainly be supported.

Used equipment vendors will usually only offer liquidation (pennies on the dollar) payment for equipment. The reason is that they must make a living off the profits that they realize through reselling the equipment to another buyer. They also must take a risk in being able to resell the equipment and pay the costs of carrying the equipment in the meantime.

COMBINATION METHODS

In smaller health care organizations in particular, it is common to use a blend of approaches. These are hybrid approaches to valuing practices, and this is quite common in health care, allowing payment for tangible assets *and* payment for goodwill.

The two approaches most often combined are an income approach and an asset approach (usually fair market value in the form of in-use value). An equipment appraisal is most often performed for the tangible assets. An income approach is usually some type of income multiplier such as 0.3 to 0.4 times "gross patient receipts." In the case of a large clinic or practice with a stable bottom line, a DCF approach to projecting income and discounted to present value with a terminal value is recommended as the most conceptually correct.

❖ Hint

Be extremely careful when you use multipliers on gross revenue because the practice management may have been so bad that there is relatively little income going to the physicians. I have seen several examples in which the gross revenue was really pretty good but when you looked at what was left for the practitioners, it was way below average. As a potential buyer, keep in mind that you are paying for a going concern—an established, running business managed by someone who (mentally) lives in the twentieth century.

If the gross income is very good or the patient base is substantial enough . . . and the buying organization thinks that it can rectify the problems of management, it may go ahead and buy the practice. That does happen a lot. Especially if the buyer is a Physician Practice Management Company (PPMC), with the ability to achieve large economies of scale and inject good management.

Instead of gross patient receipts, you may want to consider income available to the physicians. The logic is that because the physician income will be typically only 45 to 55 percent of the gross income of the practice, you can use physician income and double the appropriate multiplier to arrive at a figure. This is not a common practice, but it makes more sense than paying some unrealistic figure for a practice or clinic that is doing poorly or losing money.

CHAPTER 4

Equipment Appraisals

IN GENERAL

Equipment appraisals are usually performed by specialists in appraising machinery and equipment. The professional credentials you would look for would be a firm or individual (many are self-employed) who has earned the Accredited Senior Appraiser (ASA) professional designation from the American Society of Appraisers. There are many specialties, as you may imagine, in this society, ranging from gemologists to art objects to machinery and equipment and so on. You are interested in the machinery and equipment specialists and those who do significant medical work. Ask them what percentage of their work is health care and how much they do.

However, there are a goodly number of individuals in the marketplace who are not ASA credentialed but who do an excellent job. Clearly, the designation does not mean you will get a good appraisal, but it is one indication that the person has gone to the trouble of getting the appropriate education on the process of appraising equipment and hopefully adheres to the professional standards set by the American Society of Appraisers. Sometimes a bank or an investor might require certification (*and they will not accept an appraisal by just anyone*) based on a recognized appraisal professional society and performed by a credentialed equipment appraiser.

Last, get references from your colleagues on who they have used and who seems to be servicing health care organizations well.

EQUIPMENT "DESK" APPRAISALS

When you need furnishings and equipment appraisals, a good bet often is to have an equipment appraiser do a *desk appraisal*. It costs less than a "standard" appraisal, which requires a first-hand visit to look over the equipment. If you know it to be in working order and you do not need the appraisal for a lender, you can save the cost of travel time and inventorying time on the appraisal and ask for a desk appraisal.

❖ **Hint**

(*This type of appraisal is not often acceptable to a bank because the appraiser has not seen the equipment and is merely checking the equipment market for prices of average equipment with the same specifications and age.*) The cost of this for an average physician practice should be 25 or 30 percent less than for that of an appraisal requiring an on-site evaluation of the equipment and furnishings. If a desk appraisal will suffice for your needs, do it.

The cost of any equipment appraisal will depend on the difficulty associated with finding market sales on the equipment. I try to gauge how much I charge by the special nature of the clinic or practice. General practices are relatively straightforward. A clinic that provides other specialty types of services involves equipment that is less abundant with harder-to-find transactions. Again, that involves calling around and seeing what the same equipment has sold for recently. Once sales are located, appraisers may need to perform a PSA to determine how your equipment compares with that which has sold to come up with an estimate of value.

❖ **Hint**

A ballpark tool for estimating what a "standard" (on-site) equipment appraisal will cost for a given practice is to multiply the square footage of the practice by 50 cents. So, if you have a 3,000-square-foot office, the approximate cost for an equipment appraisal would be $1,500. Depending on the type of practice, it could certainly be more or less, but 50 cents per square foot is a good planning figure. If there are multiple sites in an appraisal project, it is common to provide a discount on the market research because although the number of a specific type of thing may be 50, you only have to do the research once and then apply that to the same items . . . assuming they are all generally in the same condition.

When shopping for equipment appraisers, firms with appraisers who are ASA members with the American Society of Appraisers are going to be a safer bet. They follow a professional set of standards, USAP, that is acknowledged by Medicare. As discussed elsewhere, many individuals call themselves appraisers but have literally no or little professional background in the discipline. When you use them, understand what you are getting. Also, they do not tend to be any less expensive than ASA Machinery and Equipment (M&E) appraisers. That leaves little reason to use others—with one exception. Sometimes, equipment may be so technically difficult to assess that you really need someone who is full-time in that particular industry (i.e., linear accelerators or simulators).

GETTING NEW COST DATA FROM EQUIPMENT MANUFACTURERS

Manufacturers can be helpful in determining what equipment costs new. You cannot use these values because you are obviously looking for the values of used pieces of equipment, but the new price data from the manufacturer will provide a valuable benchmark for gauging the validity of the information you get from used equipment vendors.

When you call the manufacturers, ask for "customer service." Usually, these people can tell you what something new costs or about the replacement equipment for the one that you are trying to find out about. Also, ask them how long the particular model that you inquired about has been made. If you have the model number or designation, this will usually be enough.

❖ **Hint**

If the equipment is no longer being made and has been out of production for five years, generally there will no longer be technical support or parts available from the manufacturer. Although you may still be able to find third-party biomedical people who will work on it, be aware that there will be growing difficulty in locating parts and that the value of such a piece of equipment is approaching "junk." (There are exceptions to this, but as a general rule, items that are out of production have a limited remaining life and limited value. In my opinion, 5 percent of new cost is probably all you should pay.) But do not forget to check the market!

When you are using information from a manufacturer representative, it is important to keep in mind that any costs do not include the (depreciated) transportation, installation, taxes, and education costs (of the staff to use the equipment). These are legitimate costs and need to be added to the used equipment market values.

In some cases, customer service representatives can refer you to company technicians or field representatives who can provide you with what they are seeing in the fair market values of equipment of specific types and ages.

In summary, manufacturers are not the best source of information, but they can usually tell you if something that their company makes is still reasonably usable and how long a given model has been in production (or how long it has been out of production) and what models have superseded it.

Because most physician practices use equipment for many, many years (the estimated useful life tables have no meaning in physician offices), it is worth repeating here that most models of medical equipment can be supported by parts and service for five to seven years after the model has been discontinued. If you learn from a company that a piece of equipment, say, a vision testing machine, has been out of production for 15 years, it is worth next to nothing (or may be less because of the cost to have it moved out) because it will die soon and cannot be supported by parts. You might be able to find a local biomedical company to try to service it, but formal manufacturer-level service is not available.

GETTING DATA FROM USED EQUIPMENT VENDORS

If you know of area used equipment vendors of different types, you can certainly call them to see if you can pry loose some value information. You will sometimes run into resistance, as with the rent brokers or the business brokers, because they sometimes do not want to spend (in their view, "waste") time assisting you.

❖ Hint

If you find this is the case, just call back later and say you are doing some price comparisons on used equipment and may be in the market to buy (whatever it is you are trying to find a value for) and thought they might be able to help. They will often ask if you are looking to buy something. You can answer however you prefer, but I usually say something like, "No, I am trying to find the market values on some types of used equipment. I appraise equipment periodically and often run into those interested in selling or buying it. Today, I am trying to locate sales. I would be glad to let you know of opportunities I think you'd be interested in—if you would be interested in being of help to me on this." Now they have a reason to assist you. It is one form of networking, and it is one way to set up symbiotic relationship with vendors.

Always ask first if the client would like to have you share the fact that he or she is in the market regarding a piece of equipment with potentially interested parties that might like to buy (or sell).

❖ Hint

To share such information without the express permission of the client could compromise negotiations and also jeopardizes your position with them. Do not ever compromise the confidentiality of a client . . . any more than you would release information on a patient.

CHAPTER 5

Valuation of Leases

A SHORT FAMILIARIZATION WITH THE ISSUES

Why concern yourself with valuing leases? There are two answers. The first is that from a business perspective, if you are thinking about buying a practice, you will probably want to keep the same location. To do that, you have to somehow switch places with the current lessor/owner or with the lessee/renter. How you approach the issue of what you pay for a new lease or assume from an existing lessee is discussed here. The objective is to pay fair market value by determining what the standard is in the market at the time.

Medical Office Space

The second issue to concern yourself with relates to the antikickback statutes. If you represent a hospital considering leasing space to physicians (or for that matter leasing space from physician property owners or subleasing space from physicians), make sure that you avoid the potential problems of red flags for inducements of referrals. You need to not only look at what you determine for a value of the practice or clinic but how you structure lease arrangements. The transaction needs to be an "arms-length" transaction.

Terms, Terms, Terms

You must look at the "terms of the lease," which means the (present) value of the lease terms: the interest rate at which you will pay/sell the practice, and the term of the lease. If a hospital leases an office, medical equipment, or anything else from a physician at terms that collectively result in lower than the then-current market rates, you are playing with the same antikickback and inducement for referrals issues discussed earlier.

What Is Included in the Rent?

Also, you should concern yourself with what type of lease you are offering—is it a triple net (NNN) lease, in which the lessee pays for everything including taxes and insurance, or is it something else? What is included in the lease or rent charges? Housekeeping? Are the medical waste hauler charges included in the lease? The telephone system? What? In summary, is the lease reasonable with respect to the market, and if not, how is that addressed in the lease payment?

What Is the Market as It Relates to Leased Space

The nitty gritty of the situation is that you must identify appropriate lease terms for the *area* (i.e., what is medical space being leased for? and what are the prevalent fair market terms?). If you are leasing medical office space, you need to compare several things in the *immediate* vicinity. Immediate is somewhat subjective, but in real estate, you cannot go 10 miles away to pull "comps." Most of your comparable transactions should be within a half-mile or mile. Sometimes, medical office space is less common, and you must expand the radius more.

Look at the following aspects of the lease. There may be more, but in the least, consider the following:

1. Cost per square foot (per year or per month—it is done both ways)
2. Escalation rates in lease increases
3. Expenses included in the lease amounts (e.g., utilities, housekeeping, waste removal, taxes, maintenance)
4. Other special benefits or below-market advantages (e.g., free rent for specified periods of time, parking space allotment)

Equipment

If equipment is being leased by hospitals to physicians, the same concepts hold. The terms of the agreements should reflect the current market and locale. The interest rates should be adequately researched and compared to develop fair market rates.

Alternatively, if the physician is leasing hard assets of his or her practice to a hospital (I do not see this too much), make sure that the rates are market rates. . . . What is being paid?

If the present value of the lease agreement to the lessor is less (coming from the physician-payer) than the current market rates, you may be cited for inducing referrals because you are offering something at a discounted rate to a physician. (If the physician is not the type to refer patients, then it may be a superfluous point because there are no referrals for Medicare to get excited about.)

CHAPTER 6

The Appraisal Report

FORM AND LENGTH

The form, length, and content of the appraisal depend on the purpose of the appraisal as well as on the audience of the report. In some cases, the report format is mandated or heavily influenced by law or convention. In other cases, the scope of the written report is largely or totally a matter of client preference.

Letter Report

Usually letter reports are only one or two pages outlining the assignment, the steps taken, the approaches used, and the conclusion. You are not likely to have occasion to see one of these in physician practice appraisals unless someone is providing you a cursory opinion based on general market conditions.

Long Letter Report

The long letter report is a more detailed (longer) letter outlining the detail and information sources used. This format provides specific numbers such as earnings, capitalization rates, and asset values used in the various approaches. It may include a few supporting tables.

Complete Formal Appraisal Report

The complete formal appraisal report could run from 15 pages to more than 100 pages, depending on the purpose of the report, how complex the appraisal was, and how great the need for a comprehensive and documented report, such as may be the case with a lender requirement.

CHARACTERISTICS OF A GOOD REPORT

What You Should Be Able to Understand from an Appraisal Report

1. Description of the assignment
   a. Who was retained by whom to do the appraisal
   b. What was the "applicable standard of value"
   c. Definition of property being appraised
   d. Purpose or purposes of the appraisal
2. Steps taken to carry it out
   a. Discussion of valuation approaches
   b. Description of the procedure, data, and results for each approach used
   c. Relative weight to be accorded to various approaches
   d. Premiums and/or discounts
3. Conclusion reached
4. Logical flow of data and rationale that led to and supported the conclusion

Report Should be Replicable

A major earmark of a quality appraisal report is that it should be replicable. This means that a second appraiser, following the assumptions and data sources provided in the report, should be able to come up with the same conclusions. If this is not the case, the person preparing the report has not provided enough clarity and "chicken tracks" back to the sources of data. This is an important test, so do not accept any "fuzzy logic." If you are the one preparing the appraisal, say what you are doing *and* why you chose to do it. You must explain your logic at every turn.

Report Should be Internally Consistent

There should be no inconsistencies in a report; no contradictions. If you find some in a report you receive, point them out at once. If a mistake is included in an important calculation, the implications could be disastrous if a transaction was based on the erroneous appraisal. (Just like in hospital bills, mistakes are occasionally made in appraisals, too.)

❖ Hint

When you receive an appraisal report, don't just go to the cover page where the value is listed to get the bottom line. Read through it, or have one of your more financially attuned colleagues or subordinates do it to check things over, especially if the appraiser is not a specialist in health care.

ACQUISITION SELECTION CRITERIA FOR PRACTICES

Physicians who are considering the sale of their practice to an area health care provider need to find out what is of interest in the market. Today, primary care practices are the most sought after practices because more and more health care procedures and care are being pushed to primary care physicians as a means to decrease higher specialist fees.

Further, primary care physicians are the ones who are the "gatekeepers" to the health care system and . . . who have the best ability to control the expenditure of health care dollars.

Types of Practices

So what are the purchasers of practices looking at? Family practices only? Strategic specialties? The answer is going to depend on the situation. Aside from having a strong primary care base, appropriate types and numbers of specialists will be important to round out the ability to service managed care contracts. The more prospective buyers have to go to other organizations to provide services, the less of the health care dollar they will be able to keep.

Geographics

What is the *Physician Referral Base Development Plan* of the hospital or other health care system/organization that is being considered as a potential purchaser? How is the referral base plan tied to the acquisition phase? To the overall corporate strategic plan? As a seller you may not be able to get a clear picture and will have to go on actions. If you are the buyer, certainly your physician referral base development program needs to be among the central issues of your long-range strategic plan.

Site Criteria

Site criteria for the practice/clinic operation is a central issue. What is buyers' health care delivery system access strategy? Do they want to control the system by using family practice gatekeepers? If you do not know their "formal" position on these issues, you may have an idea from what has been going on around you.

Financial Considerations

What terms are the sellers requiring (i.e., seller carryback, availability of funding, lender requirements, and loan to value limits)? What flexibility is there on the buyers' side or the sellers' side in financing the acquisition or sale? Do the price and/or the terms preclude the sale due to fair market value issues? The more flexibility and creativity you have on terms, whether you are a buyer or a seller, the greater success you will have.

Practice Performance Characteristics

As a buyer, are you generally willing to purchase a poorly performing practice with the expectation of increasing its profitability and patient mix or are you just interested in acquiring top practices? Are you willing to buy practices in lower socioeconomic areas because you think that under health care reform, everyone will be paying the same levels? Sometimes, this type of strategy works quite well. If (and it is a big "if") there is a national health insurance program that pays the same for all patients, whether hospital patients or clinic patients, the lower socioeconomic area practices will be more attractive than they currently are.

Our opinion is that current lower socioeconomic area practices will not likely ever be as attractive from an acquisition standpoint if capitation happens on an individual basis. Lower socioeconomic patients tend to be less compliant, have more health problems and a higher mortality rate, and basically cost more to care for. This means that they will hurt providers under a scenario in which a set amount is paid for a given population with a set payment.

Alternatively, if the form of capitation is based on a per-procedure basis, then lower socioeconomic area patients may be a source of more business and greater revenue because their use tends to be higher according to some sources. The key will be the negotiated capitated procedure rates.

Physician Characteristics

Are buyers acquiring practices of physicians who are not optimal case managers and employing them? If you are a physician and want to be employed, think about how well you use resources in the course of treating patients. There is no way you will be offered a position if you do poorly in this area.

COST OF A PHYSICIAN PRACTICE APPRAISAL

Depending on the situation, a basic physician practice appraisal price will vary from about $3,500 to $6,000 or more. I recently spoke to an appraiser on the East Coast who was charging $20,000 for a practice appraisal . . . which sounded like he was trying to make a career out of the project. I have a hard time imagining that, but it speaks to the merit of getting bids from professionally credentialed appraisers for the work you have done.

Mine tend to hover closer to the $4,000 mark because we don't try to provide the extensive (and often rather unnecessary) local health care marketplace background and history of the practice that most hospitals already know about.

In some instances, when a third party or lender is involved, thorough background research is necessary, however, requiring the higher expense. In appraisals that meet the IRS 59-60 ruling, a discussion of the practice history and the immediate area health care marketplace is important to comply with the regulations. See Appendix C for a complete discussion of these requirements.

COST OF EQUIPMENT APPRAISALS

Hint

The equipment appraisal portion of an appraisal will hover around an additional 50 cents per square foot of space, depending on the specialty and the size of the project. If the project is a large one, the price should go down from the above figure. Also, if you ask for an equipment appraisal and there are many similar or same pieces of equipment, the appraiser will have less research to do, so he or she should give you a break on that. Do not be afraid to ask for it. You should get it.

Although the above range represents what you will see most often, there really are no standardized fees for equipment appraisals, and many appraisers who perform them will basically charge what they think the client will pay.

Many appraisers charge $250 or $500 per piece of equipment as a minimum. That may be appropriate for an uncommon piece of equipment in which there is some difficulty in trying to come up with a legitimate fair market value. I have personally spent, on many occasions, the better part of a day (five to eight hours) trying to track down values for one piece of equipment. In that case, $250 to $300 or more is not unrealistic.

Further, most of the time an appraiser spends on an appraisal project is on the minority of the equipment. The 80–20 rule applies again. "Eighty percent of the time is spent on 20 percent of the equipment." That 20 percent also usually involves the higher priced items (not the chairs and desks and copiers).

When I inventory equipment and furnishings for a standard general practice office, for example, I end up with eight or so single-spaced pages of equipment, and there are about 250 items to value. The standard charge ranges from 75 to 85 cents per square foot of the leased space. My fees for existing clients are also discounted significantly by at least 20 percent, so that on a project in which there was 6,000 square feet, I might charge 50 to 60 cents per square foot, depending on the type of practice. What you will find is that the price will go down with the volume of work associated.

There is a fair amount of negotiability in rates for equipment appraisals, and although some may try to charge $500 to provide a fair market value and a liquidation value for a single piece of equipment, the price for values on an entire physician's office may not be more than two or three times the $500. There does not seem to be an industry standard on pricing, so it pays to shop. If I dare to generalize, most equipment appraisers charge $100 to $150 per hour.

If you need an equipment appraisal for a free-standing imaging service with CTs and magnetic resonance imagings (MRIs), etc., you will likely pay between $3,500 and $5,000 for an appraisal of all the equipment, fixtures, furnishings, and leasehold improvements.

Hint

Tell the equipment appraiser that you are obtaining bids (you should anyway!) and that will tend to help keep the price down. (Also, see discussion on Desk Appraisals.)

WORKING WITH APPRAISERS

What Are the Appraisal Designations and What Do They Mean?

I will preface my comments here by saying that I am not going to provide a full description of what individuals with this designation can do. I will only briefly mention what they do and why that may have meaning for you as a health care executive or physician. I also have several biases that I will disclose now.

I believe that you need to use firms that employ individuals with professional credentials in appraisal *and* with demonstrable experience in health care. Individuals who call themselves valuation "consultants" should be avoided. Knowledge and experience in business valuation in the context of the appraisal profession are absolutely vital. You do not know what you are getting if the individual is a consultant. There are no standards or requirements to be a consultant. (Half the unemployed people out there today call themselves consultants.)

What about CPAs?

Perhaps a consultant you are considering has worked in health care and is a CPA. Would you consider that person qualified to meet your appraisal needs? No, is the answer. Valuation and appraisal science is a discipline for which there is a body of knowledge and for which there are subspecialists. Certainly, health care experience is extremely valuable, and accounting is useful, but debits and credits have little to do with arriving at accurate market values.

Aside from the technical aspects of approaching an appraisal assignment, there are the regulatory concerns. The OIG and Medicare know how to analyze professional reports, and they know when they spot something that does not follow the methodologies and approaches. The IRS clearly knows when they see an appraisal whether it meets the various requirements that they have. The last thing you want to do is to find yourself in trouble with the federal government or in a litigation case with an amateur appraiser testifying on your behalf.

Some CPAs can do a good job of appraising—if they have good appraisal background or work with a valuation firm. Many CPAs go on to get an ASA business valuation designation if they plan on regularly doing business valuation. (Just remember not to rely on someone with an accounting CPA certificate for market value information.)

You do not have to settle for amateurs. Get good help. It is out there. Many of the big accounting firms have appraisal departments. If you use one of them, ask. Similarly, if they have health care departments as well, there is a good chance you will find qualified people there. Just because they are affiliates of a major accounting network, I wouldn't avoid asking them why they think they are qualified to truly appraise in the health care field. Remember, we are not talking about accounting, audits, or reimbursement assistance here—what their claim to fame is. Call around some more, if just to solicit bids to keep everyone on his or her toes and quoting competitively—and let everyone know you are gathering bids.

My smaller specialist firm recently bid $7,500 on a project for an Idaho hospital that belonged to a national chain. I bid less than half the price of what their "big four" firm did ($20,000). The chain's corporate attorneys liked the comfort of the big name and wanted to pay 60 percent more for that privilege—so the facility paid high above a competitive rate.

MAI Designation

"MAI" stands for Member-Appraisal Institute from the Appraisal Institute (Chicago, IL) and is the premier appraisal designation in real estate appraisal. Their heavy orientation is real estate, and they work in both commercial real estate and residential areas. Some MAIs do business valuation as well.

From an appraisal standpoint, the training of an MAI is second to none. By law, MAIs may appraise anything, but, of course, you should use one able to demonstrate significant experience in health care and business valuation.

ASA Designation

ASA stands for Accredited Senior Appraiser with the American Society of Appraisers. Within the American Society of Appraisers, you can find those who are members with the AM designation or those who are accredited senior members, ASAs. There is a great variety of specialties and subspecialties with this group, ranging from those who specialize in appraising jewelry, construction equipment, medical equipment, standard business valuations, etc.

More than the MAI category, individuals with the ASA designation tend to do more business valuations (what a physician practice appraisal is). This is probably the first place to look for a physician practice appraiser. ASAs specializing in business valuation do many professional practices whether they are attorney practices, dental practices, consulting practices, or physician practices. Try to find a firm that specializes in physician practices or health care. ASAs are also your best source for equipment appraisals.

SRPA Designation

An individual with an SRPA (Senior Real Property Analyst) received his or her designation from a now-extinct organization called the Society for Real Estate Appraisers, which merged with the American Institute for Real Estate Appraisers to become The Appraisal Institute. SRPAs tended to be counterparts to an MAI. They dealt with commercial properties more than residential properties and also had training to do business valuations. They are not as well regarded as MAIs but may be able to do a business valuation.

RM and SRA Designations

RM and SRA designations are professional residential appraisers and would not have a clue as to how to approach a business valuation. They may be able to provide you with a survey on leases or rents in an area, however. Although their focus is residential, if you are located in a less populated area, chances are that you will not find an MAI-, SRPA-, or ASA-designated individual. One of these designated professionals could, however, do a survey of medical space and tell you the fair market rent for an office that you are considering renting.

Other Designations

There are other designations from less known organizations. Some of them may have experience and provide a good quality service, but they are not associated with the premier professional organizations. They tend to have lesser requirements for membership.

State Licensed Appraisers

State licensed appraisers are individuals who have taken a real estate appraiser test given by the state they reside in and have taken a number of courses but who are nearly 100 percent focused on real estate. As with the RM and the SRA designation, they may be used for a local real estate appraisal or a rent study.

Valuation Software

This brings me to another related subject. You may have noticed that there are several valuation software tools on the market. What is happening is that many CPAs and consultants buy them to use if they are asked for a business valuation for a practice. These software packages miss many aspects of what appraisals include and provide no real ability to assess the nature of the practice in its market and how that has an effect on value. In fact, I recently heard of one lawsuit against a CPA in Florida who rendered an appraisal that was no more than a software valuation analysis.

The client suffered because of poor advice and went to court for a remedy. So be careful and ask if the appraising individual uses a "canned software valuation program" (I am going to avoid listing the names for my own legal benefit). Just be aware that those are in the marketplace, and although they may be considered to be a tool by some, they cannot be relied on to render any type of quality estimate of value in my opinion. So . . . garbage in—garbage out.

PROFESSIONAL FEES FOR APPRAISALS

Common Practice

Most appraisal firms base their fees on the amount of time that the engagement will require for one or several members of the staff plus out-of-pocket expenses. They usually quote an hourly or daily billing rate with an amount not-to-exceed. The range for business valuation is about $125 to $175 per hour. After 1996, increase that by a few percent a year.

Difficult Estimates

For difficult-to-estimate assignments, it is risky to quote flat fees and often even an amount not-to-exceed. Some firms may only be willing to quote an hourly rate. If you insist on a flat fee, it will probably be a big one, especially if the appraisal office is busy. A smaller office is more often willing to take the chance on working at considerably below the regular rate just to get the business. Busy appraisers are just like busy physicians. They will not accept particularly low paying managed care contracts if they have plenty of better paying insurers.

Well-Defined Assignments with Sufficient Information

Most appraisers are willing to commit to a fixed fee and out-of-pocket expenses.

Court Testimony or Arbitration

An appraiser may quote separately for the basic appraisal, the trial preparation, depositions, and court time on an hourly or daily basis. Flat fees for testifying are not appropriate for this type of work.

HELPFUL INFORMATION FOR QUOTING AN ESTIMATE AND SCHEDULING AN APPRAISAL ASSIGNMENT

1. Specific practice type
2. Location of operation
3. Form of organization (corporation, subchapter S corporation, general or limited partnerships, sole proprietorships)
4. Purpose of appraisal
5. Interest to be valued
6. Applicable valuation date(s)
7. Status of financial statements (audited, reviewed, externally compiled, tax returns only, records "in a shoe box," and whether on cash or accrual basis)
8. Any subsidiaries or financial interest in other companies
9. Annual revenues
10. Annual profits
11. Approximate book value
12. Form and extent of appraisal report desired
13. Desired schedule

YOUR PROFESSIONAL SERVICES AGREEMENT WITH (OR AS) AN APPRAISER

The agreement should cover the definition of the valuation or appraisal assignment. The cover letter to the agreement should, in the least, address the following concerns:

1. *What property is to be valued?* You need to be as specific as possible to leave no room for doubt about the specific item/practice that you are valuing.
2. *What is the purpose of the valuation?* Because the purpose of the appraisal can sometimes have an effect on the methods used or regulations for a certain type of appraisal, the purpose needs to be stated in the agreement.
3. *Effective date of the valuation.* An appraisal is technically only good for one given date. Although individuals use appraisals that were performed even a year or so earlier, the numbers you provide as an appraiser are only good for one date. That is because you have tied the numbers to accounts and liabilities as of a given date. After that date has passed, the value is no longer applicable.
4. *What is the standard of value used in the report?* You need to state whether you are being asked to provide a fair market value appraisal, a fair market value in-use appraisal on equipment, liquidation values, insurance replacement values, etc. It needs to be plainly stated. Failure to do so can be embarrassing in the least and catastrophic in some situations.
5. *Scope of the appraisal.* It is obviously important to clarify the scope of the appraisal. Appraisers are often asked to provide "qualified" appraisals or limited review appraisals, which differ in cost and scope from a regular appraisal. Similarly, valuation experts are sometimes asked to just provide an "off-the-cuff" opinion of value, which is still technically an appraisal. (It may not be a very good one, but it constitutes an appraisal as viewed by the Appraisal Institute and the American Society of Appraisers.) The bottom line is to make sure that both the client and the appraiser know exactly what is being asked for and state it in the agreement.
6. *Time frame.* Individuals asking for appraisals are always in a hurry. It never seems to fail. Often, there is pressure involved for buyers and sellers, so it is important if you are appraising a practice or clinic to not box yourself in to an impossible turnaround time. Usually, I get three to four weeks to turnaround a standard appraisal. I have done "limited" practice appraisals in two days, though, in "emergencies." State the anticipated turnaround time, and give an outside date by which it will most certainly be done.
7. *Professional fees and any other costs.* Obviously, another area that is very important is to clarify the compensation for the report. Standard procedure is to request and get one-half of the anticipated project fee in advance. I have recently found that the best practice when turning in the appraisal is to send it COD for the balance. Notify the client when the appraisal has been sent out and to have a check ready for the balance when the courier arrives. With all but the best clients, this is the only way I will bill. There is something particularly difficult about getting paid for a report once the client has it.

IF THERE ARE CHANGES TO THE PROJECT

The engagement document should be signed by the appraiser and the client and supplemented by written addenda if any of the factors are modified during the course of the project.

SOME APPRAISAL TERMS AND CONCEPTS

Appraisal: An estimate or opinion of value. *Appraisal* is the term that is used for opinions of value when valuing real property.

Valuation: An estimate of value but a term that tends to be used more in connection with valuing businesses and professional practices.

Value: The concept of value is relative to the individual and his or her relationship with the object concerned. In some cases, the value of a business or practice is worth much more to one person than the next. The following types of value are just some of the many that you may encounter.

- ***Present Value***—This is the value of the total amount that a series of future payments is worth now. In other words, present value refers to value in the present for a stream of revenue or series of payments in the future as well as terminal interests. Present value is the result of the discounted future earnings calculation in valuation (which only has two variables) in which

$$PV = \frac{\text{Earnings}}{(1+R)^i}$$

where R = required rate of return
i = number of periods

- ***Future Value***—The future value or cash balance that you want to attain after the last payment is made.

Discount Rate: The annual rate of return on investment in the purchase of a business or practice when used to discount an income stream back to present value in a DCF method.

Goodwill: There are probably more definitions for the concept of goodwill than any other valuation-related term. For your purposes, however, I will define it as *the difference* *between an established successful business and one that has yet to establish itself and achieve success.*

Going Concern: Going concern refers to an operating functional business organization. Its importance in valuation is that a going concern and its assets are worth far more in the context of an income-generating basis than as standalone tangible assets. Further, a going concern usually carries "goodwill" with it.

Going Concern Value: The concept of going concern value is a not a standard of value but speaks to the status of that business. It means that the enterprise is being valued as an operating entity. Also, in most cases, the phrase *going concern value* is used to mean the total value of the entity as a going concern.

Net Tangible Asset Value: The current value of the net assets of a practice. It involves restating all the book values of assets and liabilities to their current market value. It is usually synonymous with adjusted book value and tangible asset backing.

Book Value:

1. Value as recorded on the balance sheet
2. Net value of assets less liabilities
3. Synonymous with historical book value

Capitalization Rate: A percentage rate by which a constant income stream is divided to indicate a value. For example, if an income stream of $10,000 were to be capitalized at 25 percent, the calculation would be $10,000/0.25, which equals a capitalized value of $40,000.

Multiple: If the stream of income being capitalized over time is considered a constant stream, the *multiple is the reciprocal of the capitalization rate*. For example, if the appropriate capitalization rate is 20 percent, the equivalent multiple is 5 (1/0.20 = 5). Multiples are often used as rough measures of values against different levels of earnings such as earnings before interest, depreciation, and taxes (EBIDT). Five is a common multiple for many health care businesses including hospitals and clinics.

CHAPTER 7

Appraising Larger Clinics

Appraising larger clinics with multiple numbers of physicians is an entirely different process from appraising smaller physician practices. They are different in the following ways.

SIZE AND SOPHISTICATION

The first difference is the sense that you are valuing a big business enterprise versus a small, excuse the expression, "mom and pop"-level operation. The former is sophisticated, and the latter tends not to be. This has implications for the appraiser because it will have an impact on the ease with which one may obtain good financial and operational information. Larger operations tend to have better data and methods of maintaining it and retrieving it. Small enterprises tend to be somewhat less detail-oriented. That sometimes means a little more work in ferreting out details.

OVERALL APPROACH TO VALUATION

Large clinics tend to be valued more in terms of a standard business approach than are professional practices, whether they are medical practices, legal practices, accounting practices, or other consulting practices. They are two distinct types of valuation. In many respects, larger clinics are easier not only because of their better record keeping but because more standard approaches apply, especially income approaches.

As I have said earlier, there tends to be very little income on the bottom line of physician practices because the available income goes into the owner's income. In terms of the large clinics, there is usually a bottom line after the physicians are paid. In this latter case, then, you have something that you can capitalize and count as income to the business.

Income Approach

It is probably useful to say that you should stick to an income approach in the valuation of a large clinic. Within income approaches, most professionals would agree that the present value of an appropriately developed DCF is the primary method.

In this method, unlike physician practices in which there is a value for the goodwill and a value for the tangible assets, there is but one value here: the value based on the production of a revenue stream.

The tangible and other assets are assumed to be included in the enterprise that generates the income stream. Aside from the real estate, the assets by themselves in these instances tend not be viewed separately. They are part of an in-place activity, the worth of which is the value of the profit generated. So, this is an important consideration. Many deals, if not most, in private industry will also include the real estate. At the level of hospitals and large clinics, it may as well. That is not the case, as much, with practices.

Exhibit 7–1 is an example of a clinic income and expense projection. This model may differ from your approach of how you wish to consider the impact of taxes, depreciation, or working capital and capital expenditures, but for the sake of showing how those elements are presented when included, the above model is offered.

To use the income approach and specifically the DCF analysis, which is the primary form of income valuation, the data must be organized in a usable format. I have done so in Exhibit 7–2 for illustrative purposes.

Spreadsheet Functions

Literally every spreadsheet software program written in the past five years has a relatively sophisticated level of financial functions built in. They all require the same basic

Exhibit 7–1 Sample Clinic Income and Expense Projection

	Year 1	*Year 2*	*Year 3*	*Year 4*	*Year 5*	*Residual*
Business Done						
Dr. A	552,681	591,369	632,764	677,058	724,452	775,164
Dr. B	529,452	566,514	606,170	648,601	694,004	742,584
Dr. C	516,599	552,761	591,454	632,856	677,156	724,557
Dr. D	497,523	532,350	569,614	609,487	652,151	697,802
Total	2,096,255	2,242,994	2,400,002	2,568,002	2,747,763	2,940,107
Collection Percentage	0.95	0.95	0.95	0.96	0.96	0.96
Total Revenues	1,991,442	2,130,844	2,280,002	2,465,282	2,637,852	2,822,503
Expenses						
Staff Salaries	305,123	326,482	349,335	373,789	399,954	427,951
Maintenance & Utilities	25,465	27,248	29,155	31,196	33,379	35,716
Medical Supplies	126,589	135,450	144,932	155,077	165,932	177,548
Office Supplies	38,569	41,269	44,158	47,249	50,556	54,095
Leases	5,600	5,992	6,411	6,860	7,340	7,854
Education, Journals	15,897	17,010	18,200	19,475	20,838	22,296
Insurance	51,354	54,949	58,795	62,911	67,315	72,027
Professional Fees, Med	69,256	74,104	79,291	84,842	90,780	97,135
Professional Fees, Adm	25,894	27,707	29,646	31,721	33,942	36,318
Business Taxes	55,894	59,807	63,993	68,473	73,266	78,394
Communications	26,589	28,450	30,442	32,573	34,853	37,292
Profit Sharing	31,598	33,810	36,177	38,709	41,419	44,318
Employee Benefits	95,026	101,678	108,795	116,411	124,560	133,279
Miscellaneous	26,598	28,460	30,452	32,584	34,865	37,305
Depreciation	17,895	19,148	20,488	21,922	23,457	25,099
Total Expenses	917,347	981,564	1,050,270	1,123,792	1,202,456	1,286,627
Available for Physician Compensation	1,074,095	1,149,280	1,229,732	1,341,490	1,435,396	1,535,875
Physician Compensation						
Dr. A	225,000	238,500	252,810	267,979	284,057	301,101
Dr. B	212,584	225,339	238,859	253,191	268,382	284,485
Dr. C	187,500	198,750	210,675	223,316	236,714	250,917
Dr. D	159,689	169,270	179,427	190,192	201,604	213,700
Total Physician Compensation	784,773	831,859	881,771	934,678	990,757	1,050,203
Net Pretax Income (Debt-Free)	289,322	317,421	347,961	406,818	444,639	485,672
Less:						
Working Capital Additions	5,000	5,000	5,150	5,305	5,464	5,628
Capital Expenditures	12,000	15,000	14,500	20,000	16,000	25,000
Plus:						
Depreciation	19,196	20,348	21,569	22,863	24,235	25,689
Debt-Free Net Cash Flow	291,518	317,769	349,880	404,376	447,410	480,733

Exhibit 7–2 Putting Data Together for Calculation of Present Value

There are several steps. The first is to assemble the data in an orderly manner so that you can perform the analysis. The table below provides one example. You may use a business calculator or a spreadsheet Present Value function with the data.

CALCULATION OF DISCOUNTED PRESENT VALUE

Determine Base Discount Rate		N	Annual Income (Taken from Spreadsheet)	Apply the Following Discount Rate per the Build-Up Method on the Left
0.085	Year One	1	$291,518	0.18
plus Risk	Year Two	2	$317,770	0.18
Modifier of	Year Three	3	$349,879	0.18
0.0975	Year Four	4	$404,374	0.18
Blended	Year Five	5	$447,410	0.18
Rate				
0.18				

Calculation of DCF for Period (Terminal Value or Residual) after 5 Years

Base Discount Rate		N	Income	Rate	
0.085					
Risk	Given:	5	$480,773	0.18	This discount factor
Modifier					may be raised or
0.0975					lowered based on
Blended			($480,773/0.18)		assessment of risk
Rate					in five years.
0.18					
	then		determine Present Value for Sixth Year and Beyond		
		5	$2,670,961	0.18	

DETERMINING PRESENT VALUE WITH A BUSINESS CALCULATOR (ONE WITH PRESENT VALUE FUNCTIONS)

Computing the present values for the above individual years is a simple process. A common and inexpensive business calculator, the Texas Instruments Business Analyst II, works as follows for the first year:

	N	Future Value	*%i*
Year One	1	$291,518	0.18

(Make sure you are in the financial mode first)

Enter: 291518	The amount listed as net profit in the first year
Enter: *FV*	The symbol for future value (you are solving for the present value of this number)
Enter: 1	You are solving for the amount at the end of the first year, so enter 1
Enter: *N*	*N* is the symbol for the number of periods
Enter: 18	Because you are using 18 as the built-up discount factor in the *PV* calculation, enter it here
Enter: *%I*	This is the symbol for the percentage interest on your interest rate or discount factor
Enter: 2nd	This key in the upper-leftmost corner of the key pad is required to activate the time-value keys
Enter: *PV*	Enter *PV* next to get the present value of the amount entered at the beginning of this process

The present value is then displayed as 247049.15. This is the present value of $291,518, discounted by 18 percent over the period of a year.

Repeat this process for each of the remaining five years. Add them together for the total present value of those five income streams collectively.

continues

Exhibit 7–2 continued

DETERMINING THE TERMINAL VALUE

It is important to now calculate the value of the terminal or residual value for income past the five-year mark so that you can add this to the present value of the first five years. This is sometimes referred to as terminal value or value "in perpetuity."

Step one: Capitalize the value of the residual net profit by the discount factor that you think is most appropriate. Often, if you think that business risk will be less for the clinic as a more mature enterprise, you can reduce the discount factor by some factor, say, about 5.

Capitalize a dollar amount by dividing the discount factor into it as above.

Step two: Determine the present value of the residual amount just the same as with each of the first five years.

Note the following:

Enter: 2670961	
Enter: *FV*	
Enter: 5	Use the *N* factor of 5 for residual calculations
Enter: *N*	
Enter: 18	For the sake of the example, we are also using 18% for the terminal value calculation.
Enter: *%I*	
Enter: 2nd	
Enter: *PV*	

The present value is then displayed as 1167501.7. This is the present value of $2,670,961, discounted by 18 percent over a five-year period.

FINAL STEP: SUM THE TWO VALUES (THE TOTAL OF PRESENT VALUES FOR THE FIRST FIVE YEARS AND THE PRESENT VALUE OF THE RESIDUAL AMOUNT)

Sum of *PV* first five years	$247,049
PV of residual income	$1,167,502
Total Present Value of Clinic	$1,414,551

HP-12C

If you are using a more business-oriented calculator such as the HP-12C, the sequences for these calculators are quite similar. The HP-12C's logic compared with the present-value calculation of the residual value by the Texas Instruments calculator is as follows:

(Start by clearing all the data in memory)
Enter: 2670961
Enter: *FV*
Enter: 18
Enter: *i*
Enter: 5
Enter: *n*
Enter: *PV*

The present value readout will appear: 1,167,501.67.

input data and have roughly the same format for developing a present value. To use them, merely refer to the functions portion of the manual coming with the software to learn the specific formula and sequence of inputting the cell data.

For example, in Excel the formula used for the present value of a set of terms is **PV (rate, nper, pmt, fv, type)**, where **rate** means the spreadsheet cell with the interest or discount rate, **nper** refers to the number of periods (how many times payment is made—usually monthly or yearly), **pmt** refers to the spreadsheet cell with the amount of a regular payment in an annuity you are anticipating (if not using the pmt, you would enter the spreadsheet cell with the future value of the amount), and **fv** refers to the anticipated future value of the amount in question; next, for **type** (optional) enter a "0" if the payment is to be received at the beginning of the period or a "1" if the payment is to be received at the end.

Calculating the Algebraic Formula for Present Value

The example you read about early in the book in the Income Approach discussion provided a good basis for calculating the present value "from scratch." There are additional examples of this important tool later in Appendix B.

Market Approach

Market data should certainly be obtained as well—if there is ample market data. One form of market data to use in publicly traded securities is the P/E ratio.

Price/Earnings Ratio

The P/E comparison method of developing a capitalization rate involves identifying transactions (sales) of entities with similar income streams (of comparable medical organizations). The P/E ratios that are found in the daily newspapers represent the current market price of a given (share of) stock divided by the latest reported 12 months of earnings per share. (In the public market, these ratios are based on after-tax earnings.)

If you determine, for example, that most similar stocks are selling between four and six times their latest 12 months' earnings, you have an indication of what to use for a ballpark value. Then focus on the subject organization's characteristics relative to the comparative companies to determine how the subject compares by the financial, operations, and market characteristics that you can identify. It is advisable that more than one comparison be used (and more appropriately, several).

Another important factor to keep in mind is that you derive a different applicable capitalization rate or multiple from the public market for each measure of earning power considered in the subject company. Capitalization rates derived from transaction data should be based on the same form or method used to determine the subject's earning power. (*Compare apples with apples.*)

To summarize, then, the P/E method within the market approach uses multiples of income based on the current market price of similar company stocks.

The multiples gleaned from the selection of a highly comparable selection of companies are applied to the earnings (EBDIT) of the subject organization for an indication of value.

If, for example, your review of P/E ratios and subsequent work in determining how the subject compares with the comparable companies suggested that an appropriate multiple of cash flow would be 4.5, then you would multiply times the clinic income (after physician compensation is deducted) and deduct depreciation, interest expense, and lease/rent expense. If the final figure is \$357,000, then the multiple would merely be applied as follows:

$$\text{P/E method value } \frac{\$357{,}000 \times 4.5}{\$1{,}606{,}500}$$

In practice, you will not find a plethora of practices with a P/E ratio for one value in the range of values reviewed. The reason is because of the difficulty in finding something in the stock market that equates to traditional physician practices. It may be helpful, however, in larger group practices and clinics.

Direct Sales Comparisons

Alternatively, if there are area or regional comparable clinics that have sold, a direct market sales comparison should be made with these. Not unlike the P/E approach, a careful analysis should be made to determine if significant or even noteworthy differences exist that would have an effect on whether the subject clinic is better or worse (worth more or less) than the comparable clinic(s). See the discussion of PSA later in this book.

Cost Approach

Cost Alone—Not a Good Indicator

The cost approach, as discussed elsewhere in this book, has little to do with the market or value in general. The value of a business depends on its financial success or its usefulness in some other way. As can be readily imagined, all businesses that cost the same to build with tangible assets are not necessarily worth the same. One reason may be "location." Although it may cost the same to build a clinic and provide the same equipment and furnishings and fixtures in Tupelo, MS, as it does in Dallas, TX, the practice will be worth more in Dallas 9 out of 10 times.

Cost Approach Means Cost-New Less Depreciation

The cost approach for larger clinics is largely the same as it is for smaller physician practices. You are looking at costs . . . but a special kind of cost: "reproduction-cost-new less accumulated depreciation."

If you are a seller, do not insist to the buyer that it would take \$250,000 to replace what you have . . . so that is "what you must have." Often, I hear physicians say, "It would cost \$_____ to replace this (my) equipment," suggesting that that is what they should get for the equipment. Replacement cost is not how you value tangible assets in the market, rather (in the cost approach) it is reconstruction- or replacement-cost-new *less accumulated depreciation.* "Replacement" value tends to relate more to insurance values and things that depreciate (vs. appreciate).

Adding the Cost of Operations to Estimate Value

Some purchasers also attempt to calculate the operational costs of starting up a practice (payroll and operating expenses) to add to their own estimation of what it would take to replicate a given practice. This approach recognizes the value of "goodwill" in a way that most other approaches do not because it attempts to identify what it takes to replicate the performance of a practice or clinic.

This is not a standard or typical appraisal "cost" approach because it deals with other than the hard costs of facilities, equipment, etc. The time required to break even or achieve a level of market penetration comparable with the subject being appraised will differ exponentially, but a health care professional with an eye toward conservatism should be able to get in the ballpark. As a rough guideline, I suggest that it could take 18 to 30 months to break even and at least several more years to reach the subject's level of penetration.

This type of operating cost analysis is more typically undertaken as a pro forma income approach. (See the sample appraisal in Appendix L on projecting income and expense based on market research.)

Sum of the Fair Market Value of "Selected" Assets for an Adjusted Book Value

Once you have had the medical equipment, fixtures, and furnishings appraised for fair market value in-use, you need to replace the book value numbers in the balance sheet with the newly appraised fair market values. Bring up to date all the receivables and payables.

The simplistic (only two adjustments are provided) adjusted balance sheet in Exhibit 7–3 shows how adjustments are recorded on the balance sheet of an organization.

There is a narrow column between the current cash basis balance sheet and the adjustment column that can be used for providing a key to the adjustment. Explanations can then be provided below.

Clinics Corporation Stock Purchases versus Selected Assets

Are you are buying selected assets or the stock—*the corporation*? Based on what is happening in the market today, practices are less apt to have their liabilities assumed in a purchase. However, large entities are usually purchased through a stock sale, which means buying the assets and assuming the liabilities.

If you were to go by the balance sheet in Exhibit 7–3 and assume the liabilities of the organization, according to the data, the organization is only worth $24,785 (book value)! Unfortunately, because of how some financial statements portray the capital structure, it is seldom an acceptable means for valuing an organization. One of the few exceptions may be when a business is very new with little business activity.

Exhibit 7–3 Bailey Center Clinic Practice, Bailey Center, Minnesota

	June 95		*Adjustments*	*Revised*
CURRENT ASSETS				
Cash	$225.00		$0.00	$225.00
Trade A/R	$0.00	(a.)	$47,656.00	$47,656.00
Bank of Wilkerson	$1,147.78		$0.00	$1,147.78
Bank Tax	$1,144.99		$0.00	$1,144.99
Bank—Trust	$1,400.99		$0.00	$1,400.99
Clinton Bank—Red Wing	$0.00		$0.00	$0.00
Note Receivable Officers	$9,000.00		$0.00	$9,000.00
Inter Co Transfers—Red Wing			$0.00	$0.00
Prepaid Fed Income Tax	$4,880.00		$0.00	$4,880.00
Medical Supplies	$0.00	(b.)	$2,470.00	$2,470.00
Cash-City Bank—Red Wing	$1,820.99		$0.00	$1,820.99
Prepaid Expense	$0.00		$0.00	$0.00
Total Current Assets	$19,619.75		$50,126.00	$69,745.75
FIXED ASSETS				
Improvements	$32,155.94		$0.00	$32,155.94
Vehicles	$43,156.60		$0.00	$43,156.60
Equipment—Bailey Center	$99,257.00		$0.00	$99,257.00
Equipment—Red Wing	$35,120.97		$0.00	$35,120.97
Accumulated Depreciation	($150,634.20)		$0.00	($150,634.20)
Total Fixed Assets	$59,056.31		$0.00	$59,056.31

continues

Exhibit 7–3 continued

	June 95	*Adjustments*	*Revised*
TOTAL ASSETS	*$78,676.06*	*$50,126.00*	*$128,802.06*
CURRENT LIABILITIES			
SIT w/h	$978.03	$0.00	$978.03
FICA & W/H	($2,478.29)	$0.00	($2,478.29)
Note Payable—(Jones) B/A	$14,000.00	$0.00	$14,000.00
Current—Long-Term Debt	$15,770.24	$0.00	$15,770.24
Unemployment		$0.00	$0.00
Total Current Debt	$28,269.98	$0.00	$28,269.98
LONG-TERM DEBT			
N/P—Phillipsburg Computer	$19,242.31	$0.00	$19,242.31
N/P—Bank One	$20,722.35	$0.00	$20,722.35
N/P—Phillipsburg City Hospital	$2,517.15	$0.00	$2,517.15
N/P—Old Kent (Jones)	$10,794.94	$0.00	$10,794.94
Current—Long-Term Debt	($15,770.24)	$0.00	($15,770.24)
Total Long-Term Debt	$37,506.51	$0.00	$37,506.51
TOTAL LIABILITIES	*$65,776.49*	*$0.00*	*$75,013.02*
STOCKHOLDER'S EQUITY			
Common Stock	$21,778.00	$0.00	$21,778.00
Officer's Life Insurance		$0.00	$0.00
Retained Earnings	($16,104.90)	$0.00	$24,784.57
Profit (Loss) to Date	$7,226.47	$0.00	$7,226.47
Total Equity	$12,899.57	$0.00	$53,789.04
TOTAL LIABILITIES & EQUITY	*$78,676.06*		*$128,802.06*

(a.) Adjustment for inclusion of current accounts receivable.
(b.) Adjustment for inclusion of value of current medical supplies.

CHAPTER 8

Negotiations—From the Seller Perspective

BUYING THE PRACTICE AND EMPLOYING THE PHYSICIAN

This was probably the main type of patient base acquisition strategy as the move to capture patient populations began. The acquiring provider bought the tangible and intangible (goodwill, mostly) assets of the practice and employed the physician(s). This was and continues to be attractive to many physicians because of the unknowns in the health care marketplace.

You will most likely be considering selling the practice to the hospital or provider that you work most frequently with. Understand that hospitals have been warned that they must not pay more than fair market value for the practice. If they do, both they and you could find yourselves in trouble with Medicare, the OIG (for Medicare fraud and abuse), and the IRS. Be reasonable and go along with a process of determining fair market value. This book is not about how to get more than what is fair; it is about how to make it worth more, or at least make sure you get what you should.

Very important in this regard are the terms that you agree to. If you require a little or no down payment, offer favorable interest rates, and a longer period for payment, you will make the deal easier to swallow for the buyer. You will also make it easier to get the asking price that you want in contrast to asking for all cash at closing. (More on this later.)

ENTER THE MEDICAL SERVICE ORGANIZATION

After a while, hospitals decided that they could buy the tangible practice assets, perhaps provide a practice management service for a percentage of the practice's gross fee, and still accomplish what their interest was, namely, increasing patient population. These medical service organizations or medical foundations that were subsidiaries or otherwise related to a hospital decided that buying the practice goodwill needlessly tied up hard-to-come-by capital.

The benefits to the physician were that he or she could forget the practice management aspects because the hospital or other health care organizational provider was now performing those tasks. In many instances, the employees of the practice became employees of the hospital or its subsidiary medical service organization (MSO) or medical foundation. The equipment and supplies were purchased from the physician. Those dollars could then be used in other appropriate ways (i.e., retirement funding or other reinvestment).

Medical service organizations were introduced beginning in the mid-1980s to provide physicians with service organizations that handled all the administrative responsibilities associated with clinic practice, leaving physicians to practice medicine. The benefits to those providing the services were that they could (1) make money providing a service, and (2) not have to pay for goodwill, the far larger component in the typical "full acquisition" of physician practices.

The benefits to physicians in signing on with a medical service organization were that those duties that required expertise in negotiating contracts and collections could be provided through service bureaus. A major concern of physicians over the past 10 or more years has been how to cope under an increasingly managed care environment. MSOs answered the need and still permitted physicians to practice as independent practitioners.

Medical foundations were similar to MSOs with the exception that the foundations were tax exempt and had the benefits of that status. For example, medical foundations might be able to accept grants and tax-deductible donations.

The benefits to the hospital or to the other buyer were that they could afford to repeat this type of tangible asset and practice management relationship with many more practices if they did not have to buy practice goodwill. (For most average family practices, goodwill might hover around 30 percent of annual gross patient revenue.) If a practice grosses $400,000, an acquiring provider could save more than $100,000 each time. Further, the acquiring providers need not even employ the physicians because the physician-sellers could still function independently and operate as physician professional corporations (PCs) with the freedom they had known. Additionally, many thought that bringing physicians in as employees would diminish their productivity and create potentially significantly greater malpractice liability problems.

Still other acquirers thought and still think that *paying for goodwill* is less than appropriate in a highly personalized service business such as physician services because "goodwill walks with the physician."

So, in summary, the rewards of ownership of physician practices tend to be viewed by nonphysician-purchasers more in terms of the patients served by the practice and the future anticipated revenues from that "customer base."

Although a practice may gross $300,000, the costs of operating the practice together with salary and perks to the physician-owner usually leave nothing on the bottom line of the practice itself. Unfortunately, hospitals are required to use an approach that bases its determination largely on the income stream and fair market (or "fair market value—in-use" asset value).

SHOPPING THE MARKET—WHY YOU MAY NOT WANT TO PLAY ONE HOSPITAL AGAINST ANOTHER

Let's face it. You have to deal with the individuals whom you have worked with over the years after the "deal is done." It's important that you not dismiss the value of those relationships and how you would feel later about "selling-out" to the "enemy" (another hospital or provider) or even seriously threaten to. Unless the home team (your current hospital) is just out in left field, try to work with them. It is probably true that a competing hospital will be quite interested in working with you and offer you a very good price (sometimes, they commit to a price that will get both of you in trouble if they are not up on the requirements—and there are those), but my experience is that you will feel better about cutting a deal with "your" hospital—if it is a hospital you are selling to.

VALUE IN THE EYE OF THE BEHOLDER—OWNER'S ROSE-COLORED GLASSES

I cannot tell you how many times physicians have come up with their formula of how much they think their practice is worth based on meaningless or totally irrelevant data. One thing you need to keep in mind is that you have an emotional tie to the practice because, in most instances, you built it. You were there when you were tapping your fingers on the desk waiting for patients to show up and when the payments on the equipment came due with not enough cash flow to pay the bills, not to mention the many other types of scenarios over the years. So, for most of you, it is your baby, and because of that, your attachment to it will tend to suggest an inflated value—*not the objective one the rest of the world will use*!

SELLER: CHECK OUT THE MARKET

You are in a market. We all are, in one sense or another, and as such, it is important to get a sense of how you stack up with the competition. If you could step outside your shoes for a moment and identify the strengths and weaknesses of your practice vis-à-vis others, how would it compare? Really? You need to identify what other practices similar to yours are bringing, and you will begin to get an idea of what to start asking.

If you are comfortable about how a practice really stacks up, you will gain a sense of what kind of flexibility you must be prepared to give. If you have only been in practice for a few years and it has not matured, you are not the most prime of acquisitions. Similarly, if a practice is located in a socially disadvantaged area, it will be less desirable because of the likely unattractive mix of third payers. Alternatively, if you have a mature practice that is located in an area of relative affluence with good third-party coverage, guess how you will do.

Sometimes, the potential buyers are such that they will just write you off if you come in with a ridiculous asking price. Other times, if there is fierce competition for area practices, the reaction will be less hostile. Be advised, though, that you still are competing with other practices for sale, and there is most likely a "bottom to the well" that the purchasers can draw from.

WHO SHOULD I SELL IT TO? OTHER PLANNING CONSIDERATIONS

Part of the answer to this question will depend on what you want to do after the sale. Do you want to relocate and go into private practice again? Fewer and fewer physicians are saying "yes" to this question for many of the same reasons that you can readily imagine.

If you want to work for a hospital, the local hospital is often a prime candidate, as you no doubt know. Under health care reform and managed care, everyone is busy building patient and market base. The greater the population you can claim access to, the greater will be your negotiating strength in dealing with managed care companies and the greater the likelihood that you will be around in the future.

You will have to make some personal determination about the nature of the particular hospital as a potential employer and whether you think that you would be happy there. What is the nature of the management and board? Have you found it difficult to relate to their decisions in the past or vice versa? Think long term.

Large specialty clinics are another category of potential buyers. For some physicians, they will be better able to feel good about these organizations working with and for physicians. Accurate or not, you may believe that you can trust them more. Yet another group is the managed care companies themselves: HMOs, PPOs, and the like. What is your orientation? So, who you sell a practice to should be a function of not only how much they are going to give you for a practice or practice assets but what other tangible and intangible things you are looking for. Last, but not least, how flexible are the terms, and how do they fit your tax situation?

APPROACHING THE HOSPITAL

Because hospitals are the most likely of buyers, let's focus the discussion around that scenario. If you know for a fact that the hospital has been buying or intends to be buying practices (or practice assets), inquire preliminarily of the administrator/CEO about interest in your practice. Let him or her know that you are contemplating a change and thought that if you were to place the practice on the market that your relationship suggested that he or she be offered the first chance at making an offer. If the question of price comes up, defer and say that you would prefer to agree to a process by which you both select a qualified appraiser to arrive at a fair market value.

The next strategy in developing a negotiating position with the hospital is to answer for yourself, what do you want as a result of the negotiation and sale? Payment for tangible and intangible goodwill? A job? Cash and the ability to move to Tahiti? If you want to stay in the area and continue to practice where you are but with the security of employment, leaving practice management to someone else, there are two potential options as discussed above—depending on what the hospital is doing and what you want to do.

MOST HOSPITALS WILL BE RECEPTIVE

Because they are generally interested in buying or acquiring practices, most hospitals will respond positively to the suggestion and will relate well to the need for a fair price. Alternatively, some may say that they do not want to pay you for goodwill and would not be amenable to such an arrangement. Some administrators are of the opinion that you cannot pay for goodwill according to the federal government. That's wrong. (At least as of this date.) Goodwill can be paid for, but as I have harped, it needs to be based on a prudent investor's financial (income approach) analysis.

So, if you run into the above comment, you may want to ask for their reference on that as a means to gently educate them. Otherwise, you will have a decision to make based on the best they say they can do. Also, as noted further along in this manual, you may want to consider selling to another physician if not the hospital or another provider such as a group practice.

Assuming again for the moment that negotiations are "on" and that you have an interested buyer, try to stay away from discussing prices at the front end. Try to, instead, mutually agree on a process that will lead to a mutually satisfactory outcome for both sides. If you *focus on interests/outcomes* (not financial demands) and follow a mutually agreed-on step-by-step approach to working through the transaction, it will be a much easier task.

Once you have identified a capable and qualified appraiser who understands the medical marketplace, see if you can obtain agreement that you will use that as the basis from which to determine value. Remember that, by law, the hospital cannot pay more than fair market value or more than a physician (typically) would—in terms of the way the federal government looks at it. So, the best you are going to do is "fair." That is not to say that some hospitals will not try to pay less. (That is why I am suggesting that you get agreement from the hospital to pay the fair market value suggested by the appraisal.) This process is discussed later.

TERMS CAN MAKE ALL THE DIFFERENCE

There once was a wealthy New York businessman whose motto was, "You can name the price if I can name the terms!" His strategy was, of course, to make the prospective seller or buyer happy with the price they select and then develop a set of terms (the length of the payback term and the interest rate) that would translate back to his present-value price. The longer the term and the lower the interest rate, the lower the present value. (All appraisals are done in present-value, pretax, cash equivalents.)

Sometimes, we run into a situation in which one of the parties is locked onto a number. The way you get around that to raise or lower the real value is through structuring the terms.

This approach can also be effectively used to break through stalemated negotiations. Sometimes, it is politically or otherwise important for the other party to have the asking price/number (irregardless of the terms) he or she needs. Surprisingly, many individuals pay too little attention to the importance of terms in identifying the present value of a price. They only look at the total dollars. This is an important concept, and you might be surprised how many physicians will willingly accept the terms as long as they get the price they want.

Remain Independent or Become an Employee

You can, in the least, sell tangible assets, keep your goodwill and become part of an MSO. You will still be on your own, in terms of generating your own income, and theoretically still have your PC, but you will not have the overhead, you will not have to do any management, and you may have the benefit of other services (e.g., a group contract negotiating service) that should be of some significant value.

There are a couple of observations to make before proceeding. Equipment value for a family practice is likely to be less than $50,000. Specialists tend to have more depending on their specialty or subspecialty. Goodwill tends to be worth reasonably more than the equipment value in most cases. Therefore, if you only get paid for equipment, you will probably lose the biggest share of the value.

Alternatively, if by virtue of what you have built (in the practice) you are able to view that as creating something worthy of exchanging for a job, then you may be completely satisfied with such an offer. I am not saying here that you should not accept this. Only that some physicians are paid for goodwill and equipment and are offered a salaried position.

Payment for goodwill and being provided a salaried position is less and less the case because there is some discussion now about what the OIG calls "double dipping" (i.e., being paid for goodwill and also given a job). The federal government is still trying to find its way on most of these issues, though, and will be for some time. The only thing you can do is to do everything that you can to make sure that you are not, or not perceived as, being paid an inducement for making referrals. Just be aware that this may come up. Conservative organizations will be less likely to pay you goodwill. More liberal and aggressive ones will. Most are aware that they have to hold the line to fair market value.

If you would rather sell everything and the only interested party is only willing to buy your tangible assets, the next best bet, from a financial standpoint, is to sell to another physician who would typically pay for goodwill.

Many physicians are opting to become employees of large group practices, HMOs, or hospitals. Depending on who you talk with, they may or may not pay goodwill. To my knowledge, I have yet to hear of physicians not being paid for, at least, the equipment and supplies.

SELLERS NEED TO THINK LONG RANGE

Think long range on this particular issue of being paid for goodwill and how that can affect what you do next and the rest of your life. If your plans include getting as much as possible for the practice and leaving to practice medicine on the *Love Boat*, you will want to hold out for a buyer who will recognize the value of the goodwill that you have built up.

If you can successfully advertise a practice in the journals to someone who might be interested when the hospital or the group practice does not want to pay goodwill, you will certainly be way ahead. If a somewhat average figure of $125,000 (for a general practice, solo practitioner) for goodwill is used, consider the importance of those funds in your next career move.

CHAPTER 9

For Hospitals—How to Approach Negotiations

TANGIBLE ASSET PURCHASE VERSUS TOTAL PRACTICE PURCHASE

As time goes by, it is most noteworthy to see that fewer hospitals are buying "practices" or even both tangible and intangible assets. Instead, they are buying the tangible assets and employing physician office staff, letting the physicians keep their goodwill and continue to work as private physicians. This way, hospitals are able to keep from spending significant capital on goodwill and still satisfy themselves that they have enough of a relationship with the physicians. From a practical standpoint, if you own the assets being used by the physician and in many cases you also employ the staff in the physician office . . . and perhaps even manage the practice, many would ask, what is the point of buying goodwill? Beyond that, when goodwill is calculated it is usually, at least, several times the value of the equipment. The physician still owns the business or the practice and that may have particular interest for the physician if he or she has a strong independent streak. At one point, the OIG said that the payment of goodwill was an inducement for referrals. They have since backed off that.

A CAVEAT ABOUT EMPLOYING PHYSICIANS

I note that some physicians are not satisfied enough with selling only practice assets. They also want to be employed. For them, security is a bigger issue. That is a big issue for a growing number. My thought is that it is quite important to structure the employment contracts with an incentive for practice productivity and profitability with physicians who want to hold out for employment.

One of the problems experienced by many hospitals is that when some physicians get on the payroll, they no longer seem to have quite the motivation to be as productive as they were as owners of the practice. It is important to recognize this fact of human nature. Most people are simply not as "driven" when they are taken from "the business-owner role" to "one of many" on the corporate payroll. The direct link to work and income hazes over. It is natural and will happen. Expect it and plan for it.

Again, for this reason, I strongly suggest that an incentive formula for practice or clinic profitability be incorporated into the physician's reimbursement. (Please notice that I said practice profitability, NOT hospital profitability.) This is not an indictment against physicians interested in employment. It is only to say that it happens to be the experience of many hospitals and that it tends to be human nature to not work as hard when one's paycheck amount is not tied directly to the week's productivity.

PHYSICIAN INFLATED IDEAS OF PRACTICE VALUE

My experience is that physicians have an inflated idea of the worth of their practices. Beyond that, they usually come up with off-the-cuff formulas based on numbers of patient charts or some multiple of gross revenue that they had read in *Medical Economics* or heard what someone else sold their practice for. And they expect you to pay that.

If you are a potential purchaser, whether you are another physician or a hospital, *expect* that the physician-sellers will have an inflated (but usually sincere) notion of the value of their practices. This is a result of several phenomena. First of all, they usually have a stake of blood, sweat, and tears in the practice, so the issue is an emotional one for them. If you confront their price as ridiculous, you will probably not get a positive reaction.

This is even more a problem when you have the case of a retiring physician who has been under a misconception for quite some time about the worth of the practice and has been "counting his chickens" based on those misconceptions. Physicians, like anyone else, begin to make retirement plans a few years ahead, and when those plans are shattered six months before the retirement because there is not the value in the practice that they thought there was (which was going to finance the dream retirement), it can be very disillusioning. So, it is important for everyone to be on the same wavelength early. If you represent a hospital, periodically suggest to the medical staff that they have a speaker come in and discuss financial planning and also practice management including valuation. That will provide a forum for an objective outside source.

A PRACTICAL WIN–WIN APPROACH TO ADDRESSING PRACTICE VALUE

Getting back to the example of the hospital administrator who is considering the acquisition of a practice (and who is approached by a physician with his or her opinion of value), an appropriate response might be to say, "Look, Dr. ______, as you probably know, we are forbidden by the federal government to pay in excess of fair market value in hospital/physician transactions, so we need to establish what that fair dollar value is. We think your practice is a very valuable practice, we regard you as a valuable member of our staff, and we know that you have given the matter serious thought. What we would like to do is, *together with you*, select an appraiser who is experienced in physician practice valuations to establish fair market value so that we can move ahead. When we get the report, we will have an indication of value and then can discuss alternatives about how we can structure a 'win–win agreement.'" (Keep in mind that although hospitals must not pay more than fair market value–present-value cash equivalent, they can be flexible on terms that make a given transaction more beneficial to the physician-seller, especially in terms of minimizing the tax impact.)

Most Physicians Will Be Receptive

Most physicians will respond positively to the suggestion and understand the need for a fair price. Alternatively, some physicians may not be pleased to negotiate from another "starting" number over which they have no control and frequently say, "Well . . . we have given this substantial thought and this is what we need. If you don't want to pay it, I am sure we can find someone who will."

At that point, you will have a decision to make because they have just rattled the first saber with the implication that a competitor would be willing to pay their asking price and they will take it. Unfortunately, you cannot afford to be intimidated and are not in a position to jeopardize your organization's participation in Medicare or your nonprofit status.

My recommendation at that point is to set up a meeting with the physician(s) and hospital representatives and invite a medical valuation expert to make a presentation. The appraiser might be willing to provide a free brief presentation if he or she thinks that there is an opportunity to do the report. You should be able to get a half-hour or so of the appraiser's time.

If the setting for the meeting happens to be a hospital acquisition committee with representatives including administration, medical staff, and trustees, I believe that will strengthen the approach with potential practice sellers. Surrounded with a meeting of reasonable people and other physicians, the seller will tend to be less unrealistic and more amenable to a reasonable process.

The valuation expert should be asked to explain how he or she will approach establishing what fair value is for the practice and answer any questions from those present at the meeting. With an approach of mutually trying to achieve "fairness," you will likely be able to obtain agreement from the physician to proceed. Try to stress a win–win situation and try to make sure that the seller knows all the cards are on the table. The more you make sure everyone is comfortable with the process, the more accepting everyone will be of the value data in the completed appraisal report.

From time to time, physicians ask too little for their practices. For reasons known only to them, they may ask for book value of their assets or some other number that they think is adequate but that is significantly less than what the practice assets are worth alone. What you do in this case depends on your philosophy. Particularly if the physician will be staying on, you may want to say that your policy is to have an appraisal done and pay no more or less than fair market value. You may choose to pay for goodwill or only tangible assets, but the point is that you may end up with an employee-physician who learns later that (though his or her own fault) you took advantage of him or her.

My other experience that relates to the above is that "employees will get you back" if they perceive that you are taking advantage of them. Physicians are also human, and they too can harbor resentment, which you do not need in your organization. Treat them fairly and you will usually reap the benefit.

The Other Side's Typical Comeback

You may find yourself in the situation in which you have initially exchanged numbers for the value of the practice; your having had a legitimate appraisal done and their having merely conjured up a figure they want to inject. The response that you frequently hear is that "there are many ways to value" something and it is possible for reasonable intelligent people to differ.

That may be true, but there are only several ways to place a value on a practice correctly and ultimately only one that best applies (which was discussed earlier). Comments like this from the other side are designed to devalue the professional work that has been done and give legitimacy to their dream price. Again, one of the problems is that there has been a great deal in medical periodicals about "how to determine value" by many individuals who are technically ignorant regarding appraisals, and that often creates problems for professional appraisers when the other side has used nonprofessionals to develop values.

One last thought on negotiations with physicians: Try to stay away from discussing prices at the front end. Try to, instead, mutually agree on a process that will lead to a mutually satisfactory outcome for both sides. If you focus on interests/outcomes (not financial demands) and follow a mutually agreed-on step-by-step approach to working through the transaction, it will be a much easier task.

KNOW WHAT YOU ARE BUYING

The measure of value, it is said, is the price at which property changes hands between a willing seller and willing buyer, both knowledgeable of the relevant facts and neither being under any pressure to act. The problem is, however, that the seller undoubtedly knows more about the property (practice) than the buyer, and although he or she may have revealed every conceivable positive aspect of the property, he or she probably has not been as forthcoming about some of the more negative aspects. Therefore, the prudent buyer must obtain as much information about the selling business as possible. "Preacquisition studies" can provide the needed information, and an appraisal specialist in health care can provide an appropriate value for the business.

Also appropriate in the planning stages, short of an appraisal, you may want to perform a *valuation analysis*, which does not include all the detail found in an appraisal nor does it cost as much but it does provide what a typical practice would go for, unembellished by the pros and cons of the actual subject practice you are considering. It considers the value from a financial analysis using a variety of techniques that may, in turn, give you enough of an idea about how much a given clinic or practice will likely cost. Such an analysis would probably include (among others) a present value of DCF (a projected value based on past performance), and a comparable P/E ratio if currently available.

These studies do not need to be exhaustive. In fact, they should not be if you are in the early planning stages. To obtain the necessary information for planning, it is enough to do what I call basic "sniff tests." Alternately, farther down the line when a direction is being finalized, more comprehensive "acquisition feasibility studies" will protect your position in the case of a major acquisition.

Also, in terms of knowing what you are buying, make sure that you clarify, whether you are the buyer or the seller, what is included in the sale and what is not. This includes both assets and liabilities. For example, are cars included? Many physicians have their cars through their PC and do not want to sell them, especially if they are retiring. (Many times, hospitals will not buy the cars anyway.) Also, are cash, accounts receivable, or any liabilities included? Itemize the assets that you want to buy and the liabilities, if any, that you are willing to take on.

Probably the more typical situation is that you will have determined what the collection rate on the accounts receivable has been from the practice (usually 80 to 90 percent) and factor that against what is currently outstanding for a value. If you are buying, you should stipulate (if you are buying the accounts receivable) that you will do an accounting of them immediately before closing and apply the collection factor to them for a value at the time.

Sometimes, the cash flow is important to acquire from a business standpoint, as opposed to starting with no cash flow, so some buyers prefer to acquire them. Similarly, physicians are usually just as happy to get cashed out on them.

If you are assuming some of or all the liabilities of the practice, the negative influence of those obviously need to be determined in the net value of the practice. More often than not, hospitals have not been choosing to assume those and just buy selected assets and pay for goodwill, approaching it "cafeteria style," buying what they want.

If you want to buy the bank accounts because you can get good terms on financing them (you usually can get better terms than a loan at the bank for the same money) and think that the available cash may be needed for physical plant improvements, then buy those, too.

CHAPTER 10

Several Keys to Successful Negotiations

STEERING CLEAR OF GOVERNMENT POTHOLES

The first matter of business is to make sure that as you plan your strategy to buy or sell in health care that you design your approach to avoid the problems associated with Medicare statutes. As most health care executives have known for some time, the antikickback provisions of the Medicare and Medicaid fraud and abuse laws bar any form of remuneration to induce patient referrals. Clearly, as noted above, a prime area for scrutiny in the recent past few years by the Health Care Finance Administration (HCFA) and the OIG has been the payments to physicians from hospitals for purchase of their practices or practice assets.

This is discussed in greater length later, but what they, of course, are looking for is anything in excess of what is accurately valued at fair market value. Payments in excess of fair market value will be clearly construed as an inducement to refer patients. Obviously, there are many reasons to be prudent in obtaining solid valuation information and expending resources in transactions, but this reason gives you the most incentive to be *very* businesslike.

The Simplest and Best Answer

Although many health care executives hesitate to spend money on an appraisal, there is no excuse for not getting an appraisal for major expenditures. You can certainly use the tools this book provides to develop a good approximation of value for a practice, a clinic, or medical equipment, and to develop a range of values based on different assumptions, but it is usually worthwhile to get a professional opinion of value from those in the trade with demonstrated experience and knowledge of health care.

TERMS CAN MAKE ALL THE DIFFERENCE

Surprisingly, many people pay too little attention to the importance of terms in identifying the present value of a price. Many only fix themselves on the total dollars or the basic price. As discussed in an earlier section, this is an important concept, and you might be surprised how many buyers or sellers will willingly accept the terms as long as they get the selling/purchase price that they want.

For example, if the fair market value of a practice was $250,000, it would carry a present value of $250,000 (cash NOW on the barrelhead). Obviously, if a buyer were to pay over time, the interest rate and the term would have to be such that the future value of the present value of $250,000 would still maintain the same worth.

To use a simple example, if you wanted to buy a practice with a present value of $250,000, and the seller wanted $400,000, you could agree to pay the future value of $250,000 in five years at 10 percent, or $402,627.50 (the future value of the $250,000 in five years). Thus, if the seller "had to have" $400,000, you could pay it in a one-time balloon payment at the end of five years, and stay within the fair market value mandated by Medicare. Some sellers would go for that, depending on their particular tax or personal situation.

"TYPICAL" TERMS IN THE SALE OF A PROFESSIONAL PRACTICE

1. A cash down payment is common and is typically 20 to 35 percent of the transaction price (but it is not unusual to see 10 percent as a low figure or 50 percent as the high). Sometimes, sellers insist on "cash on the barrelhead." Determine what works for you with an

eye toward these ranges and how badly you want to buy or sell.

2. There is usually a balance of the price to be paid over some period, usually three to five years or more. The physician's income and tax situation will have a big impact on this point. It is likely that the physician's accountant will want to put his or her two cents in.
3. Contracts for the balance of the transaction price usually are interest-bearing, but the rate of interest is almost always less than a market rate. Keep in mind that the interest rate is one of the key determinants in the ultimate "present value of your transaction price." If it is lower, the principal amount can be higher and the term can be shorter.
4. Consequently, fair market value of such contracts accepted as part of the consideration in a sale usually is less than their face values. (*So be careful when you see sales prices without knowing the terms—prices are not necessarily cash or present value.*) As with the above point, the price is only one of the three main terms (interest rate, term, and principal or price).
5. Some contracts may have a contingency clause that makes the full expected amount that the seller will realize dependent on certain future events. Such an event could be the (1) level of earnings or (2) retention for some time period of the patient base. This is a good hedge against those sellers who might be inclined to relax a little too much.
6. Professional practice transactions often diverge significantly from present-value cash equivalent as the values of contracts arising from the sales of small businesses. It is not uncommon for the terms of the contract to be such that the cash equivalent value is 20 percent or more below the face value of the transaction. *A crucial aspect of negotiating a successful acquisition is the knowledge of how to calculate the present-value cash equivalent of an offer or counteroffer.* Make sure you refer to the methodology in this book to become familiar with that. As I have said elsewhere, a physician may have a fixed dollar amount in mind. Where you have some room to deal (*and often to move the acquisition into the fair market value arena when the physician is asking too much*) is via the terms (interest rate, term, and down payment) you negotiate.

CHAPTER 11

What Does Medicare Say about Appraisals and Appraisers?

PROVIDER REIMBURSEMENT MANUAL

The Medicare regulations discuss appraisal guidelines for the purchase of equipment, values on which to base your cost reports, and the selection of appraisers. There is relatively little said about business valuations per se, but the regulations do speak to the issue of American Society of Appraisers' principles as they relate to asset sales. They obviously have a vested interest in seeing professional appraisals done because of the capital reimbursement issue.

These topics are discussed in the Provider Reimbursement Manual, Chapter 1, Allowable Costs, Regulation section 100-135.16, para. 4590-4897P: appraisal, appraisal date, appraised book value, appraisal expert, appraisal guidelines, historical cost determination, standards requirements, transmittal 331, approval of an appraisal purchase of facility as an ongoing operation, goodwill, and Medicare principles regarding goodwill.

INUREMENT

Tax-exempt organizations are required to be organized and operated exclusively for charitable, religious, or other educational purposes and may not allow any part of their net earning to inure to the benefit of private individuals. This prohibition against inurement is *absolute*. No part of any tax-exempt entity's earnings may inure to any private persons who are *defined to include those persons with personal and private interest in the activities of the organization or "insiders."* This IRS definition generally considers physicians to be insiders at hospitals (although many hospitals would dispute that interpretation).

PRIVATE BENEFIT

Tax-exempt organizations must be organized and operated to serve public rather than private interests. As long as the private benefit is ruled incidental to the public benefit of a transaction, there is not a problem. The private benefit applies to everyone, *not just to insiders* as the inurement standards do.

Violation of either of these can result, as you probably already know, in the loss of tax-exempt status. The purchase of a physician group at more than fair market value could violate the inurement or private benefit prohibitions.

THE BASIC RULE

The basic rule is that "transactions between tax exempt organizations and all third parties must not exceed the fair market value of the goods or services provided." If you are not absolutely sure that you can provide this, find a pro.

DOCUMENT THE COMMUNITY NEED—ONE MORE THING YOU CAN DO TO MINIMIZE CHANCES OF BEING CHALLENGED BY THE FEDERAL GOVERNMENT

To minimize the risks to the hospital/health care system against charges of inurement or private benefit from this transaction, document, if possible, in writing the community benefit of the transaction. To the extent that your points can be demonstrated, you will be in a safer position. Also, to the extent that the minutes and records including the rationale for considering the subject transaction can be traced over time, most would agree that you would be somewhat better off.

Rural hospitals have a bit of an edge in this regard. Generally, the IRS has given hospitals and physicians in rural areas much more latitude than in urban areas due to shortages of physicians in many rural areas.

ARM'S-LENGTH TRANSACTIONS IN PHYSICIAN–HOSPITAL TRANSACTIONS

It is also important to be able to demonstrate that arm's length transactions occurred. The literature stresses the importance of having a practice valuation done as a basis for establishing a fair market value so that if any questions do arise on this transaction, the practice valuation that you had done is likely to play a critical role.

MEDICARE ANTIKICKBACK STATUTE—MEDICARE FRAUD AND ABUSE

The fraud and abuse statute calls for the imposition of criminal penalties on anyone who knowingly or willfully offers, pays, solicits, or receives any remuneration to induce or in return for the referral or arranging for the furnishing of any item or service for which payment may be made by Medicare or a state health care program. You probably knew this, but it does not hurt to hear it once in a while. Governmental remedies to the violation of the statute are meant to be attention-getters. Violations are punishable by a $25,000 fine or imprisonment for up to five years (or both—if you are particularly unlucky). Obviously, you need to take the appropriate precautions to avoid such an event. I don't think that many spouses would be very understanding about the jail part, if you were found culpable in a kickback case involving your organization.

Violation of the statute can also be grounds for exclusion of up to five years from participation in the Medicare and Medicaid programs. This is not new to you, but a discussion on the subject would not be complete without at least mentioning it. This statute has been broadly interpreted by the courts. A Court of Appeals decision held that if one purpose of a payment is to induce future referrals, then notwithstanding the presence of other permissible and totally valid purposes, the statute has been violated. What they call proof, you and I may not. Until enactment of the Medicare and Medicaid Patient and Program Protection Act of 1987, the provisions governing illegal remunerations were strictly criminal in scope and U.S. attorneys were reluctant to pursue criminal prosecutions in such cases. Now, however, the Secretary of Health and Human Services can, on his or her own, prosecute a provider civilly for violations and exclude the provider from Medicare and Medicaid.

In 1991, the OIG of the Department of Health and Human Services (DHHS) issued "safe harbors," describing business arrangements that will not be attacked. One of the "safe harbors" is for the purchase of a physician practice by another physician, with several restrictions. The purchase of a physician practice by a hospital is clearly not protected. In fact, the OIG specifically identified the purchase of physician practices by a hospital as a source of abuse subject to the fraud and abuse statute. Since that time, the OIG has backed off somewhat and has indicated that a hospital may pay what another physician would pay. In the case of a large clinic, our own discussions with the U.S. attorney at the OIG office tell us that large entities should be valued the same way that a prudent investor would, using (principally) an income approach. As I mentioned earlier, a DCF projection with discount factors identified and supported by the market, an evaluation of the subject group practice, the associated risk, and the financial return required are what you need.

THE RISKS

Hospitals face risks from both the IRS and the Secretary of DHHS in physician practice acquisitions and groups. To the extent that payment is in excess of the actual fair market value (cash equivalent, present value), I would encourage you to have legal counsel involved at all stages of the transactions.

The OIG has come out over the past several years with conflicting and obtuse statements regarding what they think is okay to pay for physician practices. Their position tends to fluctuate, leaving hospitals in a quandary of what is acceptable.

In 1993, I began to hear that paying for goodwill at all would be deemed as a payment for referrals and prosecutable under the statutes. That position was followed by what appeared to be a great deal of backsliding. A subsequent position, still in 1993, was that goodwill could be paid for but it needed to be based on the type of income method used by business investors to determine the worth of the income stream. A year later, it was said that a hospital could pay what another physician would pay for a practice.

CASE STUDY: HOW DECISIONS BASED ON POOR VALUE DATA CAN FINANCIALLY CRIPPLE A HEALTH CARE ORGANIZATION

Scenario

Hospital A becomes aware of an opportunity to purchase a nearby physician office building. The medical office building (MOB) that is for sale encroaches on hospital B's market area, and the assumption is that by purchasing the building, hospital A may be able to increase its market share over time through its new relationship with the tenants of the building. The opportunistic CEO of hospital A decides to jump in with a quick counter to the physician-owners' asking price and "strike a deal." Rather than go to the bank, the CEO borrowed the funds from the plant fund with the rationale that real estate was certainly a sound investment and the return would probably be better than the return they had been receiving on the funds as currently invested.

Within 18 months, the selling physician-owners who were delighted at the buyer's counter to their "dream price" had all moved out and built another MOB, closer to hospital B and more to their liking for less than the purchase price of their former building. They put the balance of the profit in new diagnostic facilities to compete with both hospitals A and B.

Hospital A was now the proud owner of an empty physician office building that it paid far above market for, beyond even that value supported by the income stream during the previous owners' occupancy.

The CEO was distraught. He had three options: (1) try to sell the facility somewhere near market value and sustain a sizable loss, (2) try to rent out the suites despite the fact that the area was now over-built, or (3) see what use hospital A could make of the empty facility itself.

Subsequently, despite the location, hospital A relocated some of its offices and its medical records storage, began some community and wellness programs there, and offered several suites free for one year to some newly recruited physicians. Unfortunately, there were no readily available cash reserves from the plant fund to draw on for any renovations, and the hospital had become cash poor in recent months owing to several developments.

Hospital B was hardly able to contain its glee when the weight of the purchase price, magnified and multiplied by payment terms and other financing costs, became too much for hospital A to carry. Hospital reimbursement declined when some major admitters left hospital A to move into the new medical arts building and when other new competition moved to the area, skimming off much of the most profitable diagnostic service revenue.

The debt service of the purchased and (largely empty) MOB totally eroded the hospital bottom line, plunging it into red ink. The CEO was forced to resign, and the CFO has been told to look elsewhere for his stellar leadership in the boondoggle.

A month later, the new administrator of hospital A received calls from the OIG, the IRS, and the regional HCFA office regarding the payment of above-market sums to the former physician-owners.

The OIG position was that the excess of the MOB purchase price over the fair market value was being considered as a violation of the Medicare antikickback statutes. The IRS was reviewing its options regarding the hospital's tax-exempt status and private inurement. HCFA was planning to adjust out the excess of revenue from the hospital's capital reimbursement component. In addition, the hospital legal counsel has advised the Board of Trustees of hospital A that they may be individually held liable.

The Moral of the Story

The swashbuckling days of just trusting in your negotiating skills to whittle down a seller's asking price or using your gut feeling or some rule of thumb are gone. That was fine during cost reimbursement and before the current Medicare fraud and abuse/antikickback statutes, but today it is a gamble that you cannot afford to take.

CHAPTER 12

What to Do to Prepare a Practice for Sale

LEARN THE MARKETPLACE PREFERENCES AND ACT ACCORDINGLY

If you are a physician-seller, once you know what you want to be doing for the balance of your professional career (who you may want to work for), you will be able to identify who the top candidates are to purchase the practice. It further follows that if you know who the top candidates are, you can learn what they look for in a practice and under what terms they are buying them. When you know what buyers are most interested in, you can begin to shape your practice to meet the criteria that they use.

For example, if you learn that a given hospital is more interested in the active number of patients than the clinic income stream because they think the additional complement of lives will be a great addition, you will want to make efforts to market your clinic's services. Perhaps you will want to add a new service to make your practice stand out. Do you have a particular interest in industrial medicine, allergies, sports medicine? Start to do things that attract these patients. If there is something that interests you that is a current hot topic of interest for those who pay attention to health issues, that might be a cue.

Cultivate to your satisfaction your abilities in these areas and then speak about it in community groups. Write an article in the local newspaper. Do a news release and send it to the newspaper. Get the idea? Build a broader base. Not only that, but if you do pursue a special interest and market that ability, it certainly might be the basis for a position with a health care provider organization.

In summary then, tailor your practice to meet the profile they are looking for. If you cannot find any other practices that have sold to the organization, call the administrative offices and simply ask what they are looking for and develop an initial contact. Let them know that you may be contacting them in the future.

WHAT IS INVOLVED IN PREPARING THE STAFF AND PATIENTS, LEGALLY AND MORALLY?

Inform the staff before they hear it from someplace else. This is a common sense area, but I will share some elements that may not be as obvious. The first comment is that you do not want your staff to get the news from someone else that the practice will be selling. Have a staff meeting and let them know that in a year or so you will be entertaining offers and probably selling the practice. If they understand that their employment is not necessarily at risk because of the ongoing need, especially for staff familiar with the operation, little disruption should occur. Indeed, if the practice is purchased by a hospital or hospital-related organization, there may be a host of employee benefits coming their way that were "out of reach" to the practice per se.

Their Enthusiasm May Surprise You

If they also understand that you will be preparing the practice and trying to look for ways to increase efficiency so that a premium buyer will have interest, you are likely to get their whole-hearted support in hopes of working for a substantial organization with its attendant benefits.

Notification of Patients

This comes much, much later, usually after the deal has been done. In fact, a part of the goodwill value may include a request on the part of the buyer for you to assist in retaining patients. If you are merely going to stay in the practice and work as an employee yourself, this is less of an issue.

Alternatively, if you are leaving the area, the diminution of the practice base and the value of your help in trying to keep patients coming to the practice will be of greater value. At that point, especially if you will no longer be practicing there, the buyer may ask you to write a letter informing the patients of the change and that they may certainly continue to come to the practice, also allowing them the opportunity to have their charts sent elsewhere.

As you probably know, it is considered unethical, in the least, if not downright illegal in some places, to "sell" patient medical records. But as the custodian of these records, you or the buyer may hold them in safekeeping and at the patients' request send them elsewhere. (There are certainly better sources for legal advice and interpretation of these laws than I, but I only touch on the matter as it relates to transition of the practice and what not to value.)

WHEN DO I START?

Most experts suggest that you start preparing a practice for sale one to two years ahead of time. It takes a while for the effects of change to manifest themselves in the eye of the buyer or appraiser. The truth is that most of the recommendations that we make are good practice management suggestions, so begin chipping away at areas that you find need improving anyway.

WHAT DO I DO FIRST?

Start by doing those things that will require the most time to implement and that are among the most important. Those tasks will probably be cultivating relationships with transferable benefits to subsequent owners.

If there are cost-effective measures you can incorporate, by all means do so. If your patient scheduling system and patient flow system is not set up such that the effectiveness of your time is maximized, then by all means start investigating these opportunities. Would a physician assistant or nurse practitioner allow you to deliver more and better care to patients? Guard against being too provincial and dismissing opportunities that may hold a great deal of potential. This is time to open up to suggestions.

WHAT NEEDS THE MOST WORK?

What else can you fix that is substandard or could be taken care of without a great deal of effort? Some changes will be cosmetic, and others will be more involved. The income stream is the result of doing everything else right, so by its nature, it will take a lot of time and effort. Get started on ways to generate additional income and minimize expenses that can be realistically avoided.

If you think you need an outside opinion on a practice (sometimes it is hard to see the problems if you have been living with them for a long time), ask a friend and colleague to come over and take a look at your operation. You do the same for him or her. Ask him or her to be frank because you are trying to improve any aspects you can—and what are friends for anyway, right?

If that is not possible, ask a practice management specialist to spend a couple of hours evaluating the situation, interviewing the office manager, and looking over the records. A few hours of time will cost you a few hundred dollars plus, but it will give you valuable input that can be used in getting a much better value for a practice. Do not trip over a few dollars to lose tens of thousands.

INCREASE VOLUME AND INCOME TO THE EXTENT POSSIBLE

One main approach to income deals with only the past year of practice income, income in the last 12 months. Even when it includes three to five years, the last year is weighted most heavily, so it is the most important.

If appraisers ask for previous years' financials, only provide the last three. That will satisfy most. First, these records will be most reflective of the current earnings, and you do not want to have ancient history dampening your income stream. It will have that effect if your income has been steadily rising.

Alternatively, if your income has been going down over the past five years, inclusion of the most distant but higher income would be to your advantage to include.

Make sure that your fee schedule and other charges are up to date so that you are not artificially reducing your own potential income. Often, most of your charges will be controlled by "who pays what." For the balance, though, make sure that you are current with the market.

MINIMIZE ROUTINE EXPENSES TO THE EXTENT POSSIBLE

But Don't Delay Necessary Expenses

You do not need to postpone one-time large or unusual expenses, because appraisers will generally delete those from your expenses in their "normalization" process of your financials. Just like they delete one-time or unusual expenses from the income side, they also do it for the expense side. Their objective is to provide a picture of the most predictable, most likely income stream and, in the process, unusual items are taken out of consideration.

Other ongoing expenses should be viewed with an eye toward elimination. Sometimes, especially if you are winding down, this may be possible. To the extent that you eliminate things that are really necessary, it may hurt. Just take a half-hour and take a look at what is going out the door and make some decisions.

If you get carried away with the budget knife, it will show and that could backfire, so just do what you reasonably can.

PARTICIPATION IN MANAGED CARE CONTRACTS AND STAFF PRIVILEGES

In the mid-1980s, it was considered a negative to be involved with too many managed care contracts because it meant that you would be receiving less-than-average patient revenue on those patients. Today, however, especially as we move toward health care reform and deeper and deeper into managed care as a way of life, it is more often viewed as a positive.

Managed care contracts are the next generation. That is what life is all about in many areas, and it is what life will be about in the balance of those areas that have not yet moved into managed care.

There are some managed care programs that pay better than others and some that make more sense to belong to if you can get recognized by them and accepted as a participating physician. When the health care appraiser comes along, he or she will evaluate the nature of the program and either score it as a plus or negative. Most of the time, it will be a plus.

PPMCs APPROACH TO VALUATION OF PHYSICIAN PRACTICES AND CLINICS

PPMCs use a different approach to valuing practices and clinics. Their approach is different because how they make money is somewhat different.

Although these organizations still concern themselves with a present value of DCF approach, they also use other parameters to identify whether they want to consider a practice, once the due diligence is done. They look at membership, payment caps, claims experience, and the fees for service being charged by the practice or clinic. Each of these is significant because they directly tie to the bottom line, as can easily be envisioned.

Membership

Which managed care organizations is the practice or clinic tied into (a member of)? Obviously, if a practice is only a fee-for-service practice without participation in HMOs or other insurance programs, its ability to get business is going to be extremely difficult, especially as managed care evolves and spreads farther. Beverly Hills psychiatrists may be able to work on a private-pay basis with limited numbers of exclusive patients, but most practices cannot survive, let alone be profitable enough to remain in business.

From a strategic standpoint, PPMCs' strength in the marketplace is derived from their penetration of it. With contracts for the provision of large parts of a given market or of a large number of "lives," PPMCs may command better contracts and ensure that they not be left out of the health care provider network by insurance companies and HMOs.

Suppose you decide to start a PPMC. You will need to acquire practices that collectively have a meaningful level of the patient population contracts for the market area in question. If you do not have enough, you will likely be excluded from dealing with those insurance companies and HMOs looking for practitioners to service their "insureds."

Getting back to the issue of membership, a practice needs to be reasonably connected so that it can provide service to patients from a wide variety of insurance companies. The number of companies to participate with will vary for the area but ostensibly should range somewhere from a low of 3 or 4 to a dozen or even 20+ programs (in more urbanized areas).

Payment Caps

Second, the caps placed on the procedure fees or on the "insured lives" will have something to do with the amount of income that can be realized from a practice. If your net patient income is low because of the caps your practice is living with, you may not be the prime acquisition target by a PPMC. Although there are still places where caps exist by procedure versus a global cap on lives, the latter is the growing model and is continually being refined in the more managed care mature areas.

The medical loss ratio (MLR) due to caps and other deductions from revenue generally ranges from about 65 to 75 percent. In other words, for every dollar made, you get to keep 30 to 35 cents on average.

Claims Experience

The next area of examination generally deals with the overall practice's patient population claims experience or "how much it costs to pay for the services required by the patients covered by a practice's patients." If, for example, you identify that the overall patients of a practice are much costlier, or to put it another way, if their health care services are at such a level that they do not allow the 30 to 35 percent return, then the practice is less desirable than others and is not worth as much. It all gets back to the anticipated revenue stream. This is not rocket science.

Fees for Service

Practices or clinics need to make sure that they are receiving all that they can in terms of their fees. PPMCs might use projections with higher fees for a potential acquisition (clinic) if they have other practices in the area and know that it would be reasonable to assume that they could raise the fees to fall in line with the balance of the area's practices. However, depending on the conservatism of the particular acquisition specialist, lower existing fees might continue to be used in projecting revenue, resulting in a commensurate lower value.

Lisa Bingham, senior analyst and acquisition specialist for FPA Medical Management (San Diego, CA), indicates that she often favors the more conservative, lower, in-place fees because it is frankly a safer bet to undervalue and adjust later if need be than to overvalue and try to compensate later. It is probably safe to speculate that most similar executives would think the same way. One does not stay employed long in the field of practice valuation and acquisition if projections are too "rosy" too often.

Practice Labor Overhead

Some PPMCs have guidelines about what they expect to see in terms of staff overhead. One has a rule that they do not want to see more than three staff for every physician, nurse practitioner, or physician assistant provider. These three staff might be medical assistants, receptionists, laboratory or x-ray technicians, billers, etc. So, if you have three providers, nine ancillary staff of a varied background of duties would be acceptable. Just as that is a maximum, if a practice can work with less, that would be viewed in a more favorable light. Keep in mind that many if not most PPMCs have many functions centralized. They have some economies of scale that are possible and allow them to be cost-effective organizations.

More on Medical Loss Ratios

Earlier I spoke about typical loss ratios by which practices are judged. The general ranges in Exhibit 12–1 are probably reasonable, but I agree that many might vary based on the particulars of the situation. In some situations, a 70 to 80 percent or greater loss ratio might be pretty good, everything considered, and acceptable if the market was important.

PPMCs Often Do Not Like to Assume Liabilities, Only Assets

There are many reasons why PPMCs often do not like to assume liabilities only assets. (1) Who wants to bother with liabilities? PPMCs are not in the business of financing businesses. They provide health care. (2) Assuming liabilities might be considered buying the business and that can bring a whole new set of problems to the buyer that he or she does not need. One example might be that the buyer would have to honor agreements established by the former owner, no matter how poor they were. If you are only the purchaser of assets, you do not have those problems.

If you were interested in buying a large clinic and, for some awful reason, its staff were unionized, you would have to deal with organized labor. You would not have those issues if you were just an asset buyer.

So, in a nutshell, it makes no sense to buy the business unless the existing name of a clinic is so valuable for the goodwill involved that you cannot get it any other way (and even then, I am not sure it would be the best move); then purchase of the business entity might be something to consider . . . but not usually.

Spreadsheet Templates

PPMCs and any other active acquiring organizations have their own internally developed spreadsheet tools, which are refined and embellished over time to accommodate greater and greater numbers of variables.

Just as all businesses have different issues that have an effect on the bottom line, analysts have to factor in the financial impact of different annuities or unusual expenses that are unique to different practices.

Exhibit 12–1 Medical Loss Ratio Ranges

Excellent	50–65%
Good	65–70%
Fair	70–80%
Poor	>80%

CHAPTER 13

Selling a Practice? What Appraisers Look At

INCOME AND ITS DIRECTION

Physicians need to do everything reasonable to increase the patient revenue coming in to the practice, whether that be to the practice or to their salary and benefits. The appraiser will look at the money that can be funneled to the physician, the owner. This goes beyond salary and includes vacations, cars, and meals beyond a business need. What sellers want to point out is all the money that is coming to them from the practice, no matter where it is being spent. As a physician-seller, you are not dealing with the IRS, where one would typically try to minimize the tax burden by not pointing to each and every type of expenditure on your behalf . . . but rather just the opposite. The appraisal will not go to the IRS, although they could ask to see it if there is a question of overpayment by the hospital.

Anyway, what you get as a seller or spend as a buyer for goodwill should be a direct function of the revenue stream, unless the "appraisal problem" is unusual. Many professional medical practice appraisers think it is inappropriate to consider any approach but the income approach. It is my opinion and the position of the American Society of Appraisers that you use as many approaches as the situation permits, although you ultimately go with one.

PARTICIPATION IN AREA MANAGED CONTRACTS AND WITH THIRD-PARTY INSURERS

Initially (and still in areas in which managed care is not particularly significant), some appraisers seemed to view larger percentages of patients in a physician's practice from managed care programs as a negative . . . as being of less value that those with indemnity insurance. Well, to some extent under the older model of health care delivery, that may have been true. The fact is that now we are moving through a paradigm shift, a new health care model in which, like it or not, managed care will essentially consume the marketplace.

The point of all this is that participation in managed care plans is being considered more a positive sign because you are operating more in the future.

Some managed care programs will be closed to new physicians. In those instances, physicians should either make a special trip to meet the medical director or individual responsible for new participating physicians or leave the message that they would be interested in being considered when the organization is again in need of a physician in their particular specialty.

Even if you don't get into a managed care program you like, let the appraiser know that you have an application to participate in with them when they are next accepting additional participating physicians. It is weak, but it says that you are actively marketing and looking out for your practice growth . . . even though you are planning to sell. The antithesis is the physician who is "winding down." Believe me, if that is the picture the appraiser gets, it will hurt in the report.

On the subject of managed care contracts, if the agreements are with you personally as a physician rather than with the PC, the practice will be less valuable because a new owner of the clinic will not have those patients. Some HMOs and PPOs will only contract with individual physicians, whereas others will work with medical corporations.

Many would not feel like going to meet the HMOs personally, but your chances are better than if you do not. Drop in and tell them that you were going by and just wanted to come in and touch base because you had heard that it was active in acquiring practices. Their response should tell you a lot. If they cannot wait to pour you a cup of coffee and put a pen in your hand . . . that is a good sign. Alternatively, if you get the feeling that they cannot be bothered or want to set you up with an appointment in a month . . . that's a bad sign. In any event, you need to find out, and a brief visit will provide you with the best information.

HOSPITAL PRIVILEGES

Any hospital privileges that you have are not likely to have that great an impact on the practice value unless the practice is on the boundary of the market areas of hospitals and each is vying for your business. If you are on the staff of hospital A and hospital B is also relatively close and could reasonably serve (distance considered) the needs of your patients, you may be strategically positioned to negotiate with each—if you really want to do that.

DEMOGRAPHICS

Where a practice is located obviously makes a difference, as discussed elsewhere in this manual. Practices in affluent areas are worth more than practices located in socioeconomically depressed areas. There is not a great deal that you can do about this one. The only thing that you can show the appraiser or potential buyer is that the practice is being managed effectively and that the less favorable payer mix is offset largely by the efficiency of the practice and modern account management (collection efforts).

There is another area that relates to this one rather directly. Persons living in socioeconomically depressed areas tend to be patients who are less compliant and therefore more costly to a health care system that is obligated to care for them. This is not a value judgment, just statistics. They tend not to recover as quickly (hard on the hospital's Diagnosis Related Groups [DRGs]) because their health status does not allow them to recuperate as quickly. Not only that, but because the payment is usually less than even Medicare, it is a big loss for all health care providers.

Here is your chance to shine. If you can show by virtue of progressive patient management that your patient outcomes are good and resources utilization/cost-effectiveness is above most others, *you* will be much more likely to be offered a good position and a fair price for your practice.

PRACTICE SETTING

Equipment

Keep equipment checked out and up to speed in terms of functionality. If the equipment you have is in good working shape and is an asset contributing to the income stream of the practice, you should look for "in-use" value of the equipment. In fact, it is the appropriate type of value you must insist on when selling practice assets. Mention to the appraiser (let him or her know that you are aware of the difference) that you would expect *in-use fair market value* for the equipment instead of *fair market value*. There can be a **substantial** difference. It is legitimate, and you deserve it.

Aesthetics

How your office and the patient setting looks makes a difference. If the aesthetics are less than average, it will be reflected in the practice valuation. Like fixing up a home to sell, there is nothing cheaper than a coat of paint and some pictures. There is often a vague line of distinction between where a practice will be discounted in value and where it will not be discounted based on the rather subjective aesthetic sense of the appraiser. Before he or she comes to visit the office, have it painted and looking sharp. You can't always make a silk purse out of a sow's ear, but you can make the sow's ear prettier. If it has been quite some time since you replaced the waiting room chairs and the furniture, you might consider replacing the worst ones. When I walk into a practice office, I must confess that the impressions start to register quickly and it can set the tone for the balance of the appraisal assignment. Although the value will be largely judged by the income stream, the discount factors that speak to risk and return can be influenced by how stable and professional a practice looks. It's kind of like making a good first impression with your teacher.

PRACTICE MANAGEMENT

Operations Scheduling

How is the practice run? Do you have an office manager who is a dynamo? A cracker-jack? A go-getter? A dud? Although you may feel like avoiding dealing with a termination (nobody likes it), this past year or so will be the most important, and your office manager may have a lot to do with what you get for your practice. Make sure that the individual who you have running your practice is on the ball. If he or she just needs a little more direction and understands your need to really work on any improvement possible, I am not suggesting that you start handing out pink slips. Besides hurting your unemployment insurance premiums, it may not be necessary. Not only that but high turnover is bad for appraisals. Just try getting everyone on the same wavelength.

Personnel Management

Are you satisfied that your staff is being managed well? If so, why? Make sure that this important aspect of your practice is being managed well. It can have a dramatic impact on your practice staffing costs. Don't be satisfied with high staff turnover costs because you may think those costs are less than the cost of providing reasonable and warranted regular increases and benefits. A stable, competent staff who feel like they are appreciated are worth the investment.

Financial Management–Collections

Do you know how you are doing in collections? This can be one of the easiest problems to solve in terms of increasing your net income. In fact, it is one of the most commonly overlooked. How do your collection rates compare with others in the area? If there are differences, are they explainable and justifiable? Make sure your coding and billings are maximizing what you can legitimately receive. Additionally, a good appraiser will identify your relative effectiveness in collections.

Risk Management

How do your patients feel about you? Do they think that you treat them as a real person or a symptom to be treated? Use first names and ask about the family and how they are feeling and what brings them in today. You are in the most personal of personal services businesses. Do not lose sight of that. One of the best ways to head off problems in risk management is to treat your patients as if they were your mother. Good relationships with patients are an asset.

When it comes to selling a practice, if you have five pending malpractice cases, your chances of employment with a hospital are certainly diminished. They may still buy your practice assets but will not be enthused to buy the "practice." Why? Because as the new owners of the corporation that is being sued, they find themselves paying for settlements.

Patient Relations

Related to the topic above, keep in mind that patients want to be treated as individuals. If they sense that they are treated as cattle, you have lost the public relations game and their affinity. That affinity is why they will come back to you, why they trust you, and why they will not sue you for a bad outcome.

Market

What is the market you are in? The market/area? The specialty? Again, how do you stack up to the averages contrasted with others in your specialty in the area?

Penetration of Your Practice/Active Patients

How do you stand in the market? How many active patients do you have in the ZIP codes immediately surrounding your practice?

Socioeconomic Profile/Payer Profile/Area Employers

If you are in the middle of a Medicaid area, these patients pay the least, and your practice value will reflect this. If you are in Beverly Hills and have an established practice, that is obviously on the other end of the patient socioeconomic spectrum.

Number of Competing Physicians, Density

How does your caseload of active charts compare with the competition? If you are an ophthalmologist, are there 30 ophthalmologists within a one-block area? Find out the averages and how you compare. The American Medical Association (AMA) should be able to provide you with average office visits by specialty and by region from their publication *Socio-economic Characteristics of Medical Practice.* This is published annually and costs approximately $50 for AMA members. *This information can help in negotiations.* Sellers will benefit if they can demonstrate that they are on the high side. Alternatively, physicians with less favorable averages would not benefit by such comparisons. It also provides many other tables of information that can also be used to position your practice.

Your Marketing Efforts

What can you point to in terms of effective marketing? What have you done and what are you doing to place your practice ahead of the pack? If you have been an active marketer but the business still is not coming in, you need to alter your approach to include the services attractive to the market you cater to. Give some good thought to how to reach the constituents in your market. What are their needs? Bring them in by offering services or times that appeal to them more. Consider holding office hours one or two nights a week . . . and make sure you publicize it.

Your Ability to Transfer Goodwill

One element of value that you may capitalize on is your ability to assist in the transfer of goodwill. That means helping the buyer keep the patients in your practice. What will you do? This can be of substantial value because it is deals with having a direct and significant effect on goodwill value. Patients are goodwill. If you are willing to do extraordinary things to maintain them for the new owners, this should be a leverage point. If the offer is generous, you may be inclined to continue to work in the clinic for a time after the sale on an hourly basis. This will tend to keep the practice patients coming in.

Covenant Not to Compete

As part of the purchase price, a buyer may want to assign a portion to a "covenant not to compete." Also, under most circumstances, the guarantee of a seller not to "set up shop" in the same area is worth something. The seller gives up his or her best (most developed) market in exchange for some financial consideration.

If you are planning to leave the area, it will have less perceived value to a buyer so *keep your plans to yourself.* (A covenant not to compete has little value if you are not going to be around to potentially compete, and it will be harder for the hospital to justify if they are looking for ways to justify the expense.)

Keep the Same Telephone Number and Clinic Name if Possible

For each thing that changes with the ownership, the practice will diminish. So, if the name of your practice is the Acme Clinic versus your own name, then you may be able to transfer the practice name as well.

Communicate the Highlights of the Practice to the Appraiser

Let's say that you have worked hard for quite some time in sprucing up and bringing the finances in line. Now, you must make sure that these attributes get communicated effectively to the appraiser. If he or she does not appraise practices frequently, your comments may have a particularly positive effect.

Go through an itemized checklist of things that the appraiser should note to include in the appraisal report. Provide him or her with a copy. Be just a little overbearing in your enthusiasm. You will probably see much of it turn up in the report . . . or at least indications of it. There is more than a fair amount of subjectivity in appraiser opinions of value. Your job is to point out the merits and positive trends, especially in the areas that deal with increased volume and revenue.

CHAPTER 14

In Summary

As most health care professionals have known for some time, the antikickback provisions of the Medicare and Medicaid fraud and abuse laws bar any form of remuneration to induce patient referrals. Clearly, as noted previously, a prime area for scrutiny in the recent past few years by HCFA and the OIG has been the payments to physicians from hospitals for purchase of their practices or practice assets.

From the physician-seller standpoint, if you are negotiating with a hospital and happen to be on the board of trustees or a corporate member and you are selling your practice to the hospital . . . and it sells for more than fair market value, you could find yourself being charged for private inurement and in trouble along with the hospital for having paid too much.

From the health care executive standpoint, payment in excess of fair market value carries a number of risks, not the least of which includes charges for inducing referrals.

What HCFA and OIG are looking for, of course, is anything in excess of what is accurately valued at fair market value. Payments in excess of fair market value will be clearly construed as an inducement to refer patients.

NOW THAT YOU HAVE READ THE BOOK . . .

Read through the attached appraisals and play with the enclosed spreadsheet diskette.

I want you to be most careful in several areas because they tend to be areas in which new appraisers tend to have the most difficulty. I am not going to recite the world of appraisal to you but keep the following keenly in your mind.

Cash to Accrual Basis

You must change what is typically a set of cash-based financial statements to accrual-based to provide a present value of the business. It is also an IRS requirement. You must plug in the accounts receivable and the payables and all the other items that the practice may be obligated for but which are not reflected on the cash-based statements.

Normalize the Financial Statements

You must normalize the original statements to exclude the impact of any one-time or unusual income or expenses. These tend to distort what can be expected generally from the practice so that you cannot use them in the valuation.

Uncover Hidden Income and Expenses

For various reasons, financial statements are not always truly reflective of the practice's actual financial performance particularly because they are most frequently prepared with an eye toward avoiding taxes. Your job as an appraiser is to base the value of the practice on "normal" performance. Most often, the seller will suffer if he or she is not clear about practice dollars available to the owner or physician. For example, personal expenses paid on behalf of the physician by the practice such as cars, vacations or trips, insurance policies, loans, the daughter's condo in Maui, etc. should not be counted as expenses to the practice. Those expenses decrease the value of the practice because they decrease the net practice income.

Also, in the event you are a physician who is having an appraisal done for purposes of a marital dissolution in which the practice valuation will determine what the ex-spouse will receive, be advised that appraisers usually have developed a good sense of where to look for hidden assets and for exaggerated expenses, both of which tend to decrease the value of the practice. This is not an indictment against physicians. It just is a reflection of real life and experience.

Geographic Location

I have made reference to the value of having a practice in a desirable location versus a less desirable location. This is why it is difficult to apply a flat multiplier equally to practices by specialty. Practices in San Diego are generally worth more than practices in Manhattan, Kansas. You should first try to determine your specific marketplace values.

Sometimes, there will have been so much practice acquisition activity and there is abundant knowledge of what is going on that you will know what type of factor to apply. So, no problem. (But that is not going to be the situation in most cases.) Other problems will be that the transactors will not necessarily follow any methodology in valuing or allocating portions of the allocation price—never mind what the IRS or HCFA have to say about that—and you end up with data based on what some wheelers and dealers come up with but often without the balance of the terms (interest rate and term) to provide you with a meaningful comparison.

Using the Goodwill Registry example and technique in which the family practices goodwill factor (averaged across the entire country—i.e., urban, rural, Midwest, East Coast, and all the other factors in between) is approximately 0.30 (times gross revenue), you are left in a rather "large space" in which to fine-tune that number. How will you do it?

Well, you can use the practice valuation matrix in Appendix B to help fine-tune the "average" factor by making some subjective judgments about the practice viewed from various aspects.

To deal with the impact of desirability of location, absent any market data, you can make some rough judgments about how the desirability geographic location factor may influence the value. (Remember that the financial advantage of the geographic location at this point is not a concern because that is inherently addressed by the income stream generated.) Urban is usually seen as more desirable that rural, presumably because of availability of things many people like to be around. More pleasant climates are seen as more desirable than harsh climates. Absent solid market data, do the best you can and say how you came to your conclusions.

In Appraisal Reports: Say What You Did!

To expand on the point above, the entire appraisal report should contain your rationale for every decision that you made and every figure that you used. The report needs to be internally consistent with adequate clarification so that there is no part of the report in which the reader does not know exactly where to find the figures or other clear references used to take a position. Support all your assumptions with rationale and related detail. One senior appraiser once said to me, "You can say anything you want as long as you say why you said it." That was an exaggeration, but it stressed the importance of backing up values with logic and numbers.

APPENDIX A

Health Care Valuation and Appraisal Services

A health care valuation professional can assist you in many different ways. I have listed a few of them here. Many executives and physicians tend to shy away from getting good financial valuation data. Biased as I may be, I want to emphasize that the relatively small fees charged will usually be dwarfed by what the information will save you.

1. Fair Market Values
   - Hospitals
   - Nursing homes
   - Special subacute facilities
   - Diagnostic centers
   - Medical office buildings
   - Health care/medical real estate and REITS
   - Medical businesses
   - Subsidiary spinoffs
   - Physician practices
   - Partnership buy-in or sell-out interests
   - Inventory
2. Insurance Values—Contingent Liabilities and Replacement
   - Facilities
   - Equipment
   - Supplies
3. Eminent Domain and Condemnation Appraisals
   - Municipal condemnations
   - Negotiating FEMA allowances
   - Legal—court expert witness services
4. Nonprofit In-Kind Gift Valuations
   - Hospital donations
   - Development programs
   - Health care foundations
5. Health Care Capital Formation
   - Bond appraisals
   - Securitizations
   - Due diligence for health care investors, investment bankers, and lenders
   - Refinancing existing debt
   - Cost estimating
   - Replacement cost
6. Strategic Planning Decisions
   - Clinic acquisitions
   - Divestitures
   - Highest and best health care use of facilities studies
   - Physician retirement and practice valuation assistance
   - Assistance in structuring terms of acquisitions and divestitures
   - Setting malpractice reserves
   - Liquidation, residual or reassigned lease values
   - Identification/valuation and negotiation for strategic clinics

APPENDIX B

Techniques and Tables

PROJECTING INCOME

Where to Start—Normalizing the Financials First

The following example has used the financial data from the practice's financial operation for the previous six years. I would normally weed out unusual or one-time forms of expense or income to continue to present a normalized picture for the practice income. If the physician paid for something out of the practice that either was not an appropriate expense to the business (rather a personal expense) or was just a fluke type of expense, although legitimate, it would be culled out of the financials for purposes of projecting income and expense.

Putting Together a Model

The process for projecting a future stream of income that can then be discounted back to a present value starts with listing the historical data that you have. That is, using a spreadsheet and developing an income and expense model consistent with the one used by the subject, you first create the columns that provide for the elements of income and expense and then for the months as far out as you are planning to project. I suggest five years.

The categories for physician practices are usually quite similar. The example that follows is also fairly standard. In Exhibit B–1, I have merely taken the financial statements, eliminated any unusual types of income or expense because they distort what can be routinely expected, and input the data.

Exhibit B–1 depicts a realistic set of financials from an actual rural primary care clinic with two physicians in the Midwest, neither one making very much income. In fact, they were making about only two thirds of what they should have been by all other comparisons.

Income Attributable to Physicians

Among the methods used to value practices, using the amount of income attributable to the physicians (the net income from a small professional practice) is useful for telling a prospective buyer what he or she might expect from the same amount of effort, especially if you project the income through one of several means.

As noted earlier, it is not particularly useful in using a typical goodwill factor derived from the market because those are used in conjunction with gross revenue.

(Because, however, data are available from the AMA on office and overhead expenses versus gross income, you can identify what a given physician or group of physicians is realizing as income compared with the balance of their peers in the country.) A reasonable number is that physicians can usually keep 50 to 55 percent of their gross for their own income. In other words, if the goodwill factor for GP's was 0.30 (times gross patient revenue), you might be able to interpolate that 0.6 might be an appropriate factor to use for physician income.

This may have particular merit when the gross revenue is average or better but the physician earnings are lower than usual. Does that make sense? What I am getting at is the difference between the value of gross income and the value of net income (physician income in a physician practice). *Gross income has nothing to do with profitability* for the practitioners.

DEVELOPING AN ACCOUNTS RECEIVABLE COLLECTION RATE

Once you identify an income stream based on past performance and influenced by other external influences such as reimbursement policies, the health care marketplace, and

Exhibit B–1 Sample Medical Practice Income and Expense Data Input for Six Years

INCOME	*1987*	*1988*	*1989*	*1990*	*1991*	*1992*
Consolidated Income	$401,045.30	$453,614.64	$434,059.03	$433,495.75	$446,937.17	$441,346.96
Interest Income	$152.68	$133.95	$5.09	$17.31	$295.25	$118.77
Misc Income		$720.00	$216.00	$3.00	$12.00	
Rent Income			$3,120.00	$720.00	$2,640.00	$480.00
Gain-Sale of Asset		$2,936.80	$0.00		$4,300.00	($5,979.97)
Total Income	$401,197.98	$457,405.39	$437,400.12	$434,236.06	$454,184.42	$435,965.76
EXPENSE						
Advertising	$1,422.26	$1,312.85	$883.62	$1,293.71	$2,199.48	$626.38
Professional Dues	$1,400.00	$6,739.61	$2,713.31	$6,919.74	$2,746.00	$2,998.88
Auto Expenses	$7,320.02	$6,941.61	$4,745.10	$5,999.57	$9,130.45	$9,043.75
Auto Lease				$2,456.44	$0.00	
Donations	$225.00	$250.00	$140.00	$383.00	$859.00	$2,070.00
Depreciation	$14,671.29	$20,929.29	$14,531.46	$10,333.08	$21,199.04	$20,864.49
Employee Benefits	$7,659.40	$6,713.53	$9,312.97	$2,005.31	$4,656.96	$7,224.42
Utilities	$4,507.07	$5,401.87	$4,928.32	$4,872.68	$4,727.22	$4,168.45
General Insurance	$2,273.29	$3,618.94	$9,860.41	$6,919.46	$15,611.86	$1,938.39
Workers' Comp Insurance	$403.90	$1,708.31	$797.05	$939.33	$2,381.44	$3,329.52
Malpractice Insurance	$24,405.46	$19,115.31	$13,450.11	$13,972.59	$18,326.99	$10,217.81
Officer Life Insurance			$4,517.47	$4,017.45	$2,244.00	$2,431.00
Interest Expense	$3,404.32	$3,616.14	$3,466.45	$1,677.80	$4,881.27	$7,069.41
Office Salaries	$105,569.58	$145,641.45	$101,834.43	$106,694.20	$114,211.10	$121,530.19
Officer Salaries	$134,885.00	$127,814.00	$176,624.32	$155,175.00	$128,656.09	$137,998.24
Miscellaneous	$1,181.02	$1,301.75	$606.07	$1,181.27	$2,620.90	$2,304.95
Outside Services	$2,671.20	$3,793.83	$3,904.05	$717.14	$140.30	$3,250.00
Accounting and Legal	$3,484.05	$2,727.53	$4,489.04	$6,196.92	$3,550.00	$10,861.44
Rentals	$18,512.81	$23,440.02	$17,600.28	$7,535.00	$14,160.00	$8,025.00
Rentals—Equipment		$1,206.90	$977.27	$4,443.72	$4,819.28	$4,129.35
Repairs and Maintenance	$4,382.65	$1,939.10	$3,312.99	$4,609.44	$5,149.24	$4,739.27
Medical Supplies	$17,264.45	$27,337.56	$16,209.17	$23,433.24	$25,255.95	$21,557.38
Office Supplies	$5,458.70	$5,880.81	$6,643.72	$8,426.15	$12,860.33	$9,821.42
Medical Education	$1,804.91	$888.00	$84.00	$785.00	$3,448.10	$4,026.83
Telephone	$10,092.50	$9,181.30	$10,441.45	$11,033.75	$12,957.64	$12,383.04
Travel and Lodging	$188.00	$60.57	$111.08	$40.00	$665.41	$44.64
Meals and Entertainment	$304.67	$1,102.08	$822.70	$970.47	$1,231.43	$1,242.67
Licenses	$725.00	$310.00	$110.00	$1,177.42	$586.00	$0.00
Penalties					$280.76	
Taxes—Social Security	$13,674.87	$17,824.16	$18,362.82	$18,146.16	$16,693.22	$17,530.52
Taxes—Unemployment	$2,637.11	$3,153.82	$3,055.87	$2,959.43	$1,865.53	$2,649.14
Taxes—Property	$7,899.48	$474.44	$2,587.98	$6,965.09	$763.32	$2,248.61
Taxes—Single Business	$3,382.00	$4,386.00	$4,259.00	$1,250.00	$3,790.00	$4,380.00
Taxes—Other			$1,265.00	$480.05	$15.00	$15.00
Total Expenses	$401,810.01	$454,810.78	$442,647.51	$424,009.61	$442,683.31	$440,720.19
Net Profit (Loss)	($612.03)	$2,594.61	($5,247.39)	$10,226.45	$11,501.11	($4,754.43)

continues

Exhibit B–1 (continued)

	1987	*1988*	*1989*	*1990*	*1991*	*1992*
INCOME AVAILABLE TO PHYSICIANS						
Travel and Lodging	$188.00	$60.57	$111.08	$40.00	$665.41	$44.64
Professional Dues	$1,400.00	$6,739.61	$2,713.31	$6,919.74	$2,746.00	$2,998.88
Medical Education	$1,804.91	$888.00	$84.00	$785.00	$3,448.10	$4,026.83
Auto Expenses	$7,320.02	$6,941.61	$4,745.10	$5,999.57	$9,130.45	$9,043.75
Auto Lease	$0.00	$0.00	$0.00	$2,456.44	$0.00	$0.00
Officer Salaries	$134,885.00	$127,814.00	$176,624.32	$155,175.00	$128,656.09	$137,998.24
Officer Life Insurance	$0.00	$0.00	$4,517.47	$4,017.45	$2,244.00	$2,431.00
Meals and Entertainment	$304.67	$1,102.08	$822.70	$970.47	$1,231.43	$1,242.67
TOTAL	$145,902.60	$143,545.87	$189,617.98	$176,363.67	$148,121.48	$157,786.01

other significant influences, you will need to project what will be collected.

Most physician practices operate on a cash basis versus an accrual basis accounting system. Depending on larger clinics, they will more and more tend to use accrual accounting.

One of the approaches to valuing practices involves developing a balance sheet based on an accrual method. That means you need to provide for a collection rate of the business done.

The chart below depicts an example of historical collection performance in the same type of weighted historical values chart that is used to determine a weighted average of income over the past three to five years.

	1989	*1990*	*1991*	*1992*	*1993*	*Sum/ Wtd Avg*
Weight	1	2	3	4	5	15
Year Col Rate	0.92	0.9	0.89	0.9	0.88	
Wtd Value	0.92	1.8	2.67	3.6	4.4	13.39
		13.39 div. by		15 =		**0.89**

In the above chart, you weight the most distant year the least. One has been used to weight the year 1989, whereas the most recently completed year in this example, 1993, has been given a weight of 5. The weight for each of the years is multiplied by the actual collection rate for the year. When those multiplications have been done for all years, they are summed and divided by the sum of the weights. The answer is the weighted averaged collection rate for the past five years, which you will apply to the projected income that you have developed for the clinic.

PROJECTING FUTURE INCOME AND EXPENSE

As discussed in the Income Approach section, when attempting to perform a DCF analysis, you must develop a spreadsheet model from the historical performance of the clinic to project future income. We have provided an example of a typical smaller three-physician clinic income and expense sheet with six years of projections and a present-value analysis for an appraisal (see Exhibit B–2).

In terms of mathematical functions, there is one principal method that we use in Excel for this purpose, the **[TREND]** function. It uses a regression analysis method of least squares approach for predicting future values.

Using Linear Regression to Forecast Income

The method of projecting the data that you have input will be some form of linear regression. (I tend to use the method of least squares—see section on Techniques.) It is a function that is included on literally every type of modern spreadsheet, and I refer you to the manual for the software that you have. To try to describe or teach a mini course on linear regression would take too long here and is better explained and performed by spreadsheet software vendors. (If your spreadsheet program converts Microsoft Excel and has the same functions, the optional diskette provides a ready-made model.)

In addition to the standard income and expense categories, I often also list those elements that can be considered funds available and paid to the physicians for an idea of how they are comparing with the data from regional and country-wide comparisons by specialty. They are listed directly below the income and expense sheet.

Exhibit B–2 Excess Earnings Calculation

The following spreadsheet was developed as a model to demonstrate how the spreadsheet you develop flows into a present value-discounted cash flow method (income approach). Replace the values entered in the first five years with your own data.

						Year One	*Year Two*	*Year Three*	*Year Four*	*Year Five*	*Year Six*
Mayville Med Clinic	*Actual*	*Actual*	*Actual*	*Actual*	*Actual*	*Trended*	*Trended*	*Trended*	*Trended*	*Trended*	*Trended*
INCOME	*1990*	*1991*	*1992*	*1993*	*1994*	*1995*	*1996*	*1997*	*1998*	*1999*	*2000*
Gross Patient Revenue	$657,005	$689,855	$724,348	$760,565	$798,594	$832,240	$868,825	$905,103	$940,857	$976,340	$1,012,743
Interest Income	$153	$160	$168	$177	$186	$193	$202	$210	$219	$227	$235
Misc Income	$10,568	$11,096	$11,651	$12,234	$12,845	$13,387	$13,975	$14,559	$15,134	$15,705	$16,290
Total Income	$667,726	$701,112	$736,168	$772,976	$811,625	$845,820	$883,002	$919,872	$956,209	$992,272	$1,029,268
EXPENSE											
Advertising	$584	$602	$620	$638	$657	$675	$694	$712	$731	$749	$768
Professional Dues	$2,658	$2,738	$2,820	$2,904	$2,992	$3,073	$3,158	$3,242	$3,326	$3,410	$3,495
Auto Expenses	$10,685	$11,006	$11,336	$11,676	$12,026	$12,351	$12,693	$13,034	$13,371	$13,707	$14,048
Donations	$1,200	$1,236	$1,273	$1,311	$1,351	$1,387	$1,426	$1,464	$1,502	$1,539	$1,578
Depreciation	$13,568	$13,975	$14,394	$14,826	$15,271	$15,684	$16,118	$16,551	$16,979	$17,405	$17,838
Employee Benefits	$12,654	$13,034	$13,425	$13,827	$14,242	$14,627	$15,033	$15,436	$15,835	$16,233	$16,637
Utilities	$6,521	$6,717	$6,918	$7,126	$7,339	$7,538	$7,747	$7,954	$8,160	$8,365	$8,573
General Insurance	$2,458	$2,532	$2,608	$2,686	$2,767	$2,841	$2,920	$2,998	$3,076	$3,153	$3,232
Workers' Comp Insurance	$854	$880	$906	$933	$961	$987	$1,015	$1,042	$1,069	$1,096	$1,123
Malpractice Insurance	$32,584	$33,562	$34,568	$35,605	$36,674	$37,665	$38,709	$39,747	$40,775	$41,799	$42,839
Officer Life Insurance	$3,502	$3,607	$3,715	$3,827	$3,942	$4,048	$4,160	$4,272	$4,382	$4,492	$4,604
Interest Expense	$5,025	$5,176	$5,331	$5,491	$5,656	$5,809	$5,970	$6,130	$6,288	$6,446	$6,607
Office Salaries	$100,256	$103,264	$106,362	$109,552	$112,839	$115,891	$119,101	$122,294	$125,459	$128,610	$131,810
Officer Salaries	$301,308	$310,347	$319,658	$329,247	$339,125	$348,297	$357,945	$367,542	$377,054	$386,523	$396,140
Miscellaneous	$1,205	$1,241	$1,278	$1,317	$1,356	$1,393	$1,432	$1,470	$1,508	$1,546	$1,584
Outside Services	$4,456	$4,590	$4,727	$4,869	$5,015	$5,151	$5,294	$5,436	$5,576	$5,716	$5,858
Accounting and Legal	$6,058	$6,240	$6,427	$6,620	$6,818	$7,003	$7,197	$7,390	$7,581	$7,771	$7,965
Rentals	$16,854	$17,360	$17,880	$18,417	$18,969	$19,482	$20,022	$20,559	$21,091	$21,621	$22,159
Rentals–Equipment	$268	$276	$284	$293	$302	$310	$318	$327	$335	$344	$352
Repairs and Maintenance	$8,523	$8,779	$9,042	$9,313	$9,593	$9,852	$10,125	$10,397	$10,666	$10,933	$11,205
Medical Supplies	$15,685	$16,156	$16,640	$17,139	$17,654	$18,131	$18,633	$19,133	$19,628	$20,121	$20,622
Office Supplies	$6,400	$6,592	$6,790	$6,993	$7,203	$7,398	$7,603	$7,807	$8,009	$8,210	$8,414
Medical Education	$2,568	$2,645	$2,724	$2,806	$2,890	$2,968	$3,051	$3,132	$3,214	$3,294	$3,376
Telephone	$11,568	$11,915	$12,272	$12,641	$13,020	$13,372	$13,742	$14,111	$14,476	$14,840	$15,209
Travel and Lodging	$6,852	$7,058	$7,269	$7,487	$7,712	$7,921	$8,140	$8,358	$8,575	$8,790	$9,009
Meals and Entertainment	$2,685	$2,766	$2,849	$2,934	$3,022	$3,104	$3,190	$3,275	$3,360	$3,444	$3,530
Licenses	$608	$626	$645	$664	$684	$703	$722	$742	$761	$780	$799
Taxes–Social Security	$9,606	$9,894	$10,191	$10,497	$10,812	$11,104	$11,412	$11,718	$12,021	$12,323	$12,629

Taxes–Unemployment	$3,058	$3,150	$3,244	$3,342	$3,442	$3,535	$3,633	$3,730	$3,827	$3,923	$4,020
Taxes–Property	$15,894	$16,371	$16,862	$17,368	$17,889	$18,373	$18,882	$19,388	$19,890	$20,389	$20,896
Taxes–Single Business	$6,658	$6,858	$7,063	$7,275	$7,494	$7,696	$7,910	$8,122	$8,332	$8,541	$8,754
Taxes–Other	$389	$401	$413	$425	$438	$450	$462	$475	$487	$499	$511
Total Expenses	$613,192	$631,588	$650,535	$670,052	$690,153	$708,820	$728,454	$747,984	$767,342	$786,614	$806,186
Net Profit (Loss)	$54,534	$69,524	$85,632	$102,924	$121,472	$137,000	$154,548	$171,887	$188,867	$205,658	$223,083

The formula used to trend the future income and expense based on past performance is the [TREND] function which is based on the Method of Least Squares-Linear Regression.

TO MAKE COPIES OF THIS SPREADSHEET ON THE ENCLOSED DISKETTE, ONCE YOU HAVE LOADED IT, SAVE IT UNDER ANOTHER NAME. THEN WORK WITH IT AS YOU WISH. KEEP THIS MODEL AS YOUR MASTER COPY.

The following calculations take the data from the above projections and place them in a formula to determine the present value.

	Year 1	*Year 2*	*Year 3*	*Year 4*	*Year 5*	*Five Year Total*
Revenue	$137,000	$154,548	$171,887	$188,867	$205,658	
Enter Risk Free Rate (Treas. 30 Year Bonds) >>	7.00%	7.00%	7.00%	7.00%	7.00%	
Enter The Risk Discount Factor >>	10.00%	10.00%	10.00%	10.00%	10.00%	
Enter The Investment Return You Desire >>	8.00%	8.00%	8.00%	8.00%	8.00%	
Total Discount Factor >>	25.00%	25.00%	25.00%	25.00%	25.00%	
Present Value >>	$109,600	$98,911	$88,006	$77,360	$67,390	$441,267

Terminal Value	$223,083
Divided by Total Discount Factor of	25.00%
Equals Capitalized Terminal Value of	$892,331
Discounted Back to Present Value	$292,399
First Five Years Present Value Total	$441,267
Terminal Value Present Value Total	$292,399
Total Present Value	$733,666

Exhibit B–3 (which is also provided as a working model in the diskette version) demonstrates how you can place market data regarding physician offices in a table and determine the most appropriate market price for an office according to your specifications.

The framed table in Exhibit B–3 that displays values for ***m1***, ***m2***, ***m3***, ***m4***, and ***b*** is generated by the **[LINEST]** function of Microsoft Excel. Refer to the Microsoft Function Manual for the specifics. The development of this table provides you with the statistical values needed for use in the basic linear regression formula

$$y = (m1 * x1) + (m2 * x2) + (m3 * x3) + (m4 * x4) + b$$

. . . which is in the cell providing the output value ($158,261).

In this example, I gathered data on 11 physician offices in the area and wanted to find what the market would say was the cost of a physician office with 2,500 square feet, three examination rooms, two entrances, and 25 years old. The resulting value is $158,261.

To use the model for your own applications in the diskette version, merely replace the market data and enter the desired characteristics, and the answer appears to the left.

PRACTICE MATRIX EVALUATION TOOL

In my professional practice valuations, I frequently use a multipage matrix (Exhibit B–4) that deals with the above issues and more. It is a comparative tool that renders a score at the end of the process that tells me how a given practice, according to the values I have established, stacks up against the average practice. (I assign weights to each item and to each category containing those items. *This is uniquely my approach*, but I think it recognizes the strengths and weaknesses of practices I am valuing and allows me to be more objective in determining an overall assessment.) I use "0" as average and look at practices with the attitude of how this is really different from an average practice. If there were all zeros, the subject practice would be an average practice. I have placed no comments in the comments boxes, but it

Exhibit B–3 Multiple Linear Regression to Determine What a Given Type of Physician Office Building Should Cost or Rent for

This uses the **[Linest]** *function of Microsoft Excel.*
Enter the values listed below to generate the answer

Floor Space [X1]	*Exam Rooms [X2]*	*Entrances [X3]*	*Age [X4]*	*Value [y]*
2310	2	2	20	$142,000
2333	2	2	12	$144,000
2356	3	1.5	33	$151,000
2379	3	2	43	$150,000
2402	2	3	53	$139,000
2425	4	2	23	$169,000
2448	2	1.5	99	$126,000
2471	2	2	34	$142,900
2494	3	3	23	$163,000
2517	4	4	55	$169,000
2540	2	3	22	$149,000

m4	***m3***	***m2***	***m1***	***b***
–234.2371645	2553.21066	12529.76817	27.64138737	52317.83051
13.26801148	530.6691519	400.0668382	5.429374042	12237.3616
0.996747993	970.5784629	#N/A	#N/A	#N/A
459.7536742	6	#N/A	#N/A	#N/A

Floor Space [X1]	Exam Rooms [X2]	Entrances [X3]	Age [X4]	Value [y]
2500	3	2	25	$158,261

Now **ENTER** the parameters you want to find the composite value of a Physician Office:

Enter ^	Enter ^	Enter ^	Enter ^	Answer ^

Exhibit B–4 Physician Practice Comparative Evaluation Matrix

Directions: The following tool is provided on the accompanying diskette and was developed to assist in the evaluation of physician practices. To use the matrix merely replace the values in the grid boxes currently in the example with others based on your evaluation of the subject practice. The totals and weighting will be done automatically. You may also change the weights which we have selected to meet your own situation and values.

As you consider the subject practice, think about *how it compares to the norm.* Also plan on justifying your ratings in the **Rationale for Deviation** from the Norm Box under each section.

EVALUATION CRITERIA

	Score	*Wt.*	*3*	*2*	*1*	*0*	*–1*	*–2*	*–3*	*Totals*	*Wtd Avg*
Market Position											
Amount of Competition		6								0	
Referral Sources		2								0	
Service Lines		1								0	
Practice Community Demographics		3								0	
Participation in HMO/Managed Care Pgms?		4								0	
Volume of Patients		5								0	
	Totals	21	0	0	0	0	0	0	0	0	0.00

Explanations:

Rationale for Deviation:

EXPLANATIONS OF SCORING

	Score	*Definition*
	3	*There is no competition*
	2	*There is little competition for the primary service area*
	1	*There is competition but it is less competition than most practices face*
Relative to Competition	0	*Average level of competition*
	–1	*Somewhat greater competition than average*
	–2	*Significantly less competition than average*
	–3	*Intense competition*

continues

Exhibit B–4 continued

	Score	Definition
	3	*The practice has a large, stable referral base which is continually feeding referrals*
	2	*The practice receives a significant number of referral patients*
	1	*The practice receives somewhat more referrals than average*
Relative to Referral Sources	0	*Average level of referrals*
	−1	*Somewhat lower referrals than average*
	−2	*Significantly fewer referrals than average*
	−3	*Little or no referrals*
	3	*The practice has an extremely broad range of service lines*
	2	*The practice offers significantly greater service lines than the average practice*
	1	*The practice offers somewhat greater service lines than average*
Relative to Service Lines	0	*Average types of service lines offered*
	−1	*Somewhat lower service lines than average practice*
	−2	*Significantly fewer service lines than average practice*
	−3	*Only several specific types of service*
	3	*The immediate vicinity is represented by high-use, economically upscale patients*
	2	*The immediate community is economically stable and health care coverage is excellent*
	1	*The community is superior to the average community in either the demand or funding for health care*
	0	*Average mix of payers and patients*
Relative to Demographics	−1	*Area has either less health care coverage (or financially capable) or consumes fewer services than average*
	−2	*Immediate vicinity has a poor use rate and poor health care coverage*
	−3	*The area cannot support a healthy practice because of both low demand/need and low coverage/financing of services*
	3	*Participating in all possible managed care programs and sought after by all*
	2	*Participating in most (85%) of all possible managed care programs*
	1	*Better than average (by at least 25%) level of participation*
Relative to Participation in Managed Care	0	*Average level of participation in managed care programs*
	−1	*Poorer than average level of participation with managed care*
	−2	*Low participation and significant problems in gaining access to managed care*
	−3	*Not associated with any managed care programs and closed out by most or all*
	3	*Significantly more patients per physician than others in the market*
	2	*Significantly more patients per physician than others in the market*
Relative to Volume of Patients	1	*Somewhat more patients per physician than others in the market*
	0	*Average number of patients per specialty*
	−1	*Somewhat fewer patients than that of the average physician*
	−2	*Significantly fewer patients per physician than others in the market*
	−3	*Few patients/just beginning practice*

Operations	***Score Wt.***	***3***	***2***	***1***	***0***	***–1***	***–2***	***–3***	***Totals***	***Wtd Avg***
Effectiveness/Efficiency of Operations	3								0	
Quality and Adequacy of Staffing	1								0	
Risk Management and Patient Relations	2								0	
	6	0	0	0	0	0	0	0	0	0.00

continues

Exhibit B–4 continued

Explanations:

Rationale for Deviation:

	Score	Definition
	3	*Outstanding level of sophistication with many management systems*
	2	*Very good operationally*
	1	*Better than average level of operation*
Relative to Operations	*0*	*Average operations typical of most practices*
	–1	*Poorer than average level of performance*
	–2	*Significant problem areas, operationally*
	–3	*Disorganized/no system and ineffective*
	3	*Highest possible systems management for clinic operations*
	2	*Highly effective systems to manage the patient flow and provide services*
Relative to Efficiency & Effectiveness	*1*	*Evidence of more sophisticated systems than found in most practices*
	0	*Average level of operational effectiveness. Typical systems in place*
	–1	*Somewhat less sophisticated than average practice management*
	–2	*Significantly less sophisticated than average*
	–3	*Poorly organized and run causing unnecessary losses*
	3	*Exceptionally high risk management and patient relationship systems in place*
	2	*Much better than most practices in terms of risk management systems*
	1	*Somewhat more attention to risk management than average*
Relative to Risk Management/Pt. Relations	*0*	*Average level of precautions in delivering health services*
	–1	*Somewhat less attention to risk management than average*
	–2	*Relatively little evidence of risk management*
	–3	*No evidence of attention to risk management or patient relationships*

Financial Management	***Score***	***3***	***2***	***1***	***0***	***–1***	***–2***	***–3***	***Totals***	***Wtd Avg***
	Wt.									
Profit Potential	4								0	
Liquidity	1								0	
Collection Ratio/Bad Debt %	2								0	
Quality and Health of Receivables	3								0	
	10	0	0	0	0	0	0	0	0	0.00

continues

Exhibit B–4 continued

Explanations:

Rationale for Deviation:

	Score	*Definition*
	3	*Exceptionally superior profitable opportunities*
	2	*Very good opportunities for increased profit*
	1	*Better potential than most practices for profit*
Relative to Profit Potential	*0*	*Average*
	−1	*Less than average opportunities for profit*
	−2	*Poor prospects for being able to operate profitably*
	−3	*Not possible to operate profitably*
	3	*Excellent liquidity*
	2	*Very good liquidity*
	1	*Better than average liquidity*
Relative to Liquidity	*0*	*Average*
	−1	*Less than average liquidity*
	−2	*Significant improvement required in order to operate effectively*
	−3	*No liquidity. Operation unlikely if liquidity does not improve quickly*
	3	*Excellent collections performance*
	2	*Very good collections and systems for collection*
	1	*Better collections than typical practices in the region*
Relative to Collection Ratio/Bad Debt	*0*	*Operations reflect typical collection levels and bad debts*
	−1	*Less favorable collection rates than average*
	−2	*Significant improvement required in collection levels and bad debt performance*
	−3	*Poor collection performance is currently seriously threatening viability of the practice*

Physical Facilities	***Score Wt.***	***3***	***2***	***1***	***0***	***−1***	***−2***	***−3***	***Totals***	***Wtd Avg***
Quality	1								0	
Capacity/Space	2								0	
Condition of Facilities and Equipment	1								0	
	4	0	0	0	0	0	0	0	0	0.00

continues

Exhibit B–4 continued

Explanations:

Rationale for Deviation:

	Score	*Definition*
	3	*Facilities of rare quality and scope*
	2	*Excellent facilities & equipment/unusual capabilities*
	1	*Better than average facilities and equipment*
Relative to Facilities Quality	*0*	*Average facilities and equipment*
	–1	*Less appointed office and/or marginal equipment*
	–2	*Facilities &/or equipment poorly maintained, renovation/replacement required*
	–3	*Facilities &/or equipment unacceptable in the current market*
	3	*Facilities of rare quality and scope*
	2	*Excellent facilities & equipment/unusual capabilities*
	1	*Better than average facilities and equipment*
Relative to Capacity & Space	*0*	*Average facilities and equipment in terms of capacity and space*
	–1	*Less appointed office and/or marginal equipment*
	–2	*Facilities &/or equipment poorly maintained, renovation/replacement required*
	–3	*Facilities &/or equipment unacceptable in the current market*
	3	*Excellent/new facilities & equipment condition*
	2	*Very well maintained facilities and equipment with established PM program*
	1	*Better than average facilities and equipment*
Relative to Facilities Condition	*0*	*Average condition for facilities and equipment*
	–1	*Less than average level of maintenance and slightly older equipment*
	–2	*Facilities or equipment are not maintained or generally useable, renovation/replace required*
	–3	*Facilities or equipment are generally unacceptable*

Ease of Transition / Max. of Goodwill	***Score* Wt.**	***3***	***2***	***1***	***0***	***–1***	***–2***	***–3***	***Totals***	***Wtd Avg***
Employee Retention	1				0				0	
Patient Introduction	3								0	
Use of Seller's Name and Phone Number	2								0	
Potential for Future Seller Mkt Re-entry	1								0	
	7	0	0	0	0	0	0	0	0	0.00

continues

Exhibit B–4 continued

Explanations:

Rationale for Deviation:

	Score	*Definition*
	3	*No problems transitioning; office staff stays; no loss of patient base*
	2	*Little, if any, problems transitioning with minimum patient loss*
	1	*Greater than average difficulty in transitioning and preventing erosion of patient base*
Relative to Patient Introduction	*0*	*Average level of transition problems and reestablishment*
	–1	*Greater than average difficulty transitioning, greater than average patient loss*
	–2	*Substantial difficulty in making successful transition*
	–3	*Not likely to be able to successfully transition the practice without losing most patients*
	3	*n/a*
	2	*n/a*
	1	*Name and phone number available to buyer*
Relative to Use of Name & Phone No.	*0*	*Phone number available to buyer*
	–1	*Name and phone number not available to buyer*
	–2	*n/a*
	–3	*n/a*
	3	*n/a*
	2	*n/a*
	1	*n/a*
Relative to Non-Compete	*0*	*Seller agrees to non-compete clause which precludes re-entry to market*
	–1	*n/a*
	–2	*n/a*
	–3	*Seller will not provide a non-compete clause*

CLINIC PERFORMANCE SUMMARY **LEVEL**

Revised Summary of Blended Discount (Risk) Factors		Wts.
Market Rating	[Enter]	5
Operations Effectiveness Rating	[Enter]	3
Financial Management Rating	[Enter]	4
Physical Plant and Equipment	[Enter]	2
Ease of Transition/ Max. of Goodwill	[Enter]	1

[Enter]Example Gross Pt. Revenue =
[Enter]Base Market Goodwill Multiplier = Above Subject Evaluation Score
Resulting Multiplier = Goodwill Value by this Method =
[Enter]Fair Market Value of the Assets =

would be appropriate to substantiate why you gave higher or lower marks for each item. The result of this approach is that there is a strong "magnetism" for practices' valuations to be near typical or average.

Once each category (marketing, financial management, physical plant, etc.) is tallied, then I applied a weight to each category. I then used those totals to deviate from normalcy, one direction or the other. If you like it, use it. It is one technique that forces more objectivity. There are no models for quantifying performance when it comes to qualitative measurement of practices. This is probably as good as anything. The key to its value is the requirement to justify deviation from the norm and come up with a number based on that objectivity.

One of the biggest drawbacks in using such a tool is that you have to have a perspective on what the norms are for the various categories. If you do not have a good grasp of how one practice stacks up against another one in these categories, your end result will be flawed.

When you use this, first ask yourself whether the subject practice is better than average, average, or worse than average. Then justify the answer and assign numbers. The box following each section is for justification of your ratings.

PAIRED SALES ANALYSIS

The PSA is a technique adapted from the real estate side of the appraisal industry. It may be adapted, though, to the appraisal of medical equipment and even practices if adequate data are available.

A direct sales comparison is a process whereby comparable sales transactions are compared with the subject practice, medical equipment, or a physician office. The "subject" is the base or standard for comparison purposes (see Exhibit B–5).

To make necessary adjustments for elements of difference, however, an analysis may be made between comparables to segregate the effect of specific factors. Items of difference may be categorized into those of terms of financing, location, and practice characteristics.

The simplest tool in extracting the marketplace's valuation of a specific item is the use of paired sales comparison analysis. Practices are selected with essentially similar (ideally, identical) features, except for one specifically dissimilar feature. If the practices are nearly identical in all characteristics except for one item, the difference in observed sale prices may be attributed to the one dissimilar feature.

If a matched pair cannot be found among the comparables suited for this appraisal, the appraiser can sometimes rely on a matched pair file collected in the past to evaluate the contribution to value that specific features add to a practice.

For example, if you had good transaction data on several practices and the only noteworthy difference was that one was located in an upscale shopping mall and others were in a medical office building, you would be able to identify the value of the mall location by comparing it with the otherwise comparable (by characteristic and by the sale price) practices.

Each element of comparison in the PSA is contrasted with the subject you are trying to value. If something is essentially the same, you write "same." If something is $100,000 superior to the subject you fill in "–$100,000" (no, I did not make a mistake—I meant to say minus $100,000) in the column of the superior comparable.

Again, the idea is to bring the comparable into line (up or down) with the subject. If some aspect of the comparable is better than that aspect of the subject practice you are comparing, then you place a (–) value to the extent that the comparable is better.

At the bottom, you have a total value for each comparable as adjusted to the subject property you want a value for. In trying to find the goodwill value for the practice, let's say that practice 2 is the one located in the mall and 3 is in a typical medical office building.

Let's be clear that this probably represents too many similarities for what you would find in the marketplace, even over time. I am not saying that this is the only or even the best number of characteristics to evaluate and include in a PSA. What you use will depend on the types of differences that you find in your particular area.

A word of caution. If you plan on using a PSA frequently, in developing values for various characteristics of a practice, you will want to develop a file for each type of characteristic. You can build a file rapidly by keeping on diskette the various profiles of the practices and comparables you have used so that if you are involved in a current project that does not include fairly reasonable comparables, you may be able to use ones from your file. In those instances, you may want to do some type of adjustment for time if there is evidence that time has played a role in what practices are selling for.

Perhaps you will only want to include price, terms, payer mix, physical/facilities and patient volume.

You may choose not to do anything like this at all. Most do not use this in health care appraisals, but it does help to quantify and introduce some objectivity into the process in the event the IRS or Medicare questions your rationale, which you will need to do in any event.

I have structured the above example simplistically to make a point of how to isolate one practice characteristic, how to identify a value for it, and how it helps to substantiate a value for the subject practice.

Exhibit B–5 Direct Sales Comparison

Item	*Subject*	*Practice 1*	*Practice 2*
Transaction $	Not yet sold	250,000	350,000
Terms $	20% down, Bal over 5 Years @ 9%	Same	Same
Marketing	Average	Same	Same
Physical Plant	Good	Same	Same
Financial	Average	Same	Same
Risk/Legal	Good	Same	Same
General Mgt	Good	Same	Same
Payer Mix	60% Care, 10% Caid, 25% Com 5% Pvt	Same	Same
Patient Volume	3,800 active patients	Same	Same
Profitability	$150,000 physician income	Same	Same
Location	Medical Ofc Bldg	Same	–100,000
Indicated Value		**$250,000**	**$250,000**

In this case, it is clear that, according to the market, the value for the clinic is $250,000.

Many familiar with only one way of valuing practices or clinics would say, "Just go by the financials," or *the income approach*. After all, that is what most appraisals are based on.

This is technically true, but it is always best to test your various techniques against one another for reasonableness, kind of a reality check. Additionally, you should always perform as many applicable approaches to value as available data will support. So, if market data are available, it should always be included as one of your methods. Theoretically, the market is the best measure of value.

❖ Hint

The PSA is just a technique to use in the market approach, and if you can use it, I encourage you to. This form of analysis lends itself very well to comparing major medical equipment items and their respective values. Through the techniques described above, you can also isolate the value of various features of similar types of equipment.

A very valuable tool to use in conjunction with a PSA in identifying the likely market value of a practice office or medical office building is multiplier linear regression analysis.

APPENDIX C

IRS Revenue Ruling 59–60

Revenue Ruling 59–60, Section 3, "Approach to Valuation" is the formal discussion by the IRS on how a valuation should be conducted and what it should contain with some interpretive guidelines. Let me, however, summarize the key points for you:

A. *The marketplace is the best test for value because it reflects the judgment of the investing public.* What this means for practice appraisers is that they need to do their best to find out what is really going on in the market. That is what fair market value is all about.
B. Recognition for internal and external economic factors should be a part of the valuation.
C. Factors to consider in a valuation are as follows. Eight are listed; a couple are hard to use on physician practices.
   1. Nature of the business and history of the enterprise from its inception
   2. Economic outlook in general, and condition and outlook of the specific industry in particular
   3. Book value of the stock and the financial condition of the business
   4. Earning capacity of the company
   5. Dividend paying capacity (not particularly applicable to practices)
   6. Whether the enterprise has goodwill or other intangible value
   7. Sales of stock and the size of the block of stock to be valued
   8. Market price of stocks of corporations engaged in the same or a similar line of business having their stocks actively traded in a free and open market, either on an exchange or over the counter (not particularly applicable to practices)

Weight to be accorded various factors is also discussed. The point is made that earnings should be accorded the most weight in valuing operating companies and asset values the most weight in valuing holding companies. Practices fit in the former category.

Averaging of factors. The IRS discourages the use of mathematical weighting of various factors. Their position is that such a practice excludes active consideration of other important factors. But, hey, . . . the government does it, and it really is a useful tool in effectively trending. My practice is to make sure that no one can say, by virtue of my thorough appraisal, that other important considerations were not considered.

In summary, Revenue Ruling 59–60 was written 35 years ago. It offers insight into processes for valuation. There is, however, much room for subjectiveness, and even courts have been less than consistent in their interpretations, as has the IRS.

APPENDIX D

Uniform Standards of Professional Appraisal Practice

USPAP is a set of guidelines (really professional requirements, the violation of which can get you ejected promptly from professional appraisal associations) and sets the standards for the development of appraisals. They are recognized by lenders, investors, and the government as criteria against which appraisals should be measured. The document, which was developed principally by the Appraisal Institute and the American Society of Appraisers, deals more with real estate and other real property than it does with business valuation. To that extent, medical furnishings and equipment are affected, but you will likely obtain an equipment appraisal that adheres to these principles if you use a professional appraiser.

The issue of financial valuation is discussed, in particular the DCF method. The primary issue involves making certain that the factors and rates used are substantiated with research and narrative in the report.

If you are interested in obtaining a full copy of USPAP, you may do so by writing to the Appraisal Institute, 430 N. Michigan Avenue, Chicago, IL 60611-4088.

APPENDIX E

Certification (By Appraiser)

In every appraisal, you will need to provide a statement of certification, the general conditions of which are as follows.

CERTIFICATION: The appraiser certifies and agrees that

1. The appraiser has no present or contemplated future interest in the property appraised; and neither the employment to make the appraisal nor the compensation for it is contingent on the appraised value of the property. (*You need to state that you have no conflict of interest.*)
2. The appraiser has personally inspected XYZ Clinic, and it was evaluated from documents listed in the "Sources of Information" section and information made available to the appraiser from interviews with clinic personnel and the physician-owners. To the best of the appraiser's knowledge and belief, all statements and information in this report are true and correct, and the appraiser has not knowingly withheld any significant information. (*This says that your report is thoroughly researched and that you are not trying to be tricky.*)
3. All contingent and limiting conditions are contained herein (imposed by the terms of the assignment or by the undersigned affecting the analyses, opinions, and conclusions contained in the report).
4. The appraisal report has been made in conformity with and is subject to the requirements of the Code of Professional Ethics of the Appraisal Institute and USPAP.
5. All conclusions and opinions concerning real estate that are set forth in the appraisal report were prepared by the appraiser whose signature appears on the appraisal report, unless indicated as "Review Appraiser." No change of any item in the appraisal report shall be made by anyone other than the appraiser, and the appraiser shall have no responsibility for any such unauthorized change.

CONTINGENT AND LIMITING CONDITIONS

The CERTIFICATION of the appraiser appearing in the appraisal report is subject to the following conditions and to such other specific and limiting conditions set forth by the appraiser in the report.

1. The appraiser assumes no responsibility for matters of a legal nature affecting the subject appraised or the title thereto, nor does appraiser render any opinion as to the title, which is assumed to be good and marketable. The property is appraised as though under responsible ownership. (*In case there is any misunderstanding, appraisers are not attorneys or title companies and this clarifies that.*)
2. The appraiser has personally surveyed the subject practice. (*If you do not personally inspect the practice you need to say so here.*)
3. The appraiser is not required to give testimony or appear in court because of having made the appraisal with reference to the practice in question, unless arrangements have previously been made. (*Appraisers often get called into court to defend their appraisals when a dispute breaks out. If you go to court, make arrangements to be paid for it because you could be spending a long time there.*)
4. The appraiser assumes that there are no hidden or unapparent aspects of the practice that would render it more or less valuable. The appraiser assumes no responsibility for such conditions or for efforts that might be required to discover such factors. (*You can-*

not be responsible for finding everything that may be a problem in the practice, only what may reasonably be expected of you. This is where that is clarified.)

6. Information, estimates, and opinions furnished to the appraiser and contained in the report were obtained from sources considered reliable and believed to be true and correct. However, no responsibility for accuracy of such items furnished the appraiser can be assumed by the appraiser. (*If you took the time to verify and double check everything you asked for, you would bog down and the appraisal would take an inordinate amount of time, not to mention the cost to the client.*)
7. Disclosure of the contents of the appraisal report is governed by the bylaws and regulations of the Appraisal Institute. (*This states the applicable source of standards.*)
8. Neither all nor any part of this content of the report or copy thereof (including conclusions as to the property value, the identity of the appraiser, professional designations, reference to any professional appraisal organizations, or the firm with which the appraiser is connected) shall be used for any purpose by anyone but the client specified in the report, the borrower if appraisal fee paid by the same, the mortgagee or its successors or assigns, mortgage insurance, consultants, professional appraisal organizations, any state or federally approved financial institution, any department, agency, or instrumentality of the United States or any state or the District of Columbia, without the previous written consent of the appraiser; nor shall it be conveyed by anyone to the public through advertising, public relations, news, sales, or other media, without the written consent and approval of the appraiser. (*This is important because many people tend to use the appraisal for purposes other than the purpose for which it was prepared. Not only that but there is a limited life on appraisals because they are written for a particular point in time. You do not want someone using an old appraisal or printing part of it in a newspaper ad.*)
9. The appraiser reserves the right to change or alter the appraisal report after its submission if new facts are received that, in the appraiser's opinion, warrant a change. (*If, God forbid, you make a mistake or subsequently learn new information, you want the right to amend the appraisal accordingly. Some new information will not make a material difference in the value, but other data certainly could.*)

APPRAISAL AGREEMENT FORMAT

The agreement in Exhibit E–1 is a typical agreement to undertake a simple practice appraisal. Depending on the type of appraisal, the agreement may be more complicated. Many firms do not even use an agreement but rather just a "*letter of engagement*" that is countersigned by the client if the client agrees to engage the appraiser.

If you require an appraisal of a hospital for any one of several reasons, the agreement will be significantly more detailed. The extent of the issues clarified in the agreement depend on the purpose of the appraiser and any other regulatory, lender, or investor requirements.

You will notice that this agreement requires that the report be sent COD. I have recently adopted the practice because of the tendency for a large percentage of clients to take excessive time to pay the balance owed for appraisal reports. If you are a client, do not be surprised if you see this. When I complete a report, I total the hours and fee, I telephone or fax the client that the report has been shipped, and I suggest that they have a check prepared for the deliverer on the following day. Some of our clients who are state agencies, federal agencies, and university medical groups have difficulty with this, but if you plan to be in the business of appraisal, I suggest that you adopt the practice unless it is not possible.

The items that are included on the following form represent a basic form. You can certainly add to this, but I would not suggest that you delete any of the components.

Many appraisal firms include the requirement to go through arbitration. I have chosen not to for reasons that make sense to me. Arbitration is not the inexpensive alternative that some persons believe. Depending on how much you are trying to collect from a project, the front end outlay does not seem to make sense. Also, my sense is that there tends to be more of a tendency to mediate or "split" the pie versus a ruling in your favor, even when you are clearly owed the fee.

Exhibit E–1 Appraisal Agreement

APPRAISAL AGREEMENT

Between ______________________________

and

__________________________________*[APPRAISER]*

to provide an Appraisal of a Professional Practice

A. Identification of the Subject to be Appraised. The professional practice of _______________ located at _______________. The appraisal will include the tangible and intangible values of the practice including the value of the equipment, fixtures, and furnishings as Fair Market Value In Use and the "going concern value" or goodwill of the professional practice.

B. Interest or Ownership to be Appraised. Tangible and Intangible Assets of the Subject Professional Practice.

C. Purpose and Date of the Appraisal. The effective date of the appraisal will be ____________________________________. The purpose of this appraisal is for acquisition of selected assets of the practice.

D. Limiting Conditions. The information on the appraisal report is based partly on facts uncovered by the appraisal firm during investigation, partly on representations made by others, and partly on information that is on record. The appraisal is made subject to the following limiting conditions:

1. No property survey will be made. No judgments are made as to any matter legal in nature. Information received from others is assumed to be correct; however, no guarantee is made as to its accuracy.

E. Professional Fees. Our fee for this report is $175/hour. We will guarantee a price not to exceed $4,500. The project will be commenced upon payment of a retainer amounting to $2,250 and receipt of one copy of this signed agreement. The balance of the fee will be due (C.O.D.) upon receipt of the completed report. In any action or proceeding with respect to appraisal fees arising out of this agreement, the parties agree that the prevailing party shall be entitled to recover all costs associated with such action.

F. Project Timeframe. We estimate a ten to fourteen day turnaround time for the project.

G. Report. We agree to prepare a narrative report meeting the Uniform Standards of Professional Appraisal Practice (USPAP) and the requirements of the American Society of Appraisers.

If accepted, please countersign below.

______________________________	______________________________
[CLIENT]	Date
______________________________	______________________________
[APPRAISER]	Date

APPENDIX F

Excess Earnings Method As Adapted to Physician Income

Earlier, an IRS excess earnings method was used in the income approach to determine the value of a practice. The table in Exhibit F–1 is another method, although less used, to determine the value of a physician's earnings.

RANGE OF VALUES

It is typical that a range of values is listed in a table at or near the end of the appraisal just before the final page that provides the selected, most appropriate value for the subject

Exhibit F–1 Calculation of Excess Earnings

SELBY CLINIC, P.C.—as Two-Physician Practice, 1994–1996 Revenue Base

CALCULATION OF GOODWILL USING EXCESS EARNINGS METHOD

Calculation of Selby Clinic Physicians	*Year*	*Compensation*		*Weighting Factor*	*Weighted Compensation*
Weighted Average	1994	$266,527	×	1	$266,527
Normal Compensation (See Schedule of Owner's Compensation)	1995	$288,864	×	2	$577,728
	1996	$317,442	×	3	$952,326
Total				6	$1,796,581
Divided by Sum of Weighting Factors					
Equals Selby Clinic Physician's 3-Year Weighted Average Compensation					$299,430
Calculation of Comparative Weighted Average Compensation	*Year*	*Compensation*		*Weighting Factor*	*Weighted Compensation*
(Median Physician Net Income	1994	$184,000	×	1	$184,000
after Expenses before Taxes,	1995	$196,000	×	2	$392,000
Non-Urban, Family Practice)	1996	$203,840	×	3	$611,520
Total				6	$1,187,520
Divided by Sum of Weighting Factors					
Equals Average Clinic Physician's 3-year Weighted Average Compensation					$197,920
Selby Clinic Physician Excess Earrings (Selby Income Less Average Income)					$101,510
Capitalized at 50%					0.5
Indicated Value of Clinic Physician Goodwill					$203,020
Add the Net Tangible Asset Value of the Practice (taken from Equipment Appraisal)					$54,242
Total Practice Value by This Method					$257,262

Exhibit F–2 Range of Values for Selby Clinic

Gross Earnings Multiplier	$241,704
Stock Value Minus All Liabilities	$227,646
Formal Stock Appreciation Per Stock Redemption Agreement	$236,571
Excess Earnings (Two-Man Practice)	$259,883

clinic or practice. It is helpful in providing the client (and the appraiser) with some context for the appraisal. Some individuals who perform appraisals (but not typically professional appraisers) take the position that there is *not one value* but rather a range of values depending on the buyer's needs.

Well, it is true that the worth of something is a function of the merit it has for a particular buyer. But . . . the most appropriate value is usually derived from the most appropriate approach (income, sales, or cost) and within those, the most appropriate "method." Most of the time, when businesses—no matter what kind—are bought and sold, it is because of the business stream of revenue, so an income approach is usually the most appropriate for practices and clinics. If data are abundant, the present value of the DCF is theoretically the best.

If you have good area sales data (which is not often the case), it will be important to provide that value in the range of values. The phrase *fair market value* in appraisal theory reminds us that market influences must be actively considered.

The traditional cost approach (pull the equity figure from the balance sheet) is not typically appropriate for practice or clinic valuations and usually represents the floor of values.

Depending on the purpose of the appraisal itself, the data available, and the client's needs, the range will contain different types of values. The range of values in Exhibit F–2 reflects a practice in which an appraisal was requested when there had been a recent stock re-evaluation. In this first case, that recent stock re-evaluation was recognized as a legitimate value. It was a bona fide transaction (someone was cashed out). Further, the value seemed to be supported by other techniques.

By the way, the values in Exhibit F–2 would be considered a very tight "group" of values.

Exhibit F–3 is another example of a different range of values in which the appraiser has computed a variety of income approaches and was able to develop a market-based approach as well.

This is just an example to illustrate that your approaches and methods will produce a wide variety of values. It is up to the appraiser to select the method that is most appropriate, that is best supported by data, and state why.

It is possible to interpolate values and place weights on various values in a range of values for a final estimate of value. For example, consider the case with the two following values.

Sales Approach:	$1,500,000
Income (DCF) Approach:	$1,650,000

In evaluating a range of values, it is never acceptable to merely average all your values. You may, however, weight one more than another for an ultimate estimate of value if you state why. In the above case, just as an example, you may think that it is most prudent to place slightly more weight on the sales approach because (1) the client ordering the appraisal is a hospital and it knows it can buy other prac-

Exhibit F–3 Range of Values

Market Approach—Sales Comparison	$345,088
Income Approach—DCF Method	$322,548
Income Approach—Excess Earnings	$295,000
Income Approach—Gross Patient Revenue Income Multiplier	$326,598
Income Approach—Multiplier of EBITDA	$400,500
Cost (Asset-Based)—Adjusted Book Value	$165,894

tices for the sales figure, (2) there is some subjectivity in the development of the discount factor in the DCF method used to produce, and (3) the economy and interest investment rates are in turmoil, so the income value is given less weight.

Let's modify these as follows:

Sales Approach:	$1,500,000	0.60	$900,000
Income (DCF) Approach:	$1,650,000	0.40	$660,000
Combined	Clinic Value		$1,560,000

USING COMPARATIVE DATA

The tables in Exhibit F–4 are intended to give you an idea of how to make some meaningful comparisons between your subject practice and the balance of the industry. I used these tables to assist me on an obstetrics practice. The basic data by year and column was taken directly from the *AMA Socioeconomic Characteristics of Medical Practice*. This yearly publication is quite useful in making comparisons in many ways. This type of comparison data is useful in developing the physician practice evaluation matrix covered earlier.

Exhibit F–4 Mean Office Expenses Per Self-Employed Physician

	OB/Gyn	*Urban*	*Pacific Reg*	*Solo*
Year	*4*	*2*	*1*	*3*
1982	24.90	18.30	19.40	17.40
1983	25.30	21.10	22.10	20.30
1984	31.10	24.70	26.70	23.40
1985	36.60	27.20	30.10	25.00
1986	37.80	30.80	30.20	26.70
1987	42.70	31.00	36.90	28.30
1988	43.00	35.70	38.90	32.00
1989	39.70	34.50	36.00	30.50
1990	46.20	34.20	39.80	30.50
1991	49.40	40.90	47.90	35.80
1992	52.13	42.17	48.13	36.83
1993	54.76	44.41	50.92	38.62
1994	57.39	46.65	53.71	40.40
1995	60.02	48.89	56.50	42.19
		Annual Rates of Increase/Decrease		
1982	0.02	0.15	0.14	0.17
1983	0.23	0.17	0.21	0.15
1984	0.18	0.10	0.13	0.07
1985	0.03	0.13	0.00	0.07
1986	0.13	0.01	0.22	0.06
1987	0.01	0.15	0.05	0.13
1988	–0.08	–0.03	–0.07	–0.05
1989	0.16	–0.01	0.11	0.00
1990	0.07	0.20	0.20	0.17
1991	0.06	0.03	0.00	0.03
1992	0.05	0.05	0.06	0.05
1993	0.05	0.05	0.05	0.05
1994	0.05	0.05	0.05	0.04

continues

Exhibit F–4 continued

Year	*OB/Gyn* 4	*Urban* 2	*Pacific Reg* 1	*Solo* 3
		Mean Number of Total Visits per Week		
1983	148.40	153.30	127.50	116.70
1984	139.00	150.30	123.10	113.70
1985	138.10	144.00	122.60	112.30
1986	139.20	140.00	121.30	112.20
1987	138.30	141.50	125.70	114.00
1988	145.60	153.30	124.60	115.60
1989	143.00	150.60	122.10	115.10
1990	146.00	150.10	125.30	116.00
1991	144.40	142.60	122.80	117.60
1992	138.40	148.50	114.20	110.90
1993	142.24	146.65	119.35	114.54
1994	142.28	146.51	118.70	114.56
1995	142.31	146.37	118.06	114.59
1996	142.35	146.24	117.41	114.61
		Mean Number of Office Visits per Week		
1983	106.30	97.30	77.20	76.60
1984	99.50	96.90	74.00	78.70
1985	101.80	92.90	76.60	79.20
1986	106.30	92.50	75.50	82.70
1987	106.40	97.20	78.10	84.50
1988	112.30	102.60	81.30	85.30
1989	109.10	100.10	78.80	85.60
1990	112.50	104.50	83.70	87.70
1991	111.60	96.10	80.20	82.00
1992	105.20	101.70	74.80	91.50
1993	111.85	102.19	80.37	90.35
1994	112.72	102.92	80.79	91.62
1995	113.58	103.64	81.22	92.89
1996	114.45	104.37	81.65	94.16

continues

Exhibit F–4 continued

Year	*OB/Gyn* 3	*Urban* 2	*Pacific Reg* 1	*Solo* 4
	Mean Nonphysician Personnel Payroll in Thousands of Dollars for Self-Employed Physicians			
1982	45.80	28.90	28.20	26.00
1983	33.30	25.00	27.50	24.20
1984	36.80	29.80	32.30	25.90
1985	42.80	33.80	34.50	29.20
1986	45.70	34.80	39.10	31.80
1987	48.10	38.50	45.90	35.90
1988	64.40	43.60	51.20	40.20
1989	61.00	49.20	50.20	40.90
1990	66.60	51.80	56.20	45.20
1991	83.00	58.50	65.00	49.50
1992	77.95	58.86	65.63	50.57
1993	82.54	62.40	69.74	53.42
1994	87.12	65.94	73.85	56.27
1995	91.70	69.48	77.96	59.12

Mean Number of Patient Discharges from the Hospital per Week

Year	*OB/Gyn* 4	*Urban* 3	*Pacific Reg* 1	*Solo* 2
1983	4.50	7.10	6.10	4.80
1984	4.00	6.80	6.30	4.40
1985	3.90	6.10	5.20	4.20
1986	3.30	5.50	5.00	4.30
1987	3.30	6.00	4.50	4.20
1988	3.60	5.60	4.90	4.50
1989	3.40	6.00	4.70	4.10
1990	3.50	5.50	4.70	4.10
1991	4.00	5.80	5.60	4.40
1992	3.80	5.50	5.60	3.90
1993	3.47	5.21	4.85	3.99
1994	3.43	5.07	4.77	3.94
1995	3.38	4.93	4.70	3.89
1996	3.33	4.79	4.62	3.83

APPENDIX G

Comparison of Interest Rates by Deviation from Risk-Free Securities Based on Level of Risk or Type

It is often helpful to get an idea of how interest rates generally tend to be based on the risk associated with market securities. Table G–1 shows how securities other than 30-year Treasury bonds tend to spread.

So, if you are investing in a practice that you believe to possess low risk, high risk, or average risk, you may find this table handy. It is worth noting that when building a composite discount rate, many individuals start with the 30-year Treasury bond rate because it is essentially risk-free. This serves as the basis on which to add additional percentage points for risk anticipated.

Tables G–2 and G–3 can be of assistance in gauging risk quantifiably. By associating the risk of the subject with the lengths and types of rates as they compare to the risk free rate, you can better estimate what an appropriate risk percentage may be. Most acquisitions use a longer range investment such as a thirty year bond because acquisitions tend to be longer than shorter.

Table G–1 is based on actual relationships of varying levels of investments by type and risk level. Only change it when inputting actual updated rates. It defines the relationships in Tables G–2 and G–3. Although the actual numbers will change, the "spreads" will remain approximately the same. We suggest, however, you enter current data in this table frequently to continue to make sure the "spreads" for risk level are current. The updating data can be found in numerous financial periodicals and even the newspaper.

Table G–2 shows the difference between a "risk-free investment" (30-year Treasury bonds) and other levels of investment. It is important to know what return a risk-free investment will provide so you can have a starting point for building your discount rate for risk in PVDCF calculations or developing multipliers. An acquisition with a high level of risk would carry a commensurately lower multiplier.

Table G–3 shows the deviation from normal rates (normal risk) in each category of investment when this table was compiled. In evaluating a practice, if you know that an average practice carries roughly a multiplier of say, 35 times gross revenue for goodwill, all other things being equal, one with a higher risk, say, due to less time to mature, might carry a higher risk and a lower multiplier or a higher cap rate (used to divide into the income stream).

Table G–1 Securities Spread

Enter current data in these columns to maintain accuracy in the interest rate "spreads" by risk level. This table is the one you place actual current percentages in for the other two tables to calculate from.

Market	U.S. Treasury	U.S. Agency	Hi Grade Corp.	Med. Grade Corp.	Low Grade Corp.
Target	Risk Free	Lowest Risk	Some Risk	Normal Risk	High Risk
Weight Grade	3	2	1	0	–1
Term		*Sample of Percent Ranges in Varying Levels of Securities by Risk Category*			
5 Year	7.81	8.10	8.59	9.47	11.87
10 Year	8.23	8.66	9.29	9.75	13.00
20 Year	8.38	9.09	9.52	10.03	13.30
30 Year	8.49	9.30	9.81	10.34	13.69

Table G–2 Difference from 30-Yr. Treasury Bonds by Risk Category (Percent)

Market **Target** **Weight Grade**	U.S. Treasury Risk Free 3	U.S. Agency Lowest Risk 2	Hi Grade Corp. Some Risk 1	Med. Grade Corp. Normal Risk 0	Low Grade Corp. High Risk –1
Term					
5 Year	0.68	–0.39	0.10	0.98	3.38
10 Year	0.26	0.17	0.80	1.26	4.51
20 Year	0.11	0.60	1.03	1.54	4.81
30 Year	0	0.81	1.32	1.85	5.20

Table G–3 Sample of Percent Difference Ranges From Normal in Varying Levels of Securities by Risk Category

Market **Target** **Weight Grade**	U.S. Treasury Risk Free 3	U.S. Agency Lowest Risk 2	Hi Grade Corp. Some Risk 1	Med. Grade Corp. Normal Risk 0	Low Grade Corp. High Risk –1
Term					
5 Year	–1.66	–1.37	–0.88	0	2.40
10 Year	–1.52	–1.09	–0.46	0	3.25
20 Year	–1.65	–0.94	–0.51	0	3.27
30 Year	–1.85	–1.04	–0.53	0	3.35

Appendix H

On-line Construction Cost Services

Exhibit H–1 is a print-out (modified for anonymity) of a physician office building attached to a skilled nursing facility (SNF). This service is a subscription service that you obtain for a very nominal fee plus on-line charges (which are not so nominal). You merely input the data, and you are provided with current data on the cost of the facility in question.

In addition to the exhibit, there is additional clarification as to how, exactly, the process for using the system was approached. It is required in formal appraisals for the reader to be able to duplicate what you did. It is a little more work, but the report is much better for it. Not only that but if your appraisal happens to go to a bank review appraiser, they will kick it back to you and make you do it correctly.

ADDITIONAL CALCULATION INFORMATION: MAIN FACILITY

The costs in the exhibit were generated via the on-line service with Marshall and Swift; however, the following information will allow the reader to find the same data in the Marshall Valuation Service (Manual).

For the medical office component of the costs, refer to "Office, Public Buildings, Schools"—section 15 (page 18) in the manual. For the appropriate cost information on the SNF, refer also to section 15 (page 22). For those familiar with the service and who wish to use the on-line calculation program or perform the calculations manually, the following parameters apply.

1. Use a 0.55 factor with category 330, Homes for the Elderly, and a 0.45 factor with the category 341, Medical Office Building.
2. Include a basement of 8,806 square feet, one-half of which is unfinished at 16.35 per square foot and one-half of which is finished for storage use at $16.70 per square foot.
3. Include an elevator serving the basement area of 8,806 square feet.
4. Include a kitchen facility based on 16,000 square feet (the approximate square footage of the residential area).
5. Include a 52,000-square-foot well-maintained asphalt parking lot (identifier code is PAS) at $1.55 per square foot.
6. Use a local labor multiplier of 0.96.
7. Use a construction class of C, Masonry Bearing Walls.
8. Use a region designation of 2, Central; if the handbook is used, use the Detroit cost multiplier.
9. Use a climate designation of 1, Extreme.
10. Use a cost rank of 2, Average.
11. Use a total floor area of the entire main facility including physician office add-on and the corridor between the nursing home and the home for the aged of 29,811.
12. Use a perimeter shape designation of 3, Irregular.
13. Use "1" for the number of stories.
14. Use the average story height of 10.
15. Use an effective age of 15 years.
16. Use a condition of 5, Very Good.
17. Use an exterior wall designator as "2," Brick, Block Back Up.
18. Use Radiant Hot Water, 9 as the designation for heat type.
19. Use a figure of 10,500 square feet for area sprinkled.

Exhibit H–1 Sample On-line Construction Costs

Marshall and Swift
Online Data Cost Estimation
Medical Facility Complex, Wheaton, MI
(.55 SubAcute Care, .45 Medical Offices)

COST ESTIMATE FOR:	National Bank of Michigan, Wheaton, Michigan
PROPERTY OWNER:	ABC Investors
ADDRESS:	500 E. Main Street, Wheaton, Michigan 49650
SURVEYED BY:	American Health Care Appraisal
DATA OF SURVEY:	November 23, 1993

DESCRIPTION:		
OCCUPANCY:	55.0% SNF 45.0% MEDICAL OFFICE	
FLOOR AREA:	29,811 Square Feet	
AVERAGE STORY HEIGHT:	10 Feet	CLASS: C Masonry
EFFECTIVE AGE: 15 Years	COST RANK: 2.0 Average	CONDITION: 5.0 Very good
NUMBER OF STORIES: 1.0	COST AS OF: 11/93	
EXTERIOR WALL:	Brick Block Back up (100%)	
HEATING AND COOLING:	Radiant Hot Water (100%)	
OTHER FEATURES:		
Elevator Serving	8,806 Square Feet	
Sprinklers Serving	10,500 Square Feet	
Kitchen Equipment		

	UNITS	*COST*	*TOTAL*
BASIC STRUCTURE COST	29,811	55.61	1,654,881
BASEMENT			
Unfinished	4,403	16.35	71,989
Storage	4,403	16.70	73,530
Subtotal			145,519
BUILDING COST NEW	29,811	60.39	1,800,400
EXTRAS:			
Parking Lot, Asphalt	52,000	1.55	80,600
REPLACEMENT COST NEW			1,881,000
LESS DEPRECIATION:			
Physical and Functional		<16.7%>	<314,105>
DEPRECIATED COST			1,566,895

Cost Data by MARSHALL AND SWIFT

20. Use ten percent entrepreneurial fee/profit.
21. Use $100,000 site preparation costs.
22. Use two points bank loan fee.
23. Use $13,415 legal and accounting fees.

The first model in this section depicts what the "calculator" method from Marshall and Swift looks like. You can also use a more elaborate "segregated cost" method, which provides an estimate of cost by adding together the amounts of the various materials used in the construction of the office building.

The balance of the detail shows how the ultimate construction cost figure was determined.

APPENDIX I

Analyzing Risk in an Investment

A technique used to evaluate risk in many forms of investments can also be applied to the financial valuation of practices, clinics, and hospitals. Although this may look overly intimidating, it is not.

When you develop a table of historical data as I have for a year's time and apply some analytical statistical methods, you can identify a level of risk, primarily due to the varying levels of income. As noted in Exhibit I–1, I divided the standard deviation of the income range by the mean income and arrived at a high risk factor of 0.41. I add this factor to the risk-free rate of U.S. 30-year Treasury bonds, which is about 7 to 8 percent for a return plus a factor for the type of return (i.e., 9 to 12 percent) that you want on the investment. You can see how this adds up quickly. For a total discount rate, you would normally be looking at about one-third of what this ends up totaling.

In all candor, you can tell quite a bit from merely looking at the range and the direction the numbers are going and determine intuitively that you have a business that is not exactly predictable (risky).

Exhibit I–1 Developing a Business Risk Factor

Year	*$ Avail to Physicians*	*Descriptive Statistics Based on Five Year Earnings* — *Statistic*	*Value*
1992	$368,000		
1993	$380,959	Mean	410510.2
1994	$406,387	Standard Error	17395.0437
1995	$433,564	Median	406387
1996	$463,641	Mode	#N/A
		Standard Deviation	38896.50019
		Sample Variance	1512937727
		Kurtosis	−1.29412254
		Skewness	0.42154709
		Range	95641
		Minimum	368000
		Maximum	463641
		Sum	2052551
		Count	5
		Confidence Level (95.0%)	48296.48397

Take the	$	38,896.50	Standard Deviation
Divided by	$	410,510.20	Mean Income
Equals		**0.094751605**	**Business Risk**

Like the beta used to measure risk in the stock market, we were concerned about quantifying risk in a variable income stream. We used statistics to analyze the deviation and divide by the mean income.

The above table of statistical values is a result of an analysis by Excel Data Pak accessed by highlighting Tools on the menu bar and then selecting Data Analysis on the bottom of the menu. Then pick Descriptive Statistics. Alternatively, you could just solve for the standard deviation and the mean income for the values above. The Descriptive Statistics merely provide a broader analysis with no more effort.

APPENDIX J

Quick Cheat Sheet—Gathering and Organizing Data for Physician Practice Appraisals

1. Get the most up-to-date data possible (see needs list) and find out when the client plans on making an offer so you can try to tie everything together on that date for a dated value.
2. Normalize the financial statements (eliminating one-time or unusual expenses or income items).
3. Convert the financials from cash basis to accrual basis.
4. Get the tangible assets (equipment, fixtures, furnishings, and leasehold improvements) appraised so that they can be included in the updated balance sheet.
5. Bring the financials up to date per the date you are going to date the appraisal.
6. Review the local market for sales data and marketplace dynamics as they relate to the practice you are appraising.
7. Evaluate the practice operation and management to determine how to compare it with others in the marketplace or the industry measures.
8. Perform the applicable approaches.
   Income approach—main methods
   - Present value of discounted cash flow
     - Project the income for five years based on good pro forma.
     - Perform a present-value calculation on the next five years and a value for terminal value or reversion.
   - Price-to-earnings ratio
     - Identify a current price-to-earnings ratio in the publicly traded stock market and multiply it times the earnings of the subject.
   - Excess earnings method
     - Follow the process outlined in the book.
   - Multiplier times EBIDT (three to seven average)—for total clinic value
   - Income multiplier times gross patient revenue—for goodwill only—and add selected tangible asset value
     - Obtain the goodwill factor being paid for the practice type that you are valuing and modify it according to the practice quality.
     - Multiply the modified goodwill factor times the three- to five-year historically weighted gross patient revenue.
     - Add this goodwill value to the current fair market value of the tangible assets that you want to include in the transaction.
   - Asset based—adjusted balance sheet equity
     - From the updated balance sheet, see what the *owner's equity* is as a balance sheet approach to value.
   - Sales—market comparison of similar practices
     - Obtain comparable transaction data from similar practices or clinics.
     - Perform a PSA or other technique eliminating the dissimilarities and values technique to determine the value of the subject that you are valuing.

APPENDIX K

Other Valuation Calculations

Exhibit K–1 contains several different formulas and calculations used by those in the field depending on the projects and purpose of the appraisals. I have listed the formulas for your convenience. The accompanying diskette offers these formulas and techniques. The only items needed from you are those values in Exhibit K–1.

Exhibit K–1

Going Concern - Goodwill Calculations	
Given:	
NTAV	$100,000
Gross Revenue (Latest 12 Month Period)	$750,000
Pretax Normalized Earnings (After Remun to Owner)	$150,000
Remuneration to Owner(s)	$600,000
Required Rate of Return on NTAV	15.00%
Capitalization Rate for:	
Gross Revenue	20.00%
Cash Flow to Owner Manager	15.00%
Excess Earnings	50.00%
Normalized Earnings	10.00%

METHODS OF VALUING COMMERCIAL GOODWILL, EQUIPMENT, AND SUPPLIES

A. Capitalization of Gross Revenue

Gross Revenue / Gross Revenue Capitalization Rate	$3,750,000

B. Capitalization of Excess Earnings

[(Normalized Earnings – (NTAV × Req ROR)]/ExcEarn Cap Rate	$120,000

C. Capitalization of Normalized Earnings

(Normalized Earnings / Capitalization Rate) – NTAV	$1,400,000

continues

Exhibit K–1 continued

D. Capitalization of Cash Flow

(Normalized Cash Flow + Owner Remuneration) / Cash Flow Capitalization Rate $4,150,000

E. Discounted Cash Flow Differential

Given $V = (E^t/(1 + r_1)^t - (S^t/(1 + r_2)^t$

V	=	PV value of cash flow differential between an existing practice & new practice
t	=	The time period (one year generally)
n	=	Number of periods
E	=	Projected cash flow of existing practice to the owner for period "t"
S	=	Projected cash flow of new practice to the owner for period "t"

r_1	=	Discount rate applicable to the cash flow of the existing practice	0.15
r_2	=	Discount rate applicable to the cash flow of the new practice	0.25
GR_e	=	Annual Growth Rate for Existing Practice (ie 1.03 = 3% growth rate)	1.03
GR_n	=	Annual Growth Rate for New Practice (ie 1.20 = 20% growth rate)	1.2
I_e	=	First Year Income for Years Valued, Existing Practice	$150,000.00
I_n	=	First Year Income for Years Valued, New Practice	$75,000.00

Year	Projected Income Existing Practice	Projected Income New Practice
1	$150,000	$75,000
2	$154,500	$90,000
3	$159,135	$108,000
4	$163,909	$129,600
5	$168,826	$155,520

	Present Values		Present Values	PV Difference
V_1	$130,435	less	$60,000	$70,435
V_2	$116,824	less	$57,600	$59,224
V_3	$104,634	less	$55,296	$49,338
V_4	$93,716	less	$53,084	$40,631
V_5	$83,937	less	$50,961	$32,976

Value Indicated by this approach $252,604
is the difference in the present value of the two income streams

APPENDIX L

Sample Appraisals

To assist you in your evaluation or performance of basic appraisals, I have included several types of appraisals for your reference. The appraisals included are actual appraisals that have been modified somewhat for anonymity and to provide better illustrative examples.

The first is a completed actual equipment appraisal. The appraisal sought to identify the fair market value in-use values. No goodwill was involved in this appraisal, only equipment, fixtures, and furnishings. The forms and narrative are actual language and should be largely followed by anyone performing an appraisal on equipment for you. I have seen one equipment appraisal done by a so-called big name accounting firm with an appraisal "division," which was incredibly vague and only provided groupings of equipment with singular group values. This is totally unacceptable. You need to provide detail. If you are paying for appraisals, you need to get it. If you are doing them, you need to provide it. Refer to the equipment appraisal section of the manual.

The second appraisal is a diagnostic services physician partnership that was attempting to sell the partnership before December 31, 1994, when Stark II was about to go into effect. The partnership leased the space from the hospital's imaging department. This is an interesting example that demonstrates the types of issues you can get into in some physician clinics and partnerships, when they involve cooperative services for hospitals.

The third is the business valuation portion of a valuation of a closed hospital being turned into an assisted living center and physician offices. The special merit of this appraisal is that it deals with the changing roles of health care facilities. It includes a variety of analyses and gives an idea of how to approach the valuation of a business that has not yet begun. Although this was technically a real estate appraisal (I do not provide all the real estate data), the appraisal considered the income approach based on significant research and the cost approach. There were no reasonable sales comparisons, so that approach was not included.

The fourth appraisal is a family practice clinic appraisal. For those of you who are only interested in medical practices, you will obviously want to focus more on this sample.

Appraisal #1. Medical Office Equipment Appraisal

SAMPLE EQUIPMENT APPRAISAL

January 27, 1997

Mr. Jack Daniels
FMD Corporation
101 Main Street
La Habra, CA 12345

RE: Letter of Transmittal—Appraisal of Equipment

Dear Mr. Daniels:

In accordance with your authorization, we have made an appraisal of the Equipment and Leasehold Improvements associated with Marcus Welby, M.D. located at 125 Palmer Avenue, La Habra, CA.

The appraisal was made to express our opinion of the value based on "as is" in place, also known as fair market value in continued use of the subject asset(s) as of March 7, 1995. It is our understanding that our opinion of values reported will be used to value practice equipment and leasehold improvements for sale.

We have not investigated any financial data pertaining to the earning capacity of Marcus Welby, M.D.

Based on our analysis along with the limiting conditions contained in this report, it is our opinion that the fair market value in continued use of the subject asset(s) as of March 7, 1995, are as follows:

Fifty-Nine Thousand Dollars
($59,000)

For a detailed listing of the appraised asset(s), please refer to the Addenda.

Sincerely,

AMERICAN HEALTH CARE APPRAISAL

BGK:tk

APPRAISAL
of
Equipment and Leasehold Improvements

LOCATED AT
125 Palmer Avenue
La Habra, CA

APPRAISED BY
JAMES LABRETO, ASA

AS OF
March 7, 1995

REPORT

Property Appraised:

The property appraised in this report consists of Equipment, Furnishings, Fixtures and Leasehold Improvements associated with Marcus Welby, M.D., located at 125 Palmer Avenue, La Habra, CA.

Purpose of the Appraisal:

The purpose of the appraisal is to value practice equipment and leasehold improvements for sale as of March 7, 1995.

Function of the Appraisal:

The function of this appraisal is to provide a "fair market value in continued use" appraisal of the subject assets.

Limiting Conditions

All information presented in this report is true and accurate to the best of the appraiser's knowledge and belief.

The fee for this appraisal is not contingent on the values or other conclusions reported.

Neither the appraisers nor any member of American Health Care Appraisal (AHCA) has any present nor contemplated future financial interest in the property being appraised.

The appraiser renders no opinion as to legal fees, title, or prevailing leases. Liens and other encumbrances were disregarded. The property was appraised as if free and clear, unless otherwise specifically stated.

This study was made for the purpose stated and cannot be relied on for any other purpose.

This is for the internal use of the client only and unless otherwise stated, should not be disseminated to the public or third parties in any part.

An American Health Care Appraisal appraiser has made a personal inspection of the property. All estimates of value are presented in this report as the appraiser's opinion.

Information supplied by others that was considered in the valuation is from sources believed to be reliable, and no further responsibility is assumed for its accuracy.

We reserve the right to make such adjustments to the valuation herein reported as may be required by consideration of additional or more reliable data that may become available.

Testimony or attendance in court by reason of this appraisal shall not be required unless arrangements for such services have been made previously.

Neither all nor any part of this report is to be conveyed to the public through advertising, public relations, news, sales, or other media without the express written consent and approval of American Health Care Appraisal.

No appraisals of land, land improvements, buildings, and any intangible assets that may exist were made by AHCA.

This appraisal was made in accordance with the Code of Ethics and the requirements of the Uniform Standards of Professional Appraisal Practice set forth by the American Society of Appraisers.

The appraisal did not consider the possibility of the existence of hazardous conditions with equipment or its physical locations. We suggest you retain the services of a qualified professional to determine the existence and extent of any hazardous conditions, as well as the cost associated with any required or desirable treatment, or removal.

Description of the Business

Marcus Welby, M.D., is in the business of operating a Family Medical Practice.

Description of Assets

The assets of the business consist of office furniture, fixtures, business machines, and medical equipment.

Appraisal Theory

There are three basic approaches to value that must be considered when making an appraisal.

Cost Approach

The cost approach is a technique that uses the concept of replacement cost as an indicator of market value. This is based on the *principle of substitution* (i.e., a prudent investor would pay no more for an asset than the amount necessary to replace it new).

"Reproduction Cost New" establishes the *highest amount* a prudent investor would pay for an asset. To the extent that the asset being valued provides less utility than the new one, the value of that asset is less than the Reproduction Cost New. The Reproduction Cost New is then adjusted for loss in value due to physical depreciation, functional obsolescence, and economic obsolescence.

1. **Physical Depreciation** refers to the loss in value due to factors such as wear and tear from use and exposure to damaging elements. Generally speaking, physical depreciation is largely a function of age, maintenance, and intensity of use.
2. **Functional Obsolescence** refers to the loss in value caused by such internal factors as excess capacity, inadequacy, and technological changes that affect the property itself or its relation with other assets comprising a larger property.
3. **Economic Obsolescence** refers to the loss in value caused by economic forces external to the property itself, including changes in optimum use, legislative enactments, and changes in supply and demand relationships.

Market Approach

The market approach is a technique in which value is estimated, based on market prices in actual transactions and on asking prices for assets available as of the date of valuation. The process is essentially that of comparison and correlation between the subject asset and other similar assets that have been sold to provide and indicate current value. The approach requires the appraiser to compare the comparable assets with the subject asset and make adjustment for condition, quality, etc.

Income Approach

The income approach is based on the value of future cash flows that an asset will produce over its useful life. There are several steps in applying this approach. First, a projection is made of the cash flows that the asset is expected to generate. This involves analysis of financial information and discussion with operations personnel to project future income and related expenses. The second step is to convert these cash flows to a present-value equivalent through discounting. This discounting process uses a rate of return that accounts for the risk inherent in the cash flows and the time value of money. The market value of the asset is the sum of the discounted flows plus the present value of any residual value.

Depreciation

To determine depreciation, we used two methods. The first was to determine the fair market value of an asset after researching and analyzing the used market.

The difference between the replacement cost and the fair market value is a true indicator of depreciation from all causes. When we could not find any supportable market data, we used an age/life analysis to determine depreciation. The age/life formula is the normal life of the asset over the remaining useful life of the asset, with the end result being an indicator of the fair market value ($RUL / NUL \times \text{RCN} = FMV$). This is part of a process by which an analysis establishes the arithmetic life cycle of the assets at the appraisal date, with the adjustment made for the observed condition relating to used, physical condition and obsolescence factors, if any. To support our age/life analysis, we researched the used market for recent sales or asking prices of comparable equipment.

These findings were then compared with our depreciation formula and adjustments were made, if necessary, to reflect the market conditions at the date of appraisal.

Methodology

To arrive at our opinion of fair market value in continued use for medical equipment, furniture, fixtures, and equipment, we researched the local used markets by contacting dealers in used equipment to compare what similar items have recently sold for in the open market, or asking prices of similar items offered for sale. Tax, freight, and installation were then added, when applicable, to arrive at our opinion of value.

Certifications

The undersigned does hereby certify that, except as otherwise noted in this appraisal report:

We have inspected the subject assets described in the addenda of this report.

We have no present or contemplated future interest in the assets that are the subject of this report.

We have no personal interest or bias with respect to the subject matter of this appraisal report or the parties involved.

To the best of our knowledge and belief the statements of fact contained in this appraisal report, on which the analysis, opinions, and conclusions are based, are true and correct.

The appraisal report sets forth all the limiting conditions (imposed by the terms of our assignment or by the undersigned) affecting the analysis, opinions, and conclusions contained in this appraisal report.

All data secured from dealers, vendors, auctioneers, or other companies and individuals used in this analysis, opinions, and conclusions of value were believed to be factually correct.

I am a Senior Member of the American Society of Appraisers. Disclosure of the contents of this appraisal report is governed by the by-laws and constitution of the American Society of Appraisers.

I personally inspected the subject assets on March 7, 1995.

James Labreto, ASA
Senior Appraiser

Summary and Conclusions

Based on the data presented in this report, it is our opinion that the fair market value in continued use of the described asset(s) as of March 7, 1995 are as follows:

Fifty-Nine Thousand Dollars
($59,000)

For a detailed description of subject assets, please refer to the Addenda.

ADDENDA

SOURCE LIST

Medical Optical Inc., Los Angeles, CA
ABC X-ray Equipment, Los Angeles
Anderson Medical Supply, Los Angeles
Remarketing International, San Diego, CA
Used Furniture Co., El Monte, CA
Marshall and Swift Valuation Service, Los Angeles
Orion Blue Book—Computers, 1994
Orion Blue Book—Copiers, 1994

EQUIPMENT AND LEASEHOLD VALUES

LOCATION	*ITEM*	*MFR*	*MODEL*	*S/N*	*FMVIU*
Waiting Area	Table, coffee (3.5) cube-shaped oak 20x20x20 (expensive)				$262.50
Waiting Area	Chairs, row, (14) wooden frame with cloth upholstery				$700.00
Waiting Area	Lamps, coffee table (2) vase-type (nice, expensive)				$100.00
Main Ofc	Telephone system (11 sets incl main unit)	Northern Telecom	Mdl 02b NT8B91	402179012	$4,675.00
Main Ofc	Computer	IBM 386 Clone-Hot Chip			$500.00
Main Ofc	Monitor, monochrome				$190.00
Main Ofc	Printer, dot matrix	Smith Corona	D200		$35.00
Main Ofc	Slave terminal (2)	Espirit Systems	Espirit III Color	2702438 2702736	$650.00
Main Ofc	Clock	Seth Thomas			$25.00
Main Ofc	Clock radio	General Electric	Model 7-4550A		$15.00
Main Ofc	Typewriter	IBM	Selectric II		$65.00

LOCATION	*ITEM*	*MFR*	*MODEL*	*S/N*	*FMVIU*
Main Ofc	File cabinet, vertical 4-drawer (3)	HON			$390.00
Main Ofc	Copier	Minolta	EP-4230	3155556	$640.00
Main Ofc	Chairs, steno w/casters (2)	HON			$150.00
Main Ofc	Stool w/naugahyde cover	Pedigo			$50.00
Main Ofc	FAX	Canon	Fax 230		$160.00
Main Ofc	Chart rack w/ 3 bays, lockable and fire-proof	X2 (Times 2)	Speed files		$830.00
Main Ofc	Bookcase 5-tier, steel	HON			$95.00
Main Ofc	Picture 28x20 framed and matted				$40.00
Main Ofc	Picture 13x18 framed and matted				$40.00
Main Ofc	Modems (2) 2400-baud	Multi-Tech	Multi-Modem 224E7		$40.00
Main Ofc	Computer multi (16-user) operating system, 1 gigabyte hard drive, 8 meg 68030 chip	Alpha Micro 1000			$5,000.00
Main Ofc	Software, medical management	Medical Digital			$15,200.00
Main Ofc	Monitor	Packard Bell	TriSync	PB8510SV	$190.00
Main Ofc	Monitor, VGA	Magnavox	Professional		$190.00
Main Ofc	Printer, dot matrix 24" wide carriage Anadex	Silent Scribe			$60.00
Main Ofc	Printer, dot matrix 24" wide carriage Toshiba		P1351	550238	$60.00
Main Ofc	Calculator, printing	Casio	FR-105s		$10.00
Main Ofc	Desk, pedestal 2 bays of 2 drawers, Formica top				$220.00
Main Ofc	Computer (2)	IBM Clone 386	LRB Custom		$1,000.00
Main Ofc	Surge protector, heavy-duty	ONGuard			$50.00
Main Ofc	Printer stands (2), 1 oak, 1 oak laminated				$100.00
Main Ofc	Desk, secretary 48x30, oak (inexpensive)				$80.00
Main Ofc	Desk-top book shelf, matching				$30.00
Main Ofc	Book shelf (2) 3 levels, wall-mounted, oak-laminated				$60.00
Main Ofc	File cabinet, legal, pine, stained, 5-drawer				$195.00
Main Ofc	Monitor, VGA	WIN			$190.00
Main Ofc	Book shelf, 4 levels, pine-laminated				$85.00
Main Ofc	File cabinet, 4-drawer, metal, heavy-duty				$120.00
Main Ofc	Computer, 286	Leading Edge			$360.00
Main Ofc	Monitor, VGA	Leading Edge			$110.00
Main Ofc	Chair, steno (2) w/casters				$150.00
Main Ofc	Chair, cloth w/arms, stickball				$25.00
Main Ofc	Cabinet, storage 20x20, Formica-covered				$15.00
Main Ofc	Microwave oven	Sharp	Model: Carousel		$55.00
Main Ofc	Refrigerator	Kenmore		0.4 cu ft	$80.00
Main Ofc	File cabinet, 2-drawer, legal, metal	HON			$90.00
Main Ofc	Coffee maker	General Electric	Brew starter		$20.00
Main Ofc	Peripheral port switch box	Logical Connection			$30.00
Main Ofc	Picture 28x36		Poster type		$40.00
Main Ofc	Printer, dot matrix, wide carriage	Printronix	Model 05704	55022	$730.00
Laboratory	Battery charger Nickel Cadmium	Again and Again	Model cc-8		$25.00
Laboratory	Microscope, illuminated	Olympus		237942	$270.00

LOCATION	*ITEM*	*MFR*	*MODEL*	*S/N*	*FMVIU*
Exam Room 7	Exam table 2 pieces: 1. Cushioned, flexible exam top bolted to 2. Base with steel frame, wooden sides and cabinets with electrical outlets and step	No identification			$700.00
Exam Room 7	Pictures (2) framed and matted, 30x25; 28x20				$80.00
Exam Room 7	Waste container, sharps	Monoject-Sherwood Medical		522795	$15.00
Exam Room 7	Jars, glass 1- swabs, 1- tongue depressors				$10.00
Exam Room 7	Potted plant, small				$10.00
Exam Room 7	Stool w/casters				$50.00
Exam Room 7	Chair, straight				$40.00
Exam Room 7	Magazine rack, floor				$40.00
Exam Room 7	Waste receptacle, covered				$45.00
Exam Room 7	Otoscope	Welch Allyn			$250.00
Exam Room 7	Patient bathroom framed poster				$40.00
Exam Room 7	Window blinds, venetian, horizontal, narrow (2) 40"				$60.00
Exam Room 6	Exam table, naugahyde				$200.00
Exam Room 6	Otoscope	Welch Allyn			$250.00
Exam Room 5	Exam table 2 pieces: 1. Cushioned, flexible exam top bolted to 2. Base with steel frame, wooden sides and cabinets with electrical outlets and step	No identification			$700.00
Exam Room 5	Pictures (2) framed and matted, 30x25; 28x20				$80.00
Exam Room 5	Waste container, sharps	Monoject-Sherwood Medical		522795	$15.00
Exam Room 5	Jars, glass 1- swabs, 1- tongue depressors				$10.00
Exam Room 5	Potted plant, small				$10.00
Exam Room 5	Stool w/casters				$50.00
Exam Room 5	Chair, straight				$40.00
Exam Room 5	Magazine rack, floor				$40.00
Exam Room 5	Waste receptacle, covered				$45.00
Exam Room 5	Otoscope	Welch Allyn			$250.00
Exam Room 5	Patient bathroom framed poster				$40.00
Exam Room 5	Window blinds, venetian, horizontal, narrow (2) 40"				$60.00
Exam Room 5	Tray, sterilizer, stainless steel for forceps				$20.00
Exam Room 5	Holder, stainless steel for instruments/ forceps				$20.00
Exam Room 4	Waste container, sharps	Monoject-Sherwood Medical		522795	$15.00
Exam Room 4	Scale, infant	Detecto			$150.00
Exam Room 4	Waste receptacle, covered				$45.00
Exam Room 4	Otoscope	Welch Allyn			$250.00
Exam Room 4	Stool w/casters				$50.00
Exam Room 4	Jars, glass 1- swabs, 1- tongue depressors				$10.00

LOCATION	*ITEM*	*MFR*	*MODEL*	*S/N*	*FMVIU*
Exam Room 4	Pictures, (3) 28x18				$120.00
Exam Room 4	Mirror 12x18, framed in wicker				$20.00
Exam Room 4	Typanometer	American Electromedics Corp	Model 85TT "The tymp"	540396	$755.00
Surgical Room 3	Jars, (4) stainless steel				$20.00
Surgical Room 3	Jars, (4) glass				$20.00
Surgical Room 3	Jars, (3) metal, white				$15.00
Surgical Room 3	Waste container, sharps	Monoject-Sherwood Medical		522795	$15.00
Surgical Room 3	Fan, oscillating, 3-speed	South Coast			$20.00
Surgical Room 3	Dispenser, Band Aid, plastic	Johnson and Johnson			$15.00
Surgical Room 3	Dispenser, tube gauze	Tubegaus			$20.00
Surgical Room 3	Sterilizer/Autoclave	Pelton and Crane	Omni-clave	a3-6520	$915.00
Surgical Room 3	Boot cast, large	Castaway			$75.00
Surgical Room 3	Suction machine	Schuco	Schuco-vac 5711-130	21092 32289	$400.00
Surgical Room 3	Colonoscope, 160 cm	Pentax			$1,650.00
Surgical Room 3	Light source	Pentax			$300.00
Surgical Room 3	Cart, stainless steel on casters, sml, lightweight	No name			$75.00
Surgical Room 3	Cart, stainless steel on casters (2)	Lakeside			$200.00
Surgical Room 3	Stool, cushioned w/casters				$50.00
Surgical Room 3	Chair, wooden with fabric cushions, arms	Coriander Wood Designs, Redmond, WA			$80.00
Surgical Room 3	Magazine, rack, wall-mounted, wood				$40.00
Surgical Room 3	Multipurpose table	Ritter	Model A7	728110-9	$825.00
Surgical Room 3	Tray, sterilizer (4)				$80.00
Surgical Room 3	Fulgerator	Ellman Mfg, Hewlett, NY	Surgitron, Model FR	10,203	$1,650.00
Surgical Room 3	Light, ultraviolet exam	Burton Medical Products	Model 31602	8268	$100.00
Surgical Room 3	Tray, surgical stainless steel, on casters				$75.00
Surgical Room 3	Cylinder, 80 cu in +/– for nitrous oxide with KR-Med regulator on cart				$80.00
Surgical Room 3	Cylinder, 34 cu in +/– for oxygen with MADA regulator/gauge on cart				$40.00
Surgical Room 3	Waste can, large				$45.00
Surgical Room 3	Outlet (electric) extension strip				$10.00
Surgical Room 3	Lamp, gooseneck, floor model				$40.00
Surgical Room 3	Blinds, venetian, narrow 2 sets 40" long and 36" high				$60.00
Nurse's O.R. Sub-Sta	Chair, bench, high, on casters, adjustable, fabric				$120.00
Nurse's O.R. Sub-Sta	Cart	Lakeside			$100.00
Nurse's O.R. Sub-Sta	Thermometer, electronic	Cheeseborough-Ponds Hospital Products Div	Model f-1500	L8812744/f	$300.00

LOCATION	*ITEM*	*MFR*	*MODEL*	*S/N*	*FMVIU*
Nurse's O.R. Sub-Sta	Stethoscope, dual head and dual tubing (expensive)	Regency			$100.00
Nurse's O.R. Sub-Sta	Stethoscope, standard				$25.00
Nurse's O.R. Sub-Sta	Blood pressure cuff, wall-mounted	Baumanometer			$100.00
Nurse's O.R. Sub-Sta	Waste container, sharps	Johnson and Johnson			$15.00
Nurse's O.R. Sub-Sta	Computer workstation to Alpha 1000 monitor and keyboard				$300.00
Nurse's O.R. Sub-Sta	Chair, wooden with fabric cushions, arms	Coriander Wood Designs, Redmond, WA			$80.00
Exam Room 1	Blinds, venetian, narrow, 2 sets 40" long and 36" high				$60.00
Exam Room 1	Exam table w/stirrups	Hamilton	Steeltone		$700.00
Exam Room 1	Head set (light)	Welch Allyn	79103		$200.00
Exam Room 1	Picture, 28x20, framed and matted				$40.00
Exam Room 1	Stool, chrome, w/cushion and casters	Pedigo			$50.00
Exam Room 1	Waste receptacle, metal w/cover				$45.00
Exam Room 1	Otoscope	Welch Allyn			$250.00
Exam Room 1	Waste container, sharps	Monoject-Sherwood Medical	522795		$15.00
Exam Room 1	Jar, glass				$5.00
Exam Room 1	Jar, metal, white				$5.00
Exam Room 1	Tuning (audiometric) fork				$25.00
Exam Room 1	Magazine rack, wooden, wall-mounted				$40.00
Exam Room 2	Exam table	Hamilton	Steeltone		$700.00
Exam Room 2	Picture (1) framed and matted, 28x20				$40.00
Exam Room 2	Waste container, sharps	Monoject-Sherwood Medical	522795		$15.00
Exam Room 2	Jars, glass (3)				$15.00
Exam Room 2	Stool w/casters				$50.00
Exam Room 2	Chair, straight, wooden				$40.00
Exam Room 2	Magazine rack, wooden, wall				$40.00
Exam Room 2	Waste receptacle, covered				$45.00
Exam Room 2	Otoscope	Welch Allyn			$250.00
Exam Room 2	Tuning (audiometric) fork				$25.00
Exam Room 2	Head set (light)	Welch Allyn	79103		$175.00
Exam Room 2	Blinds, venetian, narrow, 2 sets 40" long and 36" high				$60.00
Hallway	Pictures, framed, various, approximately 30x20				$80.00
Hallway	Scale, physician's	Health o meter			$180.00
Hallway	Scale, physician's (older but good)	Fairbanks Morse, Chicago	g312658		$180.00
Hallway	Stool, stepping on casters	Kik step			$15.00
Hallway	Cart, stainless steel on casters	Lakeside			$100.00
Hallway	Wastebaskets, large plastic (2)				$40.00
Hallway	Refrigerator, medicine, 0.4 cu ft	GE			$80.00
Hallway	Centrifuge	Drucker Co.	Model 611D	L91-116	$160.00

LOCATION	*ITEM*	*MFR*	*MODEL*	*S/N*	*FMVIU*
Hallway	Chart rack, wooden (11)				$165.00
Hallway	Waste container, sharps	Monoject-Sherwood Medical	522795		$15.00
Hallway	Clock, battery-operated		ZIAC		$10.00
Hallway	ECG machine	Mortara		8909023025	$1,800.00
Hallway	Portable aerosol therapy unit	Healthaire	N-600		$175.00
Hallway	Blood pressure cuff				$50.00
Dr. Kiley Ofc	Book shelf (2) oak 4′ wide 5 shelves				$170.00
Dr. Kiley Ofc	Desk, oak 40x30 secretary-type laminated oak, L-shaped				$160.00
Dr. Kiley Ofc	Chair, executive on casters, fabric				$130.00
Dr. Kiley Ofc	Chairs, guest, w/arms/fabric				$80.00
Dr. Kiley Ofc	In-out basket, wooden				$5.00
Dr. Kiley Ofc	Blinds, venetian, narrow, 2 sets 40" long and 36" high				$60.00
Ms. Anderson's Ofc	Desk, 40x30, oak				$135.00
Ms. Anderson's Ofc	Chair, high back, wooden, swivel				$130.00
Ms. Anderson's Ofc	Chairs, (2) wooden, wicker back with seat cushions				$160.00
Ms. Anderson's Ofc	Bookcase, oak, 6′ high enclosed (top half glass enclosed/ bottom wooden doors)				$130.00
Ms. Anderson's Ofc	Lamp, floor w/glass table				$60.00
Ms. Anderson's Ofc	Blinds, venetian, narrow, 2 sets 40" long and 36" high				$60.00
Dr. Welby's Ofc	Book shelf (2) 3 level, oak w/matching enclosed (deeper) bases 36x12 ea.				$170.00
Dr. Welby's Ofc	Desk, 30x60 oak w/side work area w/ matching desktop bookshelf 3 drawer				$300.00
Dr. Welby's Ofc	Chairs (2), wooden with rich upholstery				$160.00
Dr. Welby's Ofc	Chair, executive upholstered, w/arms wooden				$135.00
Dr. Welby's Ofc	Coffee table, chrome and glass 30x30				$110.00
Dr. Welby's Ofc	Blinds, venetian, narrow, 2 sets 40" long and 36" high				$60.00
2d Hall Station	Computer work station				$300.00
2d Hall Station	Wooden table/stand for computer				$35.00
2d Hall Station	Chair, bench, lab-type, chrome and fabric, adjustable				$80.00
2d Hall Station	BP cuffs (3)	Sprague Rappaport			$150.00
2d Hall Station	Cabinet, 5-drawer Formica-covered (add-on)				$120.00
General	Supplies on hand estimate				$3,000.00
General	Miscellaneous ofc supplies and materials				$250.00
					$59,222.00
					(Rounded to $59,000)

Appraisal #2. Physician Partnership

AMERICAN HEALTH CARE APPRAISAL
APPRAISAL SPECIALISTS FOR THE HEALTH CARE INDUSTRY

4130 LA JOLLA VILLAGE DRIVE, SUITE 1072
LA JOLLA, CALIFORNIA 92037
(619) 751-1450

PHYSICIAN PARTNERSHIP SAMPLE APPRAISAL
ADVANCED C.T. IMAGING
19684 HOSPITAL DRIVE
LAS BUENAS, CALIFORNIA

JUNE 1, 1994

APPRAISAL REPORT

Subject

Advanced C.T. Imaging

Property Address

19684 Hospital Drive
Las Buenas, California

Nature of Appraisal Subject

U.S. (California) Partnership
Medical Specialty Services

Date of Valuation

June 1, 1994

Appraisers for

Advanced C.T. Imaging

Appraised By

American Health Care Appraisal
4130 La Jolla Village Drive, Ste 1072
La Jolla, California 92037

June 7, 1994

William F. Dodson, M.D.
Managing Partner
Advanced C.T. Imaging
19684 Hospital Drive
Las Buenas, California 91234

Subject: *Fair Market Value Appraisal of Advanced C.T. Imaging Assets and Net Tangible Asset Value*

Dear Dr. Dodson:

In accordance with your request, we have appraised the subject partnership assets.

Your attention is invited to the attached pages indicating the data collected and analyzed by our firm in formulating an opinion of value. Also attached is the certification and statement of limiting conditions.

As a result of our investigation and analysis, some of which is described in this report, it is our opinion that the market value of the subject partnership assets including all current and fixed assets as of June 1, 1994, is:

Two Million, Three Hundred Fifty Thousand Dollars
($2,350,000.00)

Cordially,

AMERICAN HEALTH CARE APPRAISAL

BGK:tk

Attachments

Introduction—Description of the Assignment

American Health Care Appraisal has been requested by Dr. William F. Dodson, Managing Partner of Advanced CT Imaging (hereafter referred to as the Partnership) to appraise the fair market value of the Partnership located in Las Buenas, California. The valuations are as of June 1, 1994, using information available at that time. The appraisal is being conducted for the divestiture of the partners due to a recent change in the California law that requires referring physicians to divest themselves of ownership in medical diagnostic and other services from which they may receive any financial interest.

In completing the appraisal, we have followed the Uniform Standards of Professional Appraisal Practice.

Summary Description of Partnership

Advanced CT Imaging, a California Partnership headquartered in Las Buenas, California, is a for-profit medical organization specializing in the provision of diagnostic computerized axial tomography services. The Partnership operates within General Memorial Hospital, Las Buenas, California. The Partnership serves the inpatients of General Memorial Hospital and outpatients referred by partner physicians and other community physicians.

Capitalization and Ownership

The Partnership is capitalized with one class of common stock with a stated par value of $12,500 per share. As of this date, there were 46 partners holding 116 shares.

Definition of Fair Market Value

Fair market value is considered to represent a value at which a willing seller and a willing buyer, both informed of the relevant facts about the business, could reasonably conduct a transaction, neither person acting under compulsion to do so. Among other factors, this appraisal considers all elements of appraisal listed in Internal Revenue Service Ruling 59-60, which generally outlines the valuation of closely held stocks and includes the following:

1. nature of the business and history of the enterprise
2. economic outlook in general and condition and outlook of the specific industry in particular
3. book value of the stock and the financials of the business
4. company's earning capacity
5. company's dividend paying capacity
6. whether the enterprise has goodwill or other intangible value
7. sales of stock and size of the block to be valued
8. market prices of stocks of corporations engaged in the same or similar lines of business whose stocks are actively traded in a free and open market, either on an exchange or over the counter

Purpose

The purpose of this appraisal is to assist in the development of an accurate opinion of fair market value for the Partnership to divest of the business. As clarified elsewhere in this report, the Partnership must divest itself of the business by the end of the current calendar year due to legislation requiring physicians to divest of diagnostic services they refer patients to if they have a financial interest in those services. We provided opinions of value for all appropriate Partnership tangible and intangible assets that investors should be expected to pay for in assuming ownership of the business whether as an asset sale or stock purchase.

Scope and Limitations

Our opinion of value of the Partnership as it relates to the income approach is predicated on what we can generally and reasonably assume in a rapidly changing health care marketplace. It is not within the scope of this brief narrative appraisal to perform precise analyses of third-party payer reimbursement systems but rather to understand and factor in our approaches to value the general direction of declining reimbursement for services and business volume.

Our projections of business volume are a function of trending past performance to the future, and our estimate of a stabilized use rate for CT scans in the Las Buenas area is based on criteria and assumptions listed elsewhere in this report.

Our estimates of income are also based on changes in the major factors (only) that drive income, namely, adjusted use rates for services, the level at which usage will stabilize, and trends in marketplace competition and general changes in reimbursement.

We also have included our estimate of retroactive payments by the state for trauma services. We have discounted these estimated amounts heavily because their level payment by the state is questionable.

In terms of accounts receivable, accounts payable, and other current assets and liabilities, we have made estimates to update values used in adjusting the Partnership balance sheet. The latest financial statements we have are as of March 31, 1994 (balance sheet and income and expense statements). If a stock purchase versus an asset purchase is anticipated, the current asset and current liabilities should be tallied immediately before the closing to determine their value at that time.

If booked accounts receivable are to be included in the sale, they should be factored by 0.54 to reflect the current collection experience level of the Partnership.

Summary Description of the Partnership

Advanced CT Imaging is a medical general partnership formed for the purpose of providing medical imaging equipment and services management and that consists of 50 physicians located in Las Buenas, California.

Location

The location of the Partnership's professional service activity is the Imaging Department, General Memorial Hospital, 19684 Hospital Drive, Las Buenas, California 91234. The Partnership leases approximately 1,036 square feet within the facility for conducting the business of the Partnership. This address is also the official address used by the Partnership to report its financial activity to the IRS.

Market Share

As discussed earlier, the hospital's market share (53 percent) of the primary service area (173,241) consists of approximately 91,288 persons. Although it might be said that the actual market share of the CT service is smaller or larger than this due a variety of factors, it is not within the scope of this report to enumerate and evaluate each of those criteria. We assume that the market for the CT service is substantially equivalent to that of the hospital. We also add that the capabilities of the electron beam Imatron CT may broaden the service area for some diagnostic services, especially in the cardiac diagnostic areas.

Date of Inception

The Partnership medical services program was implemented on June 1, 1992. A seven-year contract was entered into between the Partnership and General Memorial Hospital.

Sources of Information

- U.S. Partnership Return of Income for the Corporation, 1991 and 1992
- First Quarterly Financial Statement, 1994
- Advanced CT Imaging Partnership Roster
- Monthly Statistics, 1992–1993
- Monthly Statistics, 1993–1994
- Patient Mix Statistical Report, May 1993–April 1994
- Financial Class Activity Report, 4/1/94
- Accounts Receivable Aged Trial Balance by Financial Class, 4/1/94
- Accounts Receivable Summary by Class, 4/1/94
- Charges by Referring Doctor Report
- A/R Aged Trial Balance by Referring Doctor and Financial Class, 4/1/94
- Minutes of Managing Partners Meetings, April 1992–February 1994
- Fee Schedule in Effect
- Depreciation Schedules for Furniture, Fixtures, and Equipment Owned by the Partnership
- National Center for Health Statistics, Washington, DC
- Ms. Kim Kooper, Office of (CA) State Health Planning and Development, Data Section
- Mr. Roger Bush, Imaging Department, Bobner Medical Center, Las Pulgas, CA
- Mr. Roger Rabbit, Manager, Physicians Imaging Center, Farnham, CA
- Mr. Patrick Presley, Memorial Hospitals, Barbarosa, CA
- Ms. Judy Schwartzenneggar, General Hospital, Mexicar, CA
- Ms. Sharon Sarbozzi, Health Care Finance Administration, Baltimore, MD
- Ms. Roy Linn, Doctor's Hospital, Los Angeles, CA
- Mr. Terry Matson, Matson and Matson, CPAs, Las Buenas, CA
- Mr. Walter Dilly, CEO, General Memorial Hospital, Las Buenas, CA
- Mr. William X. Wizner, Director, Radiology/Imaging Department, General Memorial Hospital, Las Buenas, CA

Valuation Approaches and Conclusion

We have more than just useful assets. The Partnership has a contractual right to an income stream for five years. Because of the risks in predicting what is apparently a declining income, we have placed a very high discount on all future earnings. For example, real estate future earnings might be discounted at an investor desired return of 15 percent. We consider this projected income much more risky and have used a rate of 50 percent.

The projected income stream was discounted by 50 percent based on the sum of the following cumulative rates:

a. a "base" no-risk return rate of 8 percent (comparable with current 30-year Treasury bonds)
b. a cost of capital of 10 percent
c. a business risk factor of 35 percent

(The actual business risk calculation yielded a factor of 0.40 due to the spread in income levels. We attribute some of this to the January 1994 earthquake and have adjusted our risk factor from 0.40 to 0.35.)

Based on a present value of discounted cash flow (alone) as of June 1, 1994, the value of future anticipated cash flows of the Partnership is $425,474.00. (We later blend this approach, however, with the cost approach, which reduces the impact of the present value.)

The equipment was valued as fair market in-use value ($1,200,000—Imatron Ultrafast C-100 installed and in use; $4000—Picker 600 sx installed, in use; leasehold improvements, $138,693.50; the accounts receivable, $438,307.74 [0.54 of gross receivables]).

The leasehold improvements were valued at their cost new less (straight line) depreciated value. The accounts receivable were valued at their weighted and projected value based on current collection experience (0.54) of the Partnership.

The accounts payable, the accounts receivable, the supplies, and other current assets such as cash should be valued immediately before the closing if they are to be valued and a part of the transaction.

Alternatively, if the acquisition is to be a selected asset acquisition such as the acquisition of the leasehold improvements, equipment, and income stream, then attention should be directed to those individual and collective values.

Using financial statements, Partnership tax returns, and marketplace research, we arrived at indicated values based on the following approaches:

a. present value of discounted cash flow and fair market in-use value of tangible assets
b. cost approach

Based on the analysis completed and discussed later in this report, it is our opinion that the current value of the total tangible assets of the Partnership is $2,084,168.24, or $2,100,000, rounded.

PARTNERSHIP HISTORY

Number of Partners

As stated above, there are 46 partners in the organization. One partner is the Center for Women's Health, which has four physicians who collectively have two shares in the Partnership. Of the partners, 14 partners have one share, 20 partners have two shares, 5 partners have four shares, and 7 partners have six shares, for a total of 116 shares.

Control and Management

The Partnership is managed by a committee of managing partners acting as an operating executive committee that meets regularly monthly or less often in some cases. The committee of five meets with the Imaging Department Head of their affiliated hospital who acts as an operational advisor and administrative head for the implementation of many of the decisions made.

Different managing partners are assigned specific administrative tasks, and the roles and responsibilities seem to be effective. There are no employees of the Partnership. The Partnership contracts with the hospital for services and personnel who operate the department.

We have reviewed the contracts and based on our experience, we believe that they are extremely well developed and consider not only the important issues of control and business management but also address the safeguards of the patients.

Financial Management

The office makes use of the Santa Bonita Computerized Billing System. We judge them to be professional and qualified billing experts. The accounting responsibilities are handled by Matson and Matson, CPAs, P.C., 23822 W. Las Buenas Boulevard, Suite 202, Las Buenas, CA 91234. Financial statements are made available on a quarterly basis.

The current overall collections rate is approximately 54 percent. Early operations and reports demonstrated extremely high accounts receivable with contractual allowances about 16 percent.

This leaves approximately 30 percent for bad debts. A small portion (4 percent by volume of service) of these funds is tied to the trauma service, which is paid for by the state. Each year, the state legislature determines what it is going to pay for services provided. The payment is usually about two years after the date of service.

The impact of this fact on valuation of the income stream is that some of the 30 percent falls in the state trauma services category and is paid very late. Much of the service provided when the Partnership originally began will only be coming in in the near future. We have included such a figure beginning in the third quarter of each successive year for these services but have discounted by approximately one-third of the booked receivable value. We think this is reasonable based on our experience in municipally paid services.

The Contract

Roles and Responsibilities

The Partnership responsibilities essentially include the provision of imaging equipment and the necessary ancillary equipment and tenant improvements to provide services to the patients of the medical staff at the hospital. The Partnership manages the business of patient billings, ensures that the imaging equipment is maintained in perfect operating condition, and is able to provide imaging services consistent with the community standard.

Terms

Under the agreement, the hospital provides the personnel in the Imaging Department. The director of the department assists. The Partnership originally leased the space from the hospital for which the hospital receives $2,025.17 per month. This amount is adjusted annually based on incremental increases in costs to the hospital.

The fees for rental space and personnel are not available nor indicated on any financial statement the Partnership receives. These fees are "netted out" of the income received by the hospital from gross receipts. There is a negotiated per-patient formula that the hospital and the Partnership have developed, which both sides have found to be satisfactory. If the original agreed-on fees are not adequately addressed during an interim basis, they are reconciled at the end of the billing cycle with the hospital either crediting a balance or requesting additional payment.

We did not see or otherwise review these documents. Our projections for income and expense do not include the impact of these "netting out" transactions. We only point out that they exist and should be kept in mind because they are a significant element of cost. There is a record maintained with both the Partnership and the hospital on the volume of services provided as a check on the system. Although the system appears to work and is convenient for both sides in terms of not having to issue billings and checks, it is difficult to easily identify costs and does not provide the standard kinds of documentation for auditing.

Initially, the Partnership billed a global fee for services including both the professional and the technical component. That changed on March 1, 1993, when the professional component (radiologist charges) was charged for separately. The impact is that the billings were decreased but so were the expenses to the Partnership.

As mentioned above, the current contract for providing services runs until May 31, 1999. The advent of the federal Stark legislation requiring referring physicians to divest of medical businesses has made it necessary for the partners to extract themselves from this contractual obligation.

Our analysis demonstrates that it is not just "machines" that are transferring with the sale of the Partnership but also a five-year income stream. The income stream is being generated from an established, bona fide going concern assuming the risks of operation and earning the profits from its operation.

MARKETPLACE OVERVIEW

The primary service area for General Memorial Hospital is approximately 173,241 people. It encompasses the following communities.

Primary Service Area	*Population*
Carbo County	51,618
Castillano	20,472
Newberry	25,948
Santa Bonita	1,912
Sanders	38,229
Las Buenas	35,062
Total	173,241

We noted that the primary and secondary market consists of approximately 202,000 people. Our studies did not attempt to include areas outside of the primary service area, however.

From a medical perspective and as it relates to use rates in mature managed care areas, our information suggests that this market for CT studies approximates that of southern California, according to the sources listed above.

Initially, our premise was that this market had not matured or was lagging behind others in areas that were considered to be more mature from a managed care standpoint. Research proved this to be not necessarily true.

As one prime example, we selected a hospital and its joint venture imaging company as a model in the San Diego MSA, which was much easier to isolate in terms of market for comparison purposes. This was an important factor for accuracy of comparable statistics. They also shared some similarities in terms of medical staff composition and demographics. By determining the service area and respective market shares with the volume of CT scans, we were able to come up with use rates for both organizations. Our data reveal that the comparable San Diego area hospital was performing approximately 49.9 CT studies per 1,000 population and that 48.7 per 1,000 population were being performed by the facilities at General Memorial.

Interestingly, however, we noted that service volumes in southern California do not appear to have stabilized. Their trend continues downward, with most organizations reporting declines (except one that has reduced rates and undertaken marketing efforts to capture as much of the market as possible). Our research suggests that short of such initiatives, volumes will decline. Unfortunately, we have not been able to identify a single source at the local, state, or federal levels that has any firm sense of at what level of utilization the bare minimum usage will be.

We learned late in the appraisal preparation process that the number of scans shown in the monthly statistics report from hospital finance was, in fact, not inclusive of all procedures being performed. The statistics given us were those associated with the billings. For example, similar to a DRG payment, a given patient may have had several scans performed but only had one or two reimbursed, depending on the situation, the agreement, and the payer.

Although the income projections in our report are not affected because our projections were based on actual past income trending, the utilization rate is. The hospital is actually being paid at the level that the balance of the managed care community is, but we believe that the number of scans ordered by physicians is higher.

According to a hospital source, the department had been running approximately 350 scans per month. Statistics from the finance office showed only about 190–200 being associated with a charge. To the extent possible, it will be extremely important for the present and subsequent owners to narrow this significant disparity between services provided and the reimbursement possible. This effort provides one of the best opportunities for improved profitability and hence value of the CT service. The other single largest opportunity for profit in the CT business might be an aggressively poised service. Again, this is should be possible due to the type of equipment in the department. Although net income per scan may decrease significantly, net profitability could result from a campaign aggressively pricing and marketing the service to area physicians and managed care providers.

Physicians on staff have indicated that they do not think the volume of CT scans will drop from the present level. We do think they will drop, however, as they are continuing to drop even in other "mature" managed care areas and also because of the increased competition of a new Kaiser Permanente facility offering CT services approximately one mile away. We have lowered the number of reimbursable scans from the original number (200 per month) to 154 scans per month. Normally, we would have projected 140 scans per month, but we have raised the floor of this projection 10 percent to recognize the value and uniqueness of the electron beam CT for its broader service range. As noted elsewhere, the C-100 has a 2-mm slice thickness resolution capability, which is shared by only several other machines in California. Our projections also assume no change in marketing of the service, which we think is possible with the above-mentioned capabilities.

FUTURE OF CT SCANNING

Virtually since the inception of the Partnership CT operation in mid-1992, the number of procedures has dropped precipitously. In July 1992, the first month of operation, the number of procedures performed was 363. Since that time, there has been a steady and predictable decline to the current level of 196 procedures per month, or a 46 percent drop in activity. Similarly, the billed charges for the services for the same period have gone from $182,868 to currently (February 1994) $89,318, a 51 percent drop. We acknowledged that some of the recent drop may have been from the earthquake in late January.

The reasons behind these trends are several, but most central is the impact of managed care and the declining use of high-cost diagnostic tests in favor of lower-tech, less costly methods. High-tech resources inherently mean high cost, and third-party payers and health care providers saddled with the cost of providing health care for a defined population are opting to wait or to avoid expensive testing.

The income has fallen somewhat farther than the drop in procedures themselves would suggest. This is due in part to several factors, the first of which is that the reimbursement levels have been reduced to some extent by third-party payers and managed care companies through gatekeeper primary care physicians. The standard of care in terms of diagnostic testing has taken somewhat of a backstep in favor of more conservative testing. This rather directly spells bad news for those who provide high-tech, high-cost services in the health care industry. CT scans are among those.

As a corollary, radiologist fees (professional component) are being dramatically reduced by Medicare over a three-year period 1994–1996, by approximately 25 percent per year. This has no bearing on the Partnership income, but radiologists are the other side of the imaging services equation and if they are being radically cut, many would suggest that the payment component for the equipment may also be in store for payment reductions.

The bottom line for CT scan services is that they will be a prime target of negotiating managed care contractors. There will continue to be a need for such services, and a premise of ours in this report is that the use rate will drop to 154 scans per month before stabilizing and that it will happen by the end of the first quarter 1995.

TRENDS IN REIMBURSEMENT

Compounding the problem with declining volumes, reimbursement is also declining. Our survey of payments is now suggesting average payments of $350–$400 per CT study. Lower yet, Medicare is paying a maximum (global) of $157.50 per head ($36.75 professional component and $120.75 technical component) and $178.50 ($42 professional component and $136.50 technical component) for full-body scans. We do not see Medicare paying less than they currently are, and if the past is an indication of the future, only very small incremental increases in reimbursement may be expected.

We believe that from an investment standpoint, it is important to adequately reduce our expectations of reimbursement levels for the CT service. We also believe that within five years most payers will be paying close to what Medicare will be paying at that point in time. This also recognizes the impact of the new Kaiser Permanente facility going up in the immediate area, which will be a competitor for the service.

Given the foregoing, we have developed a set of trends suggesting our best estimate of what the business volume and related income stream will be on which we will perform the present value calculations. We refer you to the appendices for those documents.

ADDITIONAL ISSUES AND CONSIDERATIONS

Obligatory Sale of Partnership Assets at 10 Percent below Market Value

The contract with General Memorial Hospital to have first right of refusal and to purchase the equipment at 90 percent of fair market value is noteworthy in that it allows the hospital to acquire the main assets (CAT scanners and auxiliary equipment) at 90 percent of fair market value.

Normally, when an agreement is made for the first right of refusal, if the value or formula for an agreed value is not at fair market value, it is at least at the level of an offer "on the table." Additionally, a "first right" option requires additional financial consideration—not less and certainly not less than what would be "fair" market value.

The other noteworthy consideration is that not only does the current services agreement provide that the hospital may exercise the option but that the Partnership must sell at the 10 percent below market rates. In our experience, a prospective buyer would normally be expected to pay more for an option, requiring, say, 10 percent more if not at least market rates.

The agreement is highly unusual, but nonetheless, for reasons conscious or otherwise, both sides agreed to the arrangement and we think that it is binding. We can only speculate as to (1) whether the hospital chooses to exercise the options it has and (2) if so, whether it will continue to insist on the draconian terms developed earlier.

Our sense is that based on the relationship that had to exist to set up this unusual bipartisan arrangement in the first place, there should be a willingness to develop an equitable approach to the sale of the assets.

Unfortunately, there are, indeed, more pivotal issues that can have a great effect on the value and the ability to negotiate a reasonable selling price for the Partnership interests. Let's explore the more cogent ones.

Concept of Goodwill and "Is This a Business?"

When one attempts to address the issue of goodwill value for an enterprise, one looks at the business activity, the nature of the growing business sophistication in the marketplace, and the degree to which there is a mature business in the marketplace. Of central consideration is the value of the customer base. What will the owner(s) have built by virtue of their efforts, and how will it be transferable to a subsequent buyer? The answer is that it depends on what future income can *reasonably* be anticipated.

Analysis

There is not goodwill in the "traditional" sense that a business has been developed with a loyal customer base or following that can be readily capitalized on by a buyer. There is, however, the current contract, which runs until May 31, 1999, that currently has a significant cash flow to the owner.

Although health care business with a growing managed care environment is not an area that many investors would consider, we do think that a reasonable health care investor would pay our estimate of value for the five years of revenue stream remaining in the contract. We did not include a terminal value calculation for the CT Partnership because the contract expires at the end of five years.

Sale of Partnership versus Partnership Assets

Given the fact that the hospital has the first right to purchase the "equipment" if and when it is for sale, we asked ourselves whether it is reasonable to believe that the Partnership may be able to sell the "partnership" instead of merely the "equipment and improvements." Does this agreement preclude the right of the partnership to assign a value to and expect payment for those aspects of their enterprise that deal with business investment and development? Conventional business suggests that there is some value here. We have somewhat likened the partnership business to a franchise. In this case, the hospital has allowed the Partnership to provide CT diagnostic services to patients of the hospital.

The Partnership leases the space and the personnel and pays all costs associated with the provision of services. The hospital ventures no capital and shares in no income outside of that it receives from the Partnership for those resources it has contracted for.

We believe that there is a factor of goodwill in a sense but not to the extent that a private business has been created that has matured with a customer base that may be enjoyed by the owner. The Partnership has in its possession a contract that is conceivably transferable to a buyer who may enjoy five years of operation and income.

From one standpoint, according to the language of the contract, the lease agreement with the hospital for the space in the imaging department requires hospital approval of any sublessee. In other words, the hospital can theoretically and effectively prevent the Partnership from transferring leasehold interests to subsequent buyers of the Partnership.

In essence, the hospital position on other potential buyers determines whether there is future income and therefore value.

Pressures and Impact on Value for Complying with the State Law

Looking at the financial impact, the value of the Partnership and the equipment by virtue of **having to sell the business** by December 31, 1994 generates additional concerns and issues.

The pressure on the Partnership will be to sell while there is still an operation to sell. If January 1, 1995, arrives and the Partnership is still running the business, we can only speculate as to the consequences it would face. We do not think this is an option. Therefore, the business must be sold. If it must be liquidated, liquidation costs of assets would be appropriate. Alternatively, the hospital has vowed to pay 90 percent of fair market value, *not liquidation value*.

Alternatively, there is clearly pressure on the part of the hospital to see negotiations and a resolution to the purchase before the end of the year. The hospital did not anticipate or ask for the Stark legislation, and they, we believe from discussions with the hospital chief executive, do not want to see disruption of the service or disruption of relations with the medical staff.

The original arrangement with the hospital to allow interested staff physicians via partnerships to own and operate the CT and MRI services suggests a very open-minded and progressive hospital administration. In our national practice, we have not encountered any other such arrangements that speak to the progressiveness and relationships that must exist at the hospital to even conceive of such an approach to health services delivery.

In summary, both the Partnership and the hospital have it in their collective best interests to structure a mutually satisfactory resolution and should be amenable to negotiations and reasonable solutions.

PROJECTING PARTNERSHIP INCOME

Term

If the current owners were able to sell the Partnership to an entity investing in medical ventures or to other physicians who were not in a conflict of interest position in terms of the law for owning the Partnership/assets, there are, roughly, another five years on the current contract with the hospital. In our analysis, we have attempted to project income over the five-year period remaining in the contract.

Present Value of Discounted Cash Flow

With the estimated net income, we can identify the value of the Partnership cash flow using a present value of the discounted cash flow for the remainder of the contract. As discussed above, we built into the calculation a series of factors that include the cost of capital, the risk in the venture based on our analysis of the operation, and the future of the business.

Volumes

Per the discussion above regarding the Las Buenas area marketplace and because we had to venture an estimate of stabilized volume at some point in the future for our income approach, we estimated that the unrelenting impact of managed care would drive volumes down from the current approximate 195–200 CT studies per month (as of February 1994) down to 154 CT studies per month in the volume before stabilization—the level at which utilization of the services will not drop due to unavoidable utilization.

The selected rate used in projecting future volume was based on a curve over the 10 months before the date of this appraisal. This period was selected because of its sustaining and consistent data trend.

Business Risk—Building an Appropriate Rate for Discounted Future Income

A key element in the development of risk discount factors is the accurate assessment of the risk (of not getting the cash flow projected). Our technique for determining the level of business risk is a standard approach of dividing the standard deviation of the range of monthly cash flows by the average income for the period.

Our approach in estimating the present value of the discounted cash flow was the build-up method, whereby one adds percentages to the discount risk factor based on what risk-free investment return rates are, to which is added a factor for the business quality and its future and an expected return rate.

To start with, we noted that the return for a 30-year Treasury bond is approximately 8 percent. This is essentially the return for a risk-free investment. To this, we added a cost of capital requirement of 10 percent. We then added a factor for the additional kind of return we would want for this investment based on the risk involved and the quality and stability of the operation. Our calculations to develop a business risk factor yielded a final figure of 40.7 percent (we rounded to 40 percent) for the premium factor. As noted earlier, we have reduced this risk factor based largely on two points: the impact of the earthquake on business volumes and the fact that the CT equipment has exceptional capabilities in the health care marketplace. Our resulting business risk component was reduced to 0.35.

This large premium for risk heavily discounts future income by looking at the volatility and trend of the income. (Please see addendum for the mathematics on standard deviation.) This method is similar to the public stock risk factor of beta, which measures change in an individual stock price compared with the Standard & Poor's 500. (If the stock goes up faster and drops faster, beta is higher.)

We believe that this business is highly volatile and that there is high risk associated with getting the projected income. The result was a 50 percent discount rate on the projected income. We normally would have used a higher figure, but our calculations have already included reasonable increases in expenses and a 20–25 percent decrease in volume levels over the coming six to seven months, with a corresponding decline in revenue.

As a side note, we believe that the discount rate to one potential buyer, General Memorial Hospital, might be able to be lowered because of the control it has over that of the operation that other investors would not. In other words, the value of the income stream should be somewhat higher to the hospital than the general model we developed for outside investors.

The income approach is typically the most appropriate approach when selling a service-oriented business. The reason is because its purpose is to generate a profit or financial benefit to the owner. We believe that the income approach coupled with the fair market value in-use of the equipment and the leasehold improvements is the most appropriate method of value determination when everything is considered.

FINANCIAL STATEMENT ANALYSIS

The practice appears to enjoy relationships with third-party payers, including what appear to be the vast majority of applicable area/regional managed care organizations. In the most recent data available (May 1993–April 1994), the payer mix was as follows:

Payer Type	Percent
Workers' Compensation	4.4
PPO	5.3
HMO	22.7
Blue Cross–Blue Shield	15.1
Trauma	4.1
Medi-Cal	9.1
Private Insurance	24.9
Private Pay	14.3
Total	100

EQUIPMENT

CAT Scanners and Additional Attachments and Modalities

The partnership owns two CT scanners, one a late-model Imatron Ultra fast C-100 and an older unit, a Picker 600 SX, approximately 12 years old. The Imatron has been upgraded to a C-150L model, which corresponds with the latest model coming off the assembly line according to company officials. Despite the fact that the unit was purchased two years ago, the service agreement at $12,000 per month and the upgrades to state-of-the-art electron beam units, the Imatron in use at General Memorial Hospital is quite current and suffers from no physical or functional obsolescence.

Our ASA Medical Equipment Appraiser has researched the medical marketplace and has determined that the fair market value in-use for the Imatron unit is $1,200,000. This higher value for in-use equipment is based on the fact that a portion of the revenue stream is attributable to the unit as a working asset and also that it is installed. Installation prices can often be 20–25 percent of the base price of such equipment. The fair market value in-use of the Picker 600 SX is $4,000.00.

Leasehold Improvements

Significant leasehold improvements were made to initiate the partnership and the department. The initial cost basis for the leasehold improvements was a total of $193,604. The value of these leaseholds, according to our depreciation schedule, is $138,526. This value should be included in the collective assets.

Current Usable Supplies

The departmental supplies were not inventoried and valued in this report. We suggest that the departmental staff perform this task or the materials management department be used to identify the inventory of supplies and use the lower of cost or current market value.

According to financial statements, approximately $600 per month of operating supplies are used. In our experience, usually one to one-and-a-half month's worth of supplies are on hand. Supplies should be valued at their cost or fair market value if older than one year.

Clearly, to be accurate, a count of supplies just before closing should be done.

APPRAISAL OF FAIR MARKET VALUE

Valuation Approaches

Several approaches for valuing closely held businesses are available. The conventional approaches tend to use some form of earning power appraisal, asset appraisal, or a combination of the two. After a review of several approaches, it is our opinion that the most appropriate approach for valuing the Partnership's fair market value is a combination of an earnings approach, which gives recognition to the future income stream, together with an asset-based approach, recognizing the value of the Partnership assets and their contribution to the income stream.

This is added to the fair market in-use value of the CTs and the cost new less depreciation of the balance of the (tangible) working assets. This approach should also be the most helpful because the most likely transaction will be a purchase of selected Partnership assets. Let's examine each of these approaches briefly.

Combination Discounted Cash Flow and Fair Market In-Use Value

Income Valuation: Discounted Cash Flow

The discounted cash flow approach is based on projected volumes with a five-year life (per the contract with the hospital). The Partnership, per se, has a limited life in two ways. When in force, the Stark legislation will require that it divest itself from all businesses and activities in which its shareholders are also referring physicians. Therefore, we could not use an approach to value that would have a life past the contract with the hospital.

The contract that the Partnership has with the hospital expires May 31, 1999. Inasmuch, one cannot use approaches that would suggest a terminal value for a business or suggest the value of an income stream beyond this timeframe. For the income valuation, our DCF approach valued the monthly income streams we identified over a period of time from June 1, 1994, through May 31, 1999.

The Partnership is a going concern with current earnings. If it were not a going concern with current (net profitable) earnings, we would have exclusively elected an asset-based cost approach method. If it were a going concern without earnings or a "start-up business," we would have placed no emphasis on an earnings component and relied on a "cost approach" for the business.

In terms of income valuation, there were no comparable statistics that we could use because of the uniqueness of this particular business, which precluded a variety of methods. Although there are free-standing diagnostic imaging companies, these are not comparable with the subject because of its location and financial and other relationships with General Memorial Hospital.

If a stable future could have been predicted for the CT service and were such comparisons possible, we could have also included in our valuation approaches a "multiples of value" approach, comparing the subject with publicly traded company securities. As an example, a multiple of (range of roughly 3–10 times) earnings can be used. A factor of 5 is common for many types of health care organizations. In this example, 1993 profit before interest, taxes, depreciation, and amortization was $947,390. Based on what we know about the business' longevity and other issues, we would have factored this business by a 3, yielding a value of $2,842,170.

Again, because the contract is too short lived, a multiples approach would be misleading. The lack of comparable entities in the active trading marketplace prohibits valuation by stock comparisons. Other income methods vary, depending on the circumstances, including the values of

Earnings before Interest
Capitalization of Earnings after Tax
Capitalization of Excess Earnings after Tax
Seller Discounted Cash

Inasmuch, the remaining approaches to valuing the income stream are a discounted cash flow approach taking into consideration those issues mentioned under the section "Business Risk," combined with an asset approach.

The sales or market approach of similar businesses was not feasible because there were no known similar entities in existence that have sold.

Finally, when similar publicly traded companies are available for comparison purposes, we are able to make comparisons of value with those similar companies, adjusting for various strengths and weaknesses. Again, unfortunately, although there are free-standing imaging companies, in our opinion they are not comparable.

Equipment Appraisal: Fair Market In-Use Value

As discussed elsewhere, the primary tangible working assets of the Partnership consist of two CT scanners and their associated auxiliary equipment. These assets and their worth are distinguished from the same equipment warehoused on the open, used medical equipment market. Their values are quite different.

The former can reasonably be assigned a portion of the revenue stream from the business itself. The latter can clearly not be associated with such an existing investor benefit.

The former is installed and is operational whereas the latter is neither. The cost associated with installation of major fixed equipment is often 10–25 percent of the base price of the equipment itself.

Unless liquidation of the assets is a reasonable prospect, the assets' value lies in the ability to generate earnings rather than being an element of value that is distinct from the company's value based on its earning power.

Cost Approach

Another approach to valuing businesses that are more production than service-oriented is the cost approach. It looks at the assets required to do the job. Its premise is that the business is worth the cost to replicate the business from the ground up and paying in the market what it would for the same equipment or facilities. It does not consider the time and effort in building and refining a business.

Equipment and Leasehold Improvements

The same values assigned in our determination of value of the CTs in the previous section also apply here versus straight line depreciated value or some other approach. We have valued the two CTs at $1,200,000 and $4,000.

Current Assets Updated

Current assets were adjusted by adding in an allowance for supplies and the latest figure for accounts receivable factored times 0.54. Other current assets are valued at their cost or cash value. This increased the March 31 balance sheet Total Current Assets from $290,451 to $729,358.74.

Total shareholder equity according to our estimates and updates is $2,059,668.24.

Valuation Summary

Based on the above approaches to value (discounted cash flow with fair market value in-use and the cost approach), we have arrived at the following indications of value for Advanced C.T. Imaging of Las Buenas Medical Group II and its various assets. For the client's convenience, we have listed various assets from both a fair market value standpoint and a cost approach. We also have included in the table the adjusted current owner's equity (net tangible asset value).

In concluding the relative weights to be accorded the various approaches, one must consider the mandates of Revenue Ruling 59-60, generally accepted appraisal practices and the appraiser's experience. Revenue Ruling 59-60 discusses weighting to be accorded various approaches as follows:

> Earnings may be the most important criterion of value in some cases, whereas asset value will receive primary consideration in others. In general, the appraiser will accord primary consideration to earnings when valuing (stocks of) companies which sell products or services to the public; conversely, in the investment or holding type of company, the appraiser may accord the greatest weight to the assets underlying the security to be valued.

Clearly, the Partnership is an operating company in the provision of services and is not a holding company or investment company. Additionally, it is an operating entity, not a start-up, and has had and will have an operating profit margin for at least several years. Inasmuch, significant weight should be placed on the earnings in the determination of value.

At the same time, CT diagnostic services is a business in rapid decline (approximately 2–3 percent per month). This suggests that the asset approach should not be discounted too much because of the distinct likelihood that a sale of assets (aside from the requirement of the Stark law) is in the future. This is compounded by the fact that the Partnership must divest within six months and the termination of a contract to provide services in five years.

Therefore, when we might otherwise have accorded 75 percent of the weighting to the income stream, we have elected to allot instead 65 percent. Thirty-five percent will be allotted to the asset-based cost approach instead of 25 percent.

Asset	*Cost Approach ($)*	*Combination Method (Fair Market Value In-Use & DCF) ($)*	*Adjusted Owner's Equity (NTAV) ($)*
Future Revenue Stream	N/A	425,474	—
Cash	288,428	288,428	—
Deposits	2,050	2,050	—
Accounts Receivable	438,308	438,308	—
Supplies	600	600	—
Imatron C-100	1,200,000	1,200,000	—
Picker 600	4,000	4,000	—
Leasehold Improvements	138,693	138,693	—
Totals	2,072,079	2,497,553	2,059,668

The following table itemizes by asset category to the overall value if one were to reallocate values according to the revised total weighted value.

Asset	*Cost Approach ($)*	*Asset Wt ($)*	*Product ($)*	*FMV In-Use and DCF ($)*	*Income Wt ($)*	*Product ($)*	*Blended Values ($)*
Future Revenue	0	0.35	0	425,474	0.65	276,558	276,558
Cash	288,428	0.35	100,950	288,428	0.65	187,478	288,428
Deposits	2,050	0.35	718	2,050	0.65	1,333	2,050
Accounts Rec.	438,308	0.35	153,408	438,308	0.65	284,900	438,308
Supplies	600	0.35	210	600	0.65	390	600
Imatron C-150L	1,200,000	0.35	420,000	1,200,000	0.65	780,000	1,200,000
Picker	4,000	0.35	1,400	4,000	0.65	2,600	4,000
Leasehold Improvs.	138,694	0.35	48,543	138,694	0.65	90,151	138,694
TOTALS	$2,072,080		$725,229	$2,497,554		$1,623,410	$2,348,638

CONCLUSION

Based on an analysis of all relevant factors surrounding the Partnership and the information made available to us, it is our opinion that the fair market value of the Partnership assets, including the present value of discounted cash flow, as of June 1, 1994, is $2,350,000, rounded. The net tangible asset value of the Partnership is $2,059,668.00.

CERTIFICATION AND STATEMENT OF LIMITING CONDITIONS

CERTIFICATION: The appraiser certifies and agrees that:

1. The appraiser has no present or contemplated future interest in the property appraised; and neither the employment to make the appraisal, nor the compensation for it, is contingent on the appraised value of the property.
2. The appraiser has personally inspected the Partnership facilities and equipment, and it was evaluated from documents listed in the "Sources of Information" section and information made available to the appraiser from interviews with clinic personnel and the physician-owners. To the best of the appraiser's knowledge and belief, all statements and information in this report are true and correct, and the appraiser has not knowingly withheld any significant information.
3. All contingent and limiting conditions are contained herein (imposed by the terms of the assignment or by the undersigned affecting the analyses, opinions, and conclusions contained in the report).
4. The appraisal report has been made in conformity with and is subject to the requirements of the Code of Professional Ethics and Standards of Professional Conduct of the Appraisal Institute.
5. All conclusions and opinions concerning real estate that are set forth in the appraisal report were prepared by the appraiser whose signature appears on the appraisal report, unless indicated as "Review Appraiser." No change of any item in the appraisal report shall be made by anyone other than the appraiser, and the appraiser shall have no responsibility for any such unauthorized change.

CONTINGENT AND LIMITING CONDITIONS

The certification of the appraiser appearing in the appraisal report is subject to the following conditions and to such other specific and limiting conditions as are set forth by the appraiser in the report.

1. The appraiser assumes no responsibility for matters of a legal nature affecting the subject appraised or the title thereto, nor does appraiser render any opinion as to the title, which is assumed to be good and marketable. The property is appraised as though under responsible ownership.
2. The appraiser is not required to give testimony or appear in court because of having made the appraisal with reference to the Partnership in question, unless arrangements have been made previously.
3. The appraiser assumes that there are no hidden or unapparent aspects of the Partnership that would render it more or less valuable. The appraiser assumes no responsibility for such conditions or for efforts that might be required to discover such factors.
4. Information, estimates, and opinions furnished to the appraiser and contained in the report were obtained

from sources considered reliable and believed to be true and correct. However, no responsibility for accuracy of such items furnished the appraiser can be assumed by the appraiser.

The most recent complete financial statements available were March 1994. This information together with other partnership documents formed the basis of the business projections.

5. Disclosure of the contents of the appraisal report is governed by the bylaws and regulations of the Appraisal Institute.
6. Neither all nor any part of this content of the report, or copy thereof (including conclusions as to the property value, the identity of the appraiser, professional designations, reference to any professional appraisal organizations, or the firm with which the appraiser is connected), shall be used for any purpose by anyone but the client specified in the report, the borrower if appraisal fee paid by the same, the mortgagee or its successors or assigns, mortgage insurance, consultants, professional appraisal organizations, any state or federally approved financial institution, any department, agency, or instrumentality of the United States, or any state or the District of Columbia, without the previous written consent of the appraiser; nor shall it be conveyed by anyone to the public through advertising, public relations, news, sales, or other media without the written consent and approval of the appraiser.
7. The appraiser reserves the right to change or alter the appraisal report after its submission if new facts are received that, in the appraiser's opinion, warrant a change.

The actual support documents are not included here but rather a schedule of the types of support data is provided for your reference.

Trended Financial Statements

A. Historical
B. Projections

Balance Sheets

A. 1991–March 30, 1994, as prepared by Matson and Matson, CPAs
B. Estimated and Adjusted to June 1, 1994, based on available data
C. Estimated and Adjusted to June 1, 1994, based on available data with adjustments to the March balance sheet to show individual depreciation levels by category of fixed asset

Chart of Projections of Estimated CT Volume

Prediction of Future CT Volumes by Using Overall Historical Drop, 1993 Decrease Rate, and Linear Regression

Comparison of Selected Financial Indicators, March 1993–February 1994

Payer Mix as of 4/94

Depreciation Schedule

Calculation of Business Risk and Premium for Discount Rate

Appraisal #3. Closed Hospital Converted to Home for the Aged and Physician Offices

APPRAISAL ON
MILLSWORTH HEALTHCARE CENTER
100 MAIN STREET
MILLSWORTH, MICHIGAN 49000

FOR
FIRST COMMERCIAL BANK OF MICHIGAN
P.O. BOX 1
INDIAN CREEK, MICHIGAN 48000

NOVEMBER 22, 1993

November 26, 1993

Ms. Barbara Jackson
Loan Officer
First Commercial Bank of Michigan
P.O. Box 1
Indian Creek, Michigan 48000

Subject: Appraisal of former Millsworth Hospital (Millsworth Healthcare Center), 100 Main Street, Millsworth, Michigan 49000

Dear Ms. Jackson:

In accordance with a request from First Commercial Bank of Michigan, Indian Creek, Michigan, we have appraised the subject property. The legal description for the property is provided in the Appendix of this report.

The property rights appraised are fee simple title, assuming no indebtedness against the property. The purpose of this appraisal is to estimate the market value of the property as a home for the aged as of November 22, 1993. We have also provided a value for the subject following the current renovations. The market value, as used in this appraisal, is defined elsewhere in this report.

Your attention is invited to the attached pages indicating the data collected and analyzed by our firm in formulating an opinion of value. Also attached are the certification and statement of limiting conditions.

As a result of our investigation and analysis, some of which is described in this report, it is our opinion that the "as-is" value of the subject property as of November 22, 1993, is One Million Five Hundred Thousand Dollars ($1,500,000.00). The value after the currently underway renovation for a home for the aged is One Million Eight Hundred Thousand Dollars, ($1,800,000.00).

Cordially,

Margaret Salisbury, MAI, SRPA, ASA
Senior Partner

BGK:tk

Attachments

SAMPLE APPRAISAL REPORT—ALTERNATE HOSPITAL USE

Owners of Record

Health Investors, L.C.
100 Main Street
Millsworth, Michigan 49000

Property Address

100 Main Street
Millsworth, Michigan 49000

Type of Property

Home for the Aged, Class C Construction
Land: Zoned "B" Commercial

Date of Value

November 22, 1993

Appraised by

American Health Care Appraisal
4130 La Jolla Village Drive
Suite 1072
La Jolla, California 92037

CERTIFICATION OF VALUE
(DELETED FROM SAMPLE REPORT)

SUMMARY OF FACTS AND CONCLUSIONS

Ownership	Health Investors, L.C.
Location of Property	100 Main Street Millsworth, Michigan 49000
Physical Age of Improvements	Forty-one years
Effective Age with Completion of Renovations	Sixteen years as a home for the aged
Date of Transmittal	November 26, 1993
Date of Valuation	November 22, 1993
Type of Property	Home for the aged Ambulance garage Well house Medical office space
Land Area	8.07 acres
Building(s) Size	30,831 square feet
Zoning	"B"—Commercial
Present Use	Physician office rental Community rental space
Highest and Best Use	Clinic/ambulatory; subacute care; elderly residence; social/health rental space
Site Value, Market Approach	$126,400
Physical Plant Value ***"As Is,"*** Cost New Less Depreciation	$1,373,600
Total Value Estimate	$1, 500,000
Physical Plant Value ***after Renovation*** Cost New Less Depreciation	$1, 673,600
Total Value Estimate	$1, 800,000

PREMISES OF THE APPRAISAL

CONTINGENT AND LIMITING CONDITIONS

The certification of the appraiser appearing in the appraisal report is subject to the following conditions and to such other specific and limiting conditions as are set forth by the appraiser in the report.

1. The appraiser assumes no responsibility for matters of a legal nature affecting the subject appraised or the title thereto, nor does appraiser render any opinion as to the title, which is assumed to be good and marketable. The property is appraised as though under responsible ownership.
2. The appraiser has made no formal "survey" of the property.
3. The appraiser is not required to give testimony or appear in court because of having made the appraisal with reference to the property in question, unless arrangements have been made previously.
4. The appraiser assumes that there are no hidden or unapparent aspects of the property that would render it more or less valuable. The appraiser assumes no responsibility for such conditions or for efforts that might be required to discover such factors.
5. Information, estimates, and opinions furnished to the appraiser and contained in the report were obtained from sources considered reliable and believed to be true and correct. However, no responsibility for accuracy of such items furnished the appraiser can be assumed by the appraiser.
6. Disclosure of the contents of the appraisal report is governed by the bylaws and regulations of the American Society of Appraisers.
7. Neither all nor any part of this content of the report, or copy thereof (including conclusions as to the property value, the identity of the appraiser, professional designations, reference to any professional appraisal organizations, or the firm with which the appraiser is connected), shall be used for any purpose by anyone but the client specified in the report, the borrower if appraisal fee paid by the same, the mortgagee or its successors or assigns, mortgage insurance, consultants, professional appraisal organizations, any state or federally approved financial institution, any department, agency, or instrumentality of the United States, or any state or the District of Columbia without the previous written consent of the appraiser; nor shall it be conveyed by anyone to the public through advertising, public relations, news, sales, or other media without the written consent and approval of the appraiser.
8. The appraiser reserves the right to change or alter the appraisal report after its submission if new facts are received that, in the appraiser's opinion, warrant a change.

PURPOSE OF APPRAISAL

In this project, we have estimated the value of the subject property as a 40-bed home for the aged (providing adult foster care services) with approximately 12,000 square feet of health care–related rental space as delineated elsewhere in the report. The purpose of this appraisal was to evaluate the feasibility via a projected income approach and, if feasible, to estimate the value of the subject property as a home for the aged as delineated under the current statutes of the State of Michigan. It is our understanding this report will be used to secure a bank loan for the subject property.

DEFINITION OF VALUE AND DATE OF VALUE ESTIMATE

The definition of value for purposes of this report is the fair market value of the subject property including its improvements as delineated on the foregoing Summary of Facts and Conclusions and the associated land as specified on the same schedule, on the Plat Map in the Appendix and within the Section Appraisal of Subject Land as though Vacant/Unimproved.

PROPERTY RIGHTS APPRAISED

The property rights appraised are unencumbered fee simple interest. The date of the valuation is November 22, 1993. No unattached personal properties with the exception of several desks and chairs that were being used by the contractor were noted in the building, and these items were not included in this appraisal.

SCOPE OF THE APPRAISAL

The objective of the appraisal assignment was to provide an accurate estimate of value of the subject land and the improvements according to as many of the three standard approaches (income, market, and cost) as possible and to select the most appropriate given the data available and the appropriate application of such. Because of the nature of the special and unique service to Millsworth County, a major focus of the appraisal became the need to verify or dispute the marketability and feasibility of such a special use service and therefore facility.

INCOME APPROACH

This approach mandated that we look closely at the historical and current usage of adult foster care services in not only Millsworth County but also neighboring counties and across the state to identify important influences that would have a direct impact on the financial feasibility of the project. We further contacted the National Association for Homes for the Aged, the American Association of Homes for the Aging, the Michigan Association of Homes for the Aging, and many Michigan state government departments and bureaus for input. The project required that certain assumptions be made about a service (home for the aged) when there had never been such a service offered in the local area.

Apart from only being able to develop an income approach from a projected feasibility pro forma of income and expense, the income approach was also handicapped rather significantly because there is little available historical data. There were no signed leases and no historical budgets or actual expenses. The only information we really knew was that there are two tenants now, Dr. Norma Clinton and Millsworth Medical Services. This required that we use the owner's budget projection as a starting point and then either verify and acknowledge or disagree with each assumption and expense or income line item. Our five-year pro forma was heavily influenced by the demographics, the current absorption level of area adult foster care services, and potential in the marketplace for a new service.

The income for the five years was discounted by factors including the interest rate (6.24 percent for 30 years current as of November 22) of risk-free Treasury securities and a risk modifier based on our analysis of the project under consideration. A present value from this approach is provided.

MARKET APPROACH

The typical market approach was intended to be used if applicable. We found that it was from the standpoint of reasonable geographic and time comparables on the land component.

Unfortunately, there are typically few transactions involving elderly housing projects. Most successful projects have not been placed on the market. Many of the sales that have occurred have been conducted as a part of bankruptcy or foreclosure proceedings or under duress, making comparability with the subject even more difficult to quantify. For this reason, value estimates using the sales comparison approach are sometimes given little or no weight. We found that there were not nearby or comparable sales, so this approach was not considered for other than vacant land.

COST APPROACH

The cost approach to value was ultimately used to complement the market approach on the land value. Significant in this approach was the determination of whether to use depreciated replacement cost or reconstruction cost new less depreciation. We had to determine if there was significant difference in the way a home for the aged would be built today from scratch compared with the renovated hospital with a change in use license. Once that determination was made it would be able to identify whether a replacement cost approach or reconstruction cost now (RCN) approach would be most appropriate.

PRESENTATION OF THE DATA

IDENTIFICATION OF PROPERTY

The main subject property improvement is a 40-year-old, 29,811-square-foot, one-story, brick with block backup masonry wall class C building. The facility that ceased operation in mid-1992 was a fully accredited acute care hospital located at 100 Main Street, Millsworth, Michigan. In addition to the main facility is a 896-square-foot pole building ambulance garage, a 946-square-foot physician's office that has been built next to the main facility on the side giving face to East Main Street, a connecting corridor to the county medical care facility that is approximately 3,339 square feet, and a 125-square-foot concrete-block utility building.

The land involved is approximately 8.07 acres and is an irregular lot (see appendix for plat of survey and lot description). The front (north) one-third of the property has a gentle slope of approximately 5–10 degrees, the remainder being relatively flat and sodded. The site is extremely well suited to the intended use. For further data, we turn your attention to the section on appraisal of the land as though vacant.

COUNTY AND CITY DEMOGRAPHICS

We have included a Marketview Comparison Report (MCR) from the National Data Planning Center on Millsworth County. It profiles populations by number and selected characteristics for 1970, 1980, 1991, and 1996 projected. There are three specific breakdowns: (1) ZIP codes 49000 (city of Millsworth) and 49001 (city of Shelton), (2) Millsworth Township, and (3) Millsworth County. We also make reference to several other percentages and statistics that make the MCR meaningful.

SUBJECT NEIGHBORHOOD AREA

The subject property is located in a quiet neighborhood on the edge of town. (It is zoned commercial B and has a variety of uses—professional offices, residential, agricultural, and a health care campus.) Population density in the neighborhood is somewhat less than in the city of Millsworth because it is on the eastern side and border of town, bordering an agricultural zone. The density is typical of smaller rural communities and unremarkable.

The first intersection to the east of subject on East Main Street is Old Highway 31, an active thoroughfare, used predominantly for secondary traffic and not a noise problem. About four miles from the facility is (New) Highway 31, which is the main arterial connecting Muskegon and Wellston.

Other neighborhood city streets, roads, or traffic patterns are not unusual and deserve no particular mention. Traffic is light. Only three (short) blocks east of the central business district, the property is in close proximity to the city's commercial activity and county seat. No nuisances were noted. A phase one (basic) environmental study has recently been conducted at the owner's expense and revealed no hazardous conditions.

Relating more to the contiguous businesses and related activities of the subject, there are two physician offices within the facility, and a clinic space of approximately 5,500 square feet will be occupied by a group from Memorial Hospital in Wellston, Michigan. Also, the county-operated skilled nursing facility physically adjoins the subject property via a connecting corridor. Further, the county-operated and -leased ambulance facility is on the grounds of the subject property. A new facility occupied by the Council on Aging is directly in front of the subject property. The collective group of elderly health care and social programs constitutes a health care complex that should work synergistically to draw clients to each of the programs, practices, or facilities.

In summary, there is ready access to medical care, banks, shopping, restaurants, and religious and recreational facilities. There is availability of public transportation. Access to and from major thoroughfares and highways is convenient. The overall quality of the neighborhood including the surrounding development, level of upkeep, and security, which is important to elderly residents, is quite good.

DESCRIPTION OF IMPROVEMENTS

The main "hospital" building is a one-story facility of approximately 29,811 square feet, with an 8,806-square-foot partial basement. The basic construction is on one-hour fire-resistive materials, metal lath, and plaster or gypsum board. The well house is a concrete-block facility. The ambulance garage is an "S" class storage garage, single metal wall construction. The corridor is made of hospital construction (and the skilled nursing facility is a code-conforming facility). The clinic building referenced above is of brick construction and is separated from the facility corridor by the exterior skin and construction. The following breakdown is illustrative:

Utilities

Water	Municipal. Also onsite four-inch-diameter well with 5 hp pump public sewer
Boilers	Two Power Master, natural gas, low-pressure (one boiler retrofitted to run on oil as well with 500-gallon storage tank. This will be removed as it is no longer in service)
	One Pierless boiler, 30 hp high-pressure (60–66 psi)
	Hot water boiler, 752,000 BTU gas-fired w/ (2) 100-gallon storage tanks (this will be removed as it is no longer in service)
	Generator (emergency) Onan 85 kW natural gas, alternate fuel is gasoline
	Fire protection—volunteer fire department connected to dispatch by radio and telephone

Zoning B - Commercial

There is a 52,000-square-foot asphalt parking lot on the property that is well maintained.

Facilities. The square footage of the property structures is as follows:

Hospital Building	25,526 square feet
Clinic Building	946 square feet
Well House	125 square feet
Ambulance Garage	896 square feet
Hospital/SNF Corridor	3,339 square feet
TOTAL PROPERTY	30,832 SQUARE FEET

Acme Engineering Corporation of Muskegon, Michigan, was consulted regarding the relative condition of the various systems within the subject facility. Their opinions of remaining effective life are incorporated in the following.

Electrical

It was the professional engineer's opinion that the current electrical systems, including the electrical distribution systems, branch wiring, and generator and considering the work that is already in progress to provide fire alarm wiring and annunciation, render an effective age of no greater than 10 years. Although codes have risen over the years in terms of conduit-carrying capacity with an increasing need for watts per square foot, the facility had already been licensed and operated as an acute care facility with much higher existing capabilities. The result is that facility now has a relatively new and capable electrical system.

Plumbing Piping

The plumbing piping has been repaired recently where it has been in need and there are no apparent problems with it. With the completion of this deferred maintenance, we believe that the effective age of the piping is 25 years and it has an effective remaining life of approximately 25 years.

Hot Water Piping

The hot water plumbing system was largely replaced 23 years ago in 1972. With the renovation/replacement of the domestic hot water system, we think that the remaining life of this aspect of the plumbing system is approximately 25 years. Formerly, gas chillers had been used to air condition areas within the facility. Those are being removed, and there is no code requiring them to be replaced and it is not under consideration. Air conditioning will not be part of the new program.

Boiler and Air Handlers

There is one gas-fired hot water boiler in active use, and we are estimating it has a remaining life of approximately 15 years. Steam hot water conversion is being planned for the resident rooms and potentially other areas within the facility, and we view this as a prudent management initiative. The air handlers within the facility appear to be in good maintained condition, and we have assigned a 30-year remaining life to them.

Structure

After renovation, we believe that the overall structure will be brought back down to 40 percent of its economic age through effective allocation of resources to achieve compliance with codes and cure long-deferred maintenance.

Zoning and Impact

As described elsewhere, the zoning of the property is commercial zoning "B," and the subject use conforms to this. The property is not in a flood plain, so there are no associated restrictions.

Assessed Values and Taxes

According to the County Assessor's Office, there is not assessed value on the property. Because the property had been a public facility and not taxable previously, there is literally nothing on the county records.

History

In January 1990, the City of Millsworth purchased approximately 8.8 acres owned by the Millsworth Hospital Association. This land was the majority of the property owned by the Hospital Association. The land not purchased was virtually the footprint on which the hospital and its other facilities were resting—approximately 0.7 acres. The total consideration for this 8.8 acres was $75,000 cash. It is our understanding that this may not have been an arm's length transaction in that the City was attempting to help a financially troubled community hospital.

Shortly after this acquisition, the City conveyed approximately 0.8 acres to the Council on Aging as an in-kind contribution for obtaining a Federal grant for the Council on Aging. The value assigned this property by the City for purposes of the grant was $10,000.

On May 18, 1993, the (closed) hospital facilities, equipment, and land were auctioned. The facilities for auction were the main hospital building and the two utility buildings on site. The land auctioned was the original hospital acreage less the 0.8 acres conveyed to the Council on Aging, or 8.07 acres. The facilities were auctioned for $230,000 and the land for $65,000 to Health Investors, L.C., Millsworth, Michigan.

Need, Market, and Demand for Services

The Need

In Millsworth County, there are 14 "family homes" where adult foster care is provided. In these foster homes, there are currently 121 beds licensed by the State of Michigan for Millsworth County. Facilities that have up to 20 beds are licensed by the Michigan Department of Social Services (DSS). Facilities with 21 or more beds are licensed by the Michigan Department of Public Health (MDPH). The kinds of clients being provided adult foster care fall into four categories: the elderly, the developmentally disabled, the physically disabled, and the mentally ill.

The MDPH, in its reluctance to grant Certificates of Need, has always maintained that by the mere existence of a new or additional level of health care service, demand will rise to meet the new capability and health care costs will rise. Our own experience is the same. The MDPH position is that demand (versus need) will have been created and health care costs will unnecessarily rise. We cannot judge with any degree of precision the market for an upscale service that has never been available or aggressively marketed in a given market, but we can view it in the context of the health department's position and our own experience.

What is unlikely is that the facility's beds will be totally filled by the historical consumers of adult foster care (AFC) in Millsworth County. We believe that most eventual residents will come forth because they have a new and better option in assisted living.

Population Shift—A Megatrend

The driving forces to increase the need for AFC and home for the aged (HFA) beds are, of course, a growing aging population. The aging of American society is widely known. The elderly represented only 4 percent of the population in 1900 and increased to 14 percent in 1990. It is estimated that by 2030, one-fourth of the American population will be 65 years old and older. Several social trends, including a decline in fertility and a rise in longevity, have combined to increase the proportion of the American population who are older than 65 years of age.

Living Arrangements

In 1988, most elderly men (77 percent) were married and living with their spouses, whereas less than half (42 percent) of elderly women were married. Many more elderly women than men were widowed (49 versus 14 percent). Five percent of both elderly men and women had never married, and 4 percent of the men and 5 percent of the women were currently divorced.

The living arrangements of elderly men and women are obviously influenced by their marital status. Most of the married individuals were living with their spouse in 1988. A sizable proportion were living alone, and 17 percent of the women and 13 percent of the men were living with other relatives. Only 2 percent of both men and women resided with nonrelatives. (Interestingly, there are 3,245 individuals in Millsworth County older than 65 years of age. Two percent of that number is 64.9, which is essentially the current number of state-licensed beds for AFCs in Millsworth County.)

There has been a trend for more elderly widowed and divorced individuals to live alone rather than to move in with children or other relatives. Residents of retirement housing facilities, like residents of nursing homes, tend to be predominantly female, reflecting gender ratios among the elderly. Residents of retirement facilities also tend to be older than 75. It is predicted that these trends will continue for the foreseeable future. The number of elderly women maintaining their own household is especially anticipated to rise during the next 20 years.

Analysts point out that most retired persons choose to settle at or near their original homes and that retirement housing options are more attractive to people closer to their original families, friends, and surroundings. In either event, retirement housing involves a change in lifestyle, and there is no question from the demographic statistics that many retired persons are choosing to relocate as a part of such a change. Regardless of whether people relocate before entering a retirement center or not, they look for housing near where they live.

There is no question that most elderly persons have the combined assets and income to afford retirement housing. At the same time, it is clear from market research and from numerous failed retirement housing facilities throughout the United States that care needs to be taken in designing and pricing such projects. In general, those that appeal to the "middle markets" of retired persons and that are priced accordingly have the greatest chances for success. Research has shown that the elderly do have assets but that they often have limited incomes, and they do not want to exhaust either their assets or their incomes on retirement housing expenses.

Models for Adult Foster Care

Although the foster care service is quite similar, there are two models: the family home model (three types, small, medium, and large group) and the medical model more common of homes for the aged. The latter is more often a facility and in close proximity to other medical resources, such as in the case of the subject of this appraisal.

Of the 13 family care adult foster care programs, the following breakdown may be helpful in understanding their nature:

Type	*Patient Capacity*	*Number in Millsworth County*
Family Home	1–6 residents	3
Small Group License (nonhome operator)	1–6 residents	3
Adult Foster Care Facility	7–12	6
Adult Foster Care Facility	13–20	1

These data show that there is a significant number of adult foster care beds in Millsworth County. Of the 127 licensed beds in October 1993, 12 beds went off line (in Shelton) due to licensure difficulties. There are approximately 50 AFC beds that care exclusively for developmentally disabled or mentally ill persons. As of this report, there are 64 licensed beds in Millsworth County that care specifically for elderly persons. Currently, there is an overall 85 percent occupancy rate for the existing programs, the same approximate occupancy of such programs nationally. Fifty-four persons are living in adult foster care homes currently. Of the 64 beds available, then, 10 are not occupied.

Temporary Suppressed Utilization

The need for adult foster care services (beds) has shown a slight decline in the State of Michigan over the past year (approximately 100 residents statewide). Similarly, there was just recently the delicensure of an adult foster care program in Shelton, only several miles to the south of Millsworth. This decrease in usage is a function of two phenomena. The first is that there is an effort by the Michigan DSS to keep the elderly living at home with the "home help services" and other support programs. The concept is to provide the services needed at the lowest cost. DSS has instituted a program that pays others who are able to look in on the elderly person, whether that be the next door neighbor or some other individual. They pay at a rate significantly less than the amounts paid to professional home health agencies and currently have about 30,000 elderly on such a program in the state of Michigan. This approach to addressing the issue of supporting the elderly and their independence has worked and allowed them to maximize their goal to keep people in their homes for as long as is possible.

Very little has changed in the Millsworth area regarding payment reform or population changes that would tend to affect the viability of a home for the aged over the past 5–10 years. Although usage of AFC-type services offered in past years may have actually been slightly higher than at the current time, we believe that this temporary slight depression in consumption of services is short-lived. We think that the need for assisted elderly residential services will increase but slowly.

Percentage of County Population Older than 65

The most relevant demographic information for these purposes relates to the size and nature of the 65-and-older population. In our survey, we determined that it would be beneficial to group Millsworth County with several other "like" rural counties in Michigan for which we could locate data, comparing Millsworth County with the others in terms of its relative economic standing and percentage of population older than the age of 65.

In reviewing the data, we find that Millsworth County actually has among the lowest number of elderly as a percentage of the total population. For example, of the range of counties surveyed, Mason County has approximately 16 percent of its population older than 65 years of age. Millsworth was the lowest in the survey, with an elderly percentage of 13.3 percent. The average for our group of six counties was 14.45 percent. This means that Millsworth County has, as derived from this comparative sample, approximately 8 percent fewer elderly residents than the average of the counties selected.

Comparing Michigan Counties and Millsworth County Ratios of AFC Beds to Overall Population

We have done an extensive analysis of homes for the aged in the State of Michigan and homes for the aged and adult foster care beds in similar counties. The results are that with the addition of 40 home for the aged beds, Millsworth County would be near the top of the 43 counties that have homes for the aged in terms of the lowest amount of population to support an HFA bed. (Thirty-nine counties have no such facilities.)

Comparing Similar Counties with Millsworth County and Its Ratio of AFC Beds to Overall Population

Also when comparing Millsworth County's ratio of population to AFC/HFA beds among similar sized counties, we find that it falls roughly close to the bottom in terms of having the most AFC and HFA beds per the population. Of the counties compared, Emmet had 360 persons for every HFA bed on the low side and Cheboygan had 1,792 for the high value. Millsworth was the middle value of 590 persons per among the range but much closer to the low end of the scale in terms of population to support HFA beds.

Review of Payer Mix, Third-Party versus Private-Pay Residents

We questioned both the MDPH and the Michigan DSS regarding the issue of payer mix for Millsworth County because this is a major variable in the projection of facility income.

In addition to the lower than usual elderly population, the analysis of the income levels by counties in Michigan is meaningful. Current information from the State of Michigan is that Millsworth County is the fourth poorest county in the state. This information confirmed some earlier data we had developed substantiating the relative economic status of the county (which actually placed Millsworth as the second poorest county in Michigan). One conclusion that might be drawn by most is that there will tend to be fewer private-paying residents in this county than typically found elsewhere. One Millsworth County DSS official suggested that, based on what they have seen in adult foster care programs, approximately 75 percent of the home for the aged residents would be covered through public assistance. It goes without saying of course that only 25 percent would be private-paying residents. In health care parlance, this would be a less than optimal "payer mix" (as contrasted with the best case scenario being heavy demand for the beds and full-charge paying residents). Residents covered by Social Security (SSI) may pay $724 per month, $613.30 from SSI and $110.70 from Medicaid.

Both state departments indicated that they viewed Millsworth County as being an economically disadvantaged county that would translate into a higher mix of patients paying for their care with their Social Security checks. These amounts can vary somewhat, but they acknowledged that $650, as used by the owner, is not a bad number to base revenue estimates on. Our research indicated that the most current number for SSI payment is $684 per month. The number of private-pay patients will probably be less than usual, however; the $900 used by the owner could be low. In the more urban and upscale facilities, monthly fees can go as high as $3,000 (or as low as $500). In summary, we find that the owners' estimates are reasonable.

Residents Requiring Assistance—Another Way To Evaluate the Potential Market

We extrapolated some national figures to identify the number of individuals requiring daily assistance. The percentages used were national; however, we applied them against the exact age categories and numbers for Millsworth County. The results were quite interesting. When including everyone needing help from age 45 up, the number of people in Millsworth County who need living assistance is approximately 468. These figures along with the others suggest that there is a much bigger need for assistance of some type than normally thought.

If one subtracts the number of nursing home beds in the county (182) and the current number of adult foster care beds—including developmentally disabled and mentally ill (115), we are left with roughly 171 individuals who need daily help of some kind. This seems to speak in favor of home for the aged beds.

Trend for AFC-Level Need

In Michigan, between the diminishing effects of the DSS efforts to minimize the use of AFC and HFA facilities and pressures of the increasing population, *the net overall result* has been a *slight downward trend* in usage. It is our opinion that there will be relatively little movement in terms of the overall *need* for AFC or HFA beds over the next five years. The increase or decrease will be a function of major but slowly moving trends. We find that there is some "built-in" economic obsolescence involved here.

Alternatively, we believe that those elderly who are particularly fragile will find the subject facility with its proximity to the onsite health care providers a major benefit and that the facility will immediately pull residents from other existing programs. We also are quick to add that the need that is evidenced by the *current usage of AFC facilities is not necessarily the same as the potential demand for a new and better positioned "product" in the market.*

Demand for Services Will Increase

This issue is discussed at length under the Market Approach section of this report, but suffice it to say that the resources that will be needed to meet the consumer demands of a growing and aging population as the parents of the Baby Boomers move into the consumer/payer position will have to be expanded and more comprehensive in terms of service options than have been in available in the past to residents of the area.

Current Market versus Potential Market

It is important to differentiate between the current market that relates to the service levels it has been presented with and the potential market that may be more demand-driven by a new service to the consumers. An example of the former or current market are the current users of AFC services. Although these individuals are all potential residents of the new facility, they still only represent one segment of the health care market.

New Clients for a New Service

A second category of potential consumers of services provided by the new facility are those who may not have felt comfortable considering the earlier AFC alternatives available but now are attracted to the converted facility and the merit or convenience of adjacent medical resources.

Still a third category of patients comes from either end of the "health care continuum" (i.e., several who were borderline nursing home patients and for whom a home for the aged is equally or more attractive [and less expensive]). Also within this category, we place those who may be referred from the Shelton hospital. Hospitals often have Medicare patients in-house whom they are no longer paid for and who have no real medical necessity to remain in an acute care or even subacute care setting but, for lack of a place to discharge the patient to, have not been able to discharge him or her. To be sure, this number of patients may not number in the double digits but certainly can be one type of resident if the owners actively pursue a relationship with the hospital and develop an approved transfer agreement.

Potential residents of the new facility are also likely to be those for whom home health or home help services are not enough, who must move on to a situation in which assistance is more available. This area will be a significant one to cultivate in terms of marketing (home health agencies and those in the county who are currently contracted by the state to provide "home help").

Finally, and important for future trends and versatility, the HFA facility has the option according to the MDPH to lease a portion of their beds to subacute care if they subsequently need to. The certificate of need process would need to be satisfied; however, this is a distinct option because very little additional cost would be incurred to provide a needed service.

Also in terms of providing more than one level of service, some of the beds, especially the four private rooms perpendicular to the main hallway, could be basic retirement center beds if the adult foster care demand lags. As long as some separation as to the level of residents was maintained, this is possible. Yet other possibilities, such as getting licensed as a special use facility for Alzheimer's patients, exist. "Fallback positions" in this mid-level assisted living/subacute care area abound.

Caution about Relying Entirely on AFC Services Utilization

The danger in suggesting that there can be no more demand than what is currently demonstrated by the consumption of AFC beds is that it does not consider the much different product that the subject represents. Neither does it take into consideration any marketing efforts. It is our position that the current market demand (54 elderly residents in county AFC facilities) represents the floor of the potential demand. Although many people would consider a more domestic setting such as an AFC program to place a relative, others would prefer a substantial or formal quasi-medical "facility" approach. Our strong feeling is that probably one-half of the current AFC residents will be willing or interested in considering the subject as a new place to live. The remainder of the individuals will not be interested in moving from the AFC locations for several reasons, including proximity to family, bonding with the current staff, friends they have made at the current location, and resistance to change.

Absorption

Projecting absorption periods and patterns for senior housing is difficult and imprecise. There are few universal guidelines regarding absorption, but the industry standard for average-sized proposed senior projects has traditionally been 18–24 months. In more populated areas where competition has become much more intense, lease-up periods of 24–48 months are not uncommon. Nonetheless, past history of even comparable properties (of which there are none) may give an inaccurate indication of absorption merely because of demographics. An example of one absorption study for a 170-bed unit facility showed the following:

	Average	*Range*
Preleasing	20%	0–50%
Absorption Pattern	6–7 units/mo	4–5 to 10–12 units/mo
Absorption Period	18–24 months	12–60 months

The application of the above preleasing and absorption pattern percentages and ranges probably would be difficult to justify using in the case of the subject because of the rural location/low density and the lower income.

One exception to the longer absorption periods has been elderly projects that are government-subsidized or government-supported. Because these projects are attractive, offering near-equal and sometimes better services for lower rents, they usually experience rapid lease-up periods of 12 months or less. The subject certainly falls into this category, as both Social Security income and Medicaid payments will subsidize resident rents.

Our pro forma uses *the most conservative absorption period of 60 months.* Although we show an initial high growth census during the first year, we show only gradual but consistent net growth in the resident population. Taking another look at guidelines, forecasting an absorption rate of 10 or more units per month is considered aggressive; 6–7 units per month is a more common and realistic estimate. Our first month provides for seven residents; the second and third months provide for three additional residents each. Months 4 through 7 each show an additional two residents. Months 8–12 add an additional resident bringing the facility to 70 percent occupancy. After the first year of activity, we have only allowed for small incremental increases in net occupancy level.

We also believe that, based on statistical experience, annual turnover will be approximately 10 percent.

Importance of Marketing

Perhaps, the *single largest factor* regarding the overall success and occupancy of the subject facility will be the quality and the scope of marketing effort put forth by the owners. If the effort is strong and the market is wide, we believe the new entrant into the elderly residential field will be a successful one, breaking even in approximately six months. Another trend discovered during our research was that building homes for the aged immediately adjacent to skilled nursing facilities was a fast-growing trend.

Efforts made to publicize these advantages and the availability of quality facilities and their proximity to other important medical care resources including the Council on Aging will be a strong market differentiation decision factor for consumers. Just before the facility opening, a pre- "open house" held specifically for potential sources of referral such as DSS officials, hospital representatives, and elderly program social agency personnel, should be held to elicit their support and ensure that they are fully aware of the merits of the facility and programs. Another "open house" can be held for the general public.

Inasmuch, we think the subject program and facility have an excellent opportunity to play a meaningful, profitable, and rewarding role as a home for the aged and transcend the otherwise "less-than-average" demographics.

ANALYSIS AND CONCLUSIONS

HIGHEST AND BEST USE OF THE PROPERTY AS IMPROVED

We find that many nonacute health care–related uses are best placed in the facilities of former hospitals. This certainly appears to be the case with the subject property. It has the space and roughed-in facilities that would allow it to fill many roles. It is our opinion that the optimal use of this health care property would be a residential care facility.

If there were *not* another (competing) nursing home immediately adjacent, we suggest that this use would be the highest and best use. If either the population demographics change or the existing skilled nursing facility (SNF) changes in some way to allow, the subject's highest and best use could become a nursing home. We see no signs that this will be occurring in the near future, however.

The next most acute service to a nursing home–type facility is an assisted living elderly residential facility. It would be this type of facility that would be the most cost-effective and offer the best return on the investment. This apparently is largely the approach as shared with us by the owners. The fact that the owners are opting to maximize the facility to its fullest by renting to other health care and social programs and services eliminates what would otherwise be a superadequacy condition.

HIGHEST AND BEST USE OF THE LAND AS THOUGH VACANT

Given the variety of medical and elderly-related successful activities, programs, and businesses immediately contiguous to the subject property, it is our strong opinion that the highest and best use is a health care use and specifically as that intended, a home for the aged.

Experience suggests that most land used to develop elderly projects has a value approximating vacant. Theoretically, vacant land available for its highest and best use as elderly housing is worth more than vacant land available for its highest and best use as a conventional high-density residential use. Higher rents, higher allowed densities, and lower parking requirements are three potential reasons why buyers would be willing to pay more for an elderly housing site. There appears, however, to be insufficient evidence in the market to support this except in circumstances in which project approvals have been achieved before sale.

LAND VALUE

As discussed in the Reconciliation, we were able to locate three properties that were comparable but for size in the immediate area of the subject property for developing a paired sales analysis and resultant value. Although the parcels were in the 2–3-acre range and the subject is approximately 8 acres, the other properties, due to their location and general nature required only relatively minor and straightforward adjustments in the grid.

Of course, the market approach was the only appropriate approach to value the land as though vacant. The income and cost approach did not apply, and there is no value registered with the County Assessor.

APPROACHES TO VALUE

Introduction

Elderly housing can be appraised by three traditional approaches to value: the cost approach, the income capitalization approach, and the sales comparison approach. In most cases, the purpose of the appraisal is an estimate of market value derived from a reconciliation of the three approaches. As with many sophisticated property types, appraising elderly housing includes the development's going concern or business value. Consequently, a senior project's worth is more than just the value of the real estate assets; it also includes furniture and equipment (not included in this project), licenses, and the reputation or goodwill established by the business in the community. Therefore, in a reconciliation of the three approaches, the income capitalization approach, which incorporates business value, is usually given the greatest weight.

In this project, there is no goodwill because the business has not yet been developed to the point of opening or generating an income stream as a home for the aged (although there is approximately $1,100 per month income from two onsite physician office rentals). All these realty and nonrealty components are reflected in the revenues produced by a project, but they are difficult to segregate individually using the cost or sales comparison approach. To comply with current appraisal standards, nonrealty components must be separately identified.

Cost Approach

Background on Code Compliance and Regulatory Requirements

We reviewed the construction requirements for homes for the aged that we obtained in part from the State Fire Marshall, the American Association of Homes for the Aging, and the MDPH. The facility falls under the 1991 standards, which consist of the 1985 Life Safety Code and some additional State of Michigan amendments. The facility was able to use the old (still existing) hospital license to operate because it had not yet expired and requested designation as a home for the aged. A change in use from an existing license within the health care field is allowable and permits the owner to not have to qualify under the new requirements. In other words, it was grandfathered and avoided having to do several costly physical plant upgrades. This factor alone provides the owners with a great deal of financial leverage in terms of value over their cost to renovate and use.

The MDPH and the Michigan State Fire Marshall have been working closely with the owner. We were informed by the owner during a tour of the facility and on viewing the plans for renovation now underway that these items have been addressed and are further addressed in the renovation cost breakdown.

Additionally AHCA has reviewed the existing individual MDPH regulations on homes for the aged and has determined that the facility and renovation plan address all physical plant requirements.

In summary, because the facility is moving to a less acute level of care and is not being required to meet the newest fire safety codes, we believe that the facility will be in quite acceptable condition for its intended use as a home for the aged when the current renovation program is complete. Unless the facility plans a major expansion, it will continue to be grandfathered and not have to conform with the most current published requirements (i.e., providing sprinklers for the entire facility).

Cost Model

AHCA uses the Marshall and Swift Construction Cost Estimation Service in the development of the cost approach. The primary factors used in arriving at our cost estimate were the building type of class C average construction, the degree of depreciation, the local labor index and the appropriate designations for the shape of the facility, the climate, and the square footages as appropriate.

We developed a model for a current-day 40-bed home for the aged. It is critical to distinguish that this facility is not, in Marshall and Swift vernacular, a "convalescent hospital," which requires provisions for rehabilitative therapy and approximately another $10 per square foot cost.

We thought that based on our study of the current requirements for HFAs and how the current facility will compare when complete, as well as indications from state officials that there was little or no difference from a functional or physical depreciation standpoint between the subject property and how a new home for the aged would be designed. This fact also suggested that a *reconstruction cost new less depreciation* model was appropriate in lieu of a replacement cost model.

Basic Cost Determinants

Inasmuch, we selected the Marshall and Swift Cost Estimating Service to develop a reconstruction cost new less depreciation value. The resulting factor for the total main facility of 29,811 square feet including the corridor connecting with the nursing home was based on a 55 percent use as a home for the aged and a 45 percent use as medical office rental space. We based our construction cost estimates on a one-story, irregular-shaped, class C facility with a 8,806-square-foot basement. We noted that there was an elevator adjacent to the kitchen and that the method of heating was hot water radiant heat/boiler. We listed the condition of the facility as very good and cost rank as average. For depreciation purposes, we listed **a 16-year effective age** based on **a 40-year economic life.** We identified approximately 10,500 square feet of sprinkled area.

We included additional structural costs for the attached physician office used by Millsworth Medical Services, the ambulance garage, and a 52,000-square-foot asphalt parking lot.

This is how we evaluated the facility "by system" for its remaining effective life to reach an appropriate value of reconstruction cost new less depreciation:

In the case of the mechanical and electrical systems' effective ages, we have accepted the opinions of Rhodes Engineering Corporation of Muskegon, Michigan. They believe that the electrical system, which had the distribution system replaced in 1980–81, has at least a remaining effective life of 25 years or an effective age of no more than 15 years. The branch wiring would be the oldest component (1952); however, the circuit loading capacity, which was constructed to meet acute care demands, is well suited to be able to meet the increased need of the 1990s for a home for the aged.

For the plumbing piping, we have given a remaining effective life figure of 25 years. For the hot water piping, we assigned a 30-year remaining life. For the remaining boiler/heat source that will be used, Rhodes has suggested a 15-year remaining life. The gas chillers are not going to be used in the future, so we have not rated them. The revised mechanical air ducts, sheet metal, and air coil fans were estimated to have an age of 15 years.

From a structural standpoint, one of the most significant physical plant problems has been the deferred maintenance of the facility roof. Evidence of internal ceiling leakage testifies to the advanced deterioration of the roof. The cost to cure the roof condition involves the replacement of the existing roof and represents approximately one-third of the projected renovation expense. It is our opinion that the physical structure will be restored to an effective age of 24 years on a 40-year economic life. As documented elsewhere in this report, we have found various regulatory physical plant requirements and deferred maintenance to be "curable" (i.e., the costs of correcting the conditions are more than offset by an equal or greater increase in value).

Functional Obsolescence

We have reviewed architectural plans developed by Mr. Tom Stone, Architect, Pelman, Michigan, converting the facility to the use as a home for the aged and for health care–related rental space. Although if one were building a home for the aged from "scratch," it may well be laid out differently (e.g., having the cafeteria more central to the resident rooms or having the staff "station" more central on the patient floor), we have no substantive objective criticisms of the plan or application to this use. Inasmuch, we find little functional obsolescence in the design of the facility as renovated.

Resulting Effective Overall Life

Considering the regulatory compliance and related functional compliance achieved through the cost-effective renovation program of meeting applicable Life Safety Code, Handicapped Access Requirements, and MDPH Code, we believe the effective economic age of the facility to be 16 years. This would not have been possible if the facility had not been allowed to be literally grandfathered forever from having to meet very costly code requirements for new facilities.

Value According to Cost Approach

The initial value of the subject based on the cost approach alone but including the land, we found to be $2,047,064 (unrounded).

Income Approach

Background

As stated earlier, there is no income or expense data on this project on which to base a reliable approach. We thought, however, that there was merit in attempting a pro forma projection based on reasonable resident rates, SSI and Medicare reimbursement levels, conservative expenses, and a phased-in plausible occupancy rate.

In a book written by Arthur E. Gimmy, MAI, and Michael G. Boehm in 1988, *Elderly Housing, A Guide to Appraisal, Market Analysis, Development and Financing*, the authors provided the following data on expenses as a percentage of effective gross income. We interpolated and updated the data they used to identify the same ratio for the subject. In 1988, the expense per unit for a 40-bed personal care facility was 60 percent, or $7,250. (For purposes of this study, we interpreted that to mean a full facility over which to spread costs.) In 1994, those expense numbers adjusted upward 5 percent per year would be $9,715. If we use the year end expenses for the subject when it is nearly full at the end of two years in 1996, its expense as a percentage of effective gross income would only be 48 percent. Further, its expense per unit would only come to $7,711. As an ongoing rule of thumb, 60 percent can be used as a comparison with the industry for this type of performance.

Although these numbers can only be viewed as rough ballpark estimates, it certainly does give comfort to those who concern themselves about operating overhead.

The following are the assumptions we made in developing the pro forma:

a. We increased all but the lease with Memorial Hospital by 5 percent annually. (This special "no base lease escalation" provision was an inducement extended the hospital to secure this "anchor" tenant.) It was noted that they will pay annual increases in insurance, utilities, and maintenance.
b. We thought that it was reasonable to include the leasing of the currently unoccupied spaces at specified intervals, the first in six months from the opening of the facility, the second one year after the opening. The third space was leased some 18 months after opening. At 12-month intervals, we increased each of these lease rates by 5 percent. We did not perform an area-wide rent market survey for this pro forma but rather relied on what the existing rent data and agreements were and what the letters of intent indicated.
c. We included the $200.00 monthly bequest for the dedication of the library from an arrangement with the administrators of a local trust.
d. We included an annual 2 percent increase in the rates for resident income, which tends to be consistent with what Medicaid has been doing. We acknowledge that the private payers could easily be increased more annually than the SSI-Medicaid residents; however, we have not included this differentiation.
e. We increased the various expense categories by 5 percent annually with several exceptions as follows:
    1. Utilities were increased at 3 percent annually.
    2. We used the principal and interest payments on the original loan and renovation loan as the owner and his accountant have provided us.

Currently, there are several letters of intent to rent space from the facility. Two of the letters of intent are from current renters, Dr. Norma Clinton and Millsworth Medical Care, a group of medical specialists from Wellston. One letter of intent is from Memorial Hospital in Wellston to lease 5,500 square feet for $32,000 per year and represents the facility's "anchor" tenant. Finally, the Millsworth County Ambulance Authority has filed a letter of intent to continue renting an 896-square-foot pole barn/garage from the owner.

Aside from the space that will be allocated to residential living space, approximately 4,021 square feet within the facility is leasable. One of the prime areas includes 672 square feet of space currently labeled as "gift shop" in the front section of the facility, which would be an ideal location for a satellite pharmacy from a community drug store and health care supply retail facility. We believe that this area will likely be leased within one-half year of the opening of the home for the aged.

In addition to the foregoing area, there is an additional 2,736 square feet, not including circulation corridors, which would be appropriate for community psychosocial services or other health care/elderly service use. Some of this area includes the former hospital laboratory. In our opinion, this diagnostic ancillary use should be the first use considered for the space. Aside from a laboratory in Shelton or what minor laboratory capabilities may be available through adjacent physicians' offices, there are no other laboratory facilities between Muskegon and Wellston. Millsworth is roughly halfway between them.

Normalization / Modification of Operating Income and Expense Projections

Line Item Income and Expenses. Second, the pro forma developed by the owner on the following page was developed to portray a typical monthly typical income and expense statement further along into the business's operation and not particularly a phased-in projection. We have included our version in the appraisal which provides a phased-in cash flow statement. We see the facility breaking even in the sixth month, which we consider quite good. This was possible due to the relatively low overhead of the facility principal and interest. We have also provided a phasing-in of revenue associated with the remaining rental space over 18 months.

Resident Food Costs. Resident food costs were an initial concern and may be slightly understated, but after consultation with various state agency officials, we found that the $1.00 per resident per meal is not an unreasonable cost to budget for resident groceries/food. Nursing home patients currently cost approximately $1.50 per meal. The cost savings lies in the scale of economies from congregate meal preparation and bulk food purchases.

Utilities Expense. We researched the utility cost with the local utilities provider, the City of Millsworth. Records of the former hospital utilities usage were not available; however, we used current billings to the former hospital and current billings to the medical care facility to which the subject is attached. Although neither usage is the same as what the intended use will be, we were able to interpolate some costs based on the intensity of use of both current billings. The figure used by the owner was approximately $2000 per month for utilities. We agreed with the owner and thought that this was a good estimate of what the fully rented and occupied facility will be. The number represents approximately six times the current "under renovation" figures and about one-third of the level of the attached nursing home usage. Nursing homes, by their nature, provide a much higher intensity of care, and this translates directly into the demand on utilities.

Rental Space. As stated above, we used the letters of intent to construct the pro forma that we developed for the income approach. We included 5 percent escalations in each except for the lease with Memorial Hospital. Except for this particular lease, all were treated as triple net leases using the insurance, maintenance, and taxes by space allocation provided by the owners. The hospital's lease, although not reflecting a base rental rate increase, does include a provision for recouping the other costs typically found in a triple net lease. The remaining two areas that are currently unoccupied were both included as leased over the course of one year. (See the pro forma for the specific times, amounts, and increases.)

Defining What Was Reasonable to Expect

In creating an income approach, the initial task was to first develop a reasonable revenue stream based on the base pro forma expenses provided, our projected occupancy (volume) rates, payer mix projections, and reimbursement levels. We reviewed the individual line item costs and found them to be quite reasonable so did not "normalize" them except for inflation. We projected the net revenue (both office lease and resident payments) for five years, which we considered as the holding period.

Calculation of Income Approach Value

The result was a five-year projection of income and expense for the subject property and business. To these numbers we applied a blended discount rate of 16 percent based on the current 30-year Treasury bonds and a risk factor for the investment. In our risk factor analysis for the subject, we reviewed market position, management, financial management, physical facilities, and quality of service/uniqueness. The revenue was then discounted back to a present value to provide an income approach value. The discount rate was lowered to 13 percent in the sixth year to reflect the reduction in risk of a stabilized going concern. The result of these calculations was an income approach value of $1,267,092 unrounded.

Influences on Demand and the Census Establishing the volume or census of the facility posed the greatest problem. On the one side, there were data that suggested that the county was less apt to support a home for the aged than most others, not only in terms of the percentage of elderly but also in terms of a higher welfare portion of the population. Added to this was the fact that there remains a 15 percent vacancy of the overall licensed adult foster care beds. Finally, in most comparisons that we made, there was less overall population to support HFA beds than in most counties in the state.

On the other side of the equation, however, was the fact that this market has not been provided the more upscale option of a home for the aged, not to mention one that is next to a nursing home, the Council on Aging, the biggest cluster of physician offices in the county, and mental health clinics. Downtown is about one block away. Clearly, this option for those seeking assisted living accommodations or adult foster care living arrangements will be the choice elderly residential facility in the county. If only one-third of the currently AFC recipients select the new facility for essentially the same dollars they are spending in group homes, the subject will fill nearly half its current beds.

Further, we looked closely at the paucity of homes for the aged in adjoining other counties. Muskegon County to the immediate south, has an abundance of such facilities, but we reviewed the Michigan Association of Homes for the Aging and found none in Mason, Newaygo, or Lake counties. We estimated a total elderly population for the four counties (none of which currently has a home for the aged, according to the data we have) of approximately 15,250.

Although the largest component will come from the Millsworth/Shelton/Pelman area, it seemed plausible that some residents could certainly come from these areas, especially from Wellston in Mason County, a town of approximately 9,000. For example, although there is a home for the aged on the east side of Newaygo County, people in Mason County have to travel two counties away to the north and four away to the east before finding another HFA facility.

By using data we obtained from a Laventhol and Horwath study, we learned that approximately 20 percent of the residents of such elderly residential facilities come from more than 25 miles away; 88 percent come from within 25 miles of the facility.

Additionally, using a variety of established utilization rates that relate to various age groups within a given population, we were able to determine the number of persons by age category who were likely to require the help of another person for daily living. For Millsworth County, it meant that there was a total of 468 persons, to a maximum of 545, who fell into this category.

Additionally, the medical care facility that is physically connected to the home for the aged will be a source of residents on an ongoing basis. As elderly recuperating patients progress, they will require a less intense level of supervision and care. The home for the aged is "in the right place" to work synergistically with the largely full nursing home.

How we arrived at the level of occupancy was a function of many of the considerations mentioned above together with our experience of what is more or less likely with a relatively aggressive marketing and public awareness program. Many if not all county private and public social agencies are aware of the facility's new role, and we believe they will support and refer to it.

Statistics played a big part in our projecting a slower occupancy than that projected by the owner. To begin with, we estimated an average of seven residents the first month. Those who come first will be those who are currently in an AFC home but who are more medically "brittle" and who feel comfort in being closer to medical help. The months immediately after the opening of the facility should be marked with fairly rapid activity and growth. We anticipate that the social agencies, the area nursing homes, and the social services directors of the hospitals in Wellston and Shelton will all serve as conduits for the facility's census in a way that is uncommon in more populated areas.

We concede that the volume question was/is an evasive one with many dynamic forces at work, as we have described. We also state here as we have in other parts of the report that it will not be the "need" but rather the demand that can be created with public awareness efforts that will be the engine that most propels the occupancy. If the public is not informed about the new service, the road to profitability will be lengthened. The critical issue in our minds was the fact that not only Millsworth but also the surrounding counties to the east and north were underserved in the proposed service. We believe there is the critical mass of population and market necessary to succeed and generate a reasonable profit and service the debt.

The return on equity for retirement or elderly residential facilities is not typically a high one, often ranging from 2 to 5 percent. With the relatively low end investment, this facility should perform significantly better and much sooner.

Sources of Research

As noted earlier an extensive amount of research was conducted to develop income projections. Among other sources, we interviewed personnel at the MDPH, Division of Health Facilities Development, Division of Licensing and Certification, Grand Rapids Licensing and Certification, Bureau of Health Systems, Michigan DSS, Directors Office, Division of Reimbursement, and Millsworth County DSS. We also obtained significant information and insight from the American Association of Homes for the Aging, the Michigan Association for Homes for the Aging, Arbor Associates, Inc. (Petoskey, MI), *The U.S. Census*, *Survey of Residential Retirement Facilities* (Laventhol and Horwath, 1987), *Elderly Housing—A Guide to Appraisal, Market Analysis, Development and Financing*, Arthur E. Gimmy, MAI, et al., and *The Handbook of Statistics on American*

Family Life. Data from these sources were needed to develop a pro forma income and expense projection to further estimate a demand for the services being offered by the subject facility.

Market Approach (Land Only)

The market approach for health care facilities is an extremely difficult, and more often than not, an impossible task due to the relatively infrequent sales. Additionally, these often do not occur in even remotely close geographic areas. Further, unlike standard residential or commercial real estate, it is most often not possible to obtain accurate data on all the relevant terms. For these reasons, it was not possible to provide a reliable market approach to the improvements on this project.

The market approach was used and deemed as the most appropriate for valuing the land component of the property because of its sensitivity to the market and applicability. The cost approach is not applicable to vacant land, and for reasons discussed elsewhere in this report, the derivation of a land value based on a percentage of income attributable was not considered. A standard appraisal approach for valuing land as though vacant, using a paired sales analysis, was used.

Three somewhat smaller (2–3 acre) relatively recent and geographically comparable properties were found for our analysis. Adjustments in time from sale, location, utility, and other factors were made to arrive at the value for the subject property.

Our opinion of the value of the land as though vacant by the method above and as described in the land valuation section is $126,400.

RECONCILIATION OF VALUE INDICATIONS

MARKET APPROACH

As discussed above, because of the lack of adequate data on sales of elderly assisted living facilities and their geographic dispersion, we do not believe that a paired sales analysis or other comparative analysis is worthwhile in the valuation of the property improvements. Inasmuch, the market approach for purposes of valuing the subject improvements was not used for this purpose. As noted in the previous pages, however, it was used as the predominant method in the valuation of the land.

Our rationale for using the market approach for the land value was because it provided the most market-sensitive and timely data. Although there are some esoteric income approaches possible, certainly the cost approach would be inappropriate to apply to the land component.

The income approach might have been able to be used to determine a rough land value by apportioning a part of the income based on area land to improvement ratios; however, this was not considered to be reliable for two reasons. The first was that the income approach in this report could only be our best guess based on what our experience, our research, and the owner's projections would suggest a most likely financial pro forma would look like. The second reason is that using rough land/improvement ratios may provide a ballpark idea of value at best, but when compounded with the present value of a best guess income stream, it could not be realistically presented as the strongest of approaches.

INCOME APPROACH

What is normally the most relied-on approach was of more limited value because it is based on educated speculation, particularly with regard to the occupancy rates of the facility, which is the single biggest factor in the projections. The income approach per se was never intended to be our selected approach for the reasons stated above. It was, however, viewed as a feasibility test as to whether the intended use would allow us to assign a value to the property as a home for the aged, the value intended. If our feasibility pro forma showed the home for the aged not feasible, it certainly would have overridden our ability to give the property *any* value for an HFA purpose. Indeed, our initial (and continued) position on the highest and best use would have changed.

So although we did not select the income approach as a final best estimate of value, it played an extremely important role in suggesting whether the project as envisioned by the owners was possible and a was major influence in the final opinion of value. We refer you to the following section on the cost approach for more discussion on this influence.

Short of an in-depth market telephone interview survey of a legitimate sampling of the population regarding the place in the market for a home for the aged, there is simply not enough solid data to be able to project actual volumes, income, and expense and arrive at a legitimate *value*.

Additionally, although the letters of intent from likely leaseholders are in hand and provide us with some assurance that there will be that level of income, the uncertainties of the market preclude us from considering the approach as one for use in this appraisal report. Inasmuch, again, we did not select the income approach for use in the valuation.

COST APPROACH

The cost approach is used much more for insurance, reimbursement, and taxation purposes. In the case of acute care facilities, the practice tends to be a combined asset-based approach of present value/discounted cash flow technique and fair market value for a revised net tangible asset value.

Unfortunately, we were not able to use the market or sales approach for the building improvements because of the paucity of data. Also, the income approach was based on good although not historical or market-tested data.

For these reasons, the main approach we relied on was the reconstruction of "cost new less depreciation" cost approach. It is also our opinion that "cost" does not necessarily equal value and that the cost information needed to be balanced with what we could say about the current demographics and their influence on the final value. Also, our opinion of value was guided by the income approach and feasibility work we had done. This resulted in a value less than that suggested by the cost approach but still more than the (weaker) income approach. The *cost approach alone* suggested a value of $1,694,121 (unrounded) "as is" at the highest and best use and $2,047,064 (unrounded) after the renovations currently underway.

RECONCILIATION

As a result of our investigation and analysis, it is our opinion that the market value of the identified interest in the property *as is*, on November 22, 1993, is

One Million, Five Hundred Thousand Dollars
($1,500,000.00)

which may be allocated as follows:

Land	$ 126,400
Improvements	$1,373,600
TOTAL	$1,500,000

It is our opinion that the market value of the identified interest in the property *after the current renovation program by the owner* will be

One Million, Eight Hundred Thousand Dollars
($1,800,000.00)

which may be allocated as follows:

Land	$ 126,400
Improvements	$1,673,600
TOTAL	$1,800,000

QUALIFICATIONS OF THE APPRAISERS
(DELETED FROM SAMPLE)

ADDENDA - DOCUMENTS
(LISTED ONLY)

A. Marketview Comparison Reports for Millsworth County and Millsworth, Michigan (National Planning Data Corporation)
B. Number of Adults by Category Who Need the Help of Another Person/1,000 Persons in Millsworth County
C. Home for the Aged Beds by County and Population per Bed
D. Adult Foster Care Facilities in Millsworth County, September 1993
E. Rate and Composition of Occupancy, Projected
F. Occupancy (Increase) Rate: Home for the Aged, Millsworth, Michigan
G. Comparable Counties (Population to Support Each HFA Bed)
H Percentage of Elderly/County
I. Homes for the Aged and Adult Foster Care Beds by County and Population
J. Living Arrangements of Persons 65 and Older, 1988
K. Michigan Department of Public Health Physical Plant Requirements for Homes for the Aged
L. Letter of Ability to Convert License, State Fire Marshall, Michigan State Police
M. Letter Regarding Code Compliance, Michigan Department of Public Health
N1. Cost Estimates—Main Facility (Including Site Value)
N1.a.Estimate Reconstruction Cost New
N1.b.Estimate Reconstruction Cost New, Prerenovation
N1.c.Estimate Reconstruction Cost New, Prerenovation w/Owner Renovation Allowance Added
N1.d.Estimate Reconstruction Cost New, Post Renovation
N2.Depreciation by System and Effective Age, Prerenovation
N3.Depreciation by System and Effective Age, Postrenovation
N4.Projected Renovation Costs by Owner
O. Cost Estimate—RCN Less Depreciation—Storage (Ambulance) Garage
P. Cost Estimate—RCN Less Depreciation—Utility Shed (Well House)
Q1. Five-Year Pro Forma for Subject Business Volume, Income and Expense
Q2. Expense as a Percentage of Effective Gross Income
R1. Blended Discount Rate Development—Qualitative Model
R2. Blended Discount Rate Development—Build-Up Model
S. Discounted Cash Flow and Resulting Present Value of Income Stream
T. Letter of Intent to Lease, Memorial Hospital, Wellston, Michigan
U. Letter of Intent to Lease, Norma Clinton, M.D., Millsworth, Michigan
V. Letter Regarding Transfer of Patients from Millsworth County Medical Care Facility
W. Letter of Interest, The Woman's Shelter, Wellston, Michigan
X. Letter of Interest, Planned Parenthood Centers of West Michigan
Y. Letter Regarding Bessie E. Jones Living Trust
Z. Plat Survey of Subject Land
AA. New Floor Plan of Subject Facility
AB. Percentage of Residents Originating within 25 Miles (One Table, Two Graphs)
AC. Main Facility Perimeter Lengths
AD. Paired Sales Analysis and Supplemental Narrative for Market Approach, Subject Land as Though Vacant, Frank M. LeFoutre, State Certified Appraiser
AE. Flood Map City of Millsworth, Michigan, Department of Housing and Urban Development, Federal Insurance Administration

Appraisal #4. Family Practice Clinic

AMERICAN HEALTH CARE APPRAISAL
APPRAISAL SPECIALISTS FOR THE HEALTHCARE INDUSTRY

4130 LA JOLLA VILLAGE DRIVE, SUITE 1072
LA JOLLA, CALIFORNIA 92037
(619) 751-1450

APPRAISAL REPORT
ON
MAYVILLE CLINIC
MAYVILLE, MICHIGAN

APRIL 1, 1995

SAMPLE PHYSICIAN PRACTICE APPRAISAL

SCOPE

American Health Care Appraisal has been requested by Gotham City Hospital to appraise the medical practice known as Mayville Clinic, Mayville, located at 150 S. Front Street, Mayville, Michigan 12345. The appraisal includes the value of the "practice," including goodwill and net tangible asset value and not the real estate associated.

The purpose of the valuation was for the purpose of acquiring the medical practice.

In completing this appraisal, we have followed the Standards of Professional Practice of the Appraisal Institute.

SUMMARY DESCRIPTION OF THE PRACTICE

The Mayville Clinic is located at 150 S. Front Street, Mayville, Michigan 12345, a community of 6,500 people, approximately 30 miles NNE of Metropolis, Michigan. As stated above, the clinic is operated by two general practice physicians, Dr. Dennis Williamson and Dr. Roger Davis, each owning 50 percent of the corporation.

SOURCES OF INFORMATION

In preparing this report, we have reviewed the following documents:

1. Annual *compiled* financial statements prepared by the (Mayville Clinic, Inc.) corporation's independent certified public accounting firm for the fiscal years 1990 through 1994. We have also reviewed the financial statements for January and February 1995.
2. U.S. Corporate Income Tax Returns (for the Mayville Clinic, Inc.) for fiscal years 1990 through 1994.
3. U.S. Individual Income Tax Returns for Dennis and Barbara Williamson for the years 1990 through 1994.
4. U.S. Individual Income (Partial) Tax Returns for Roger and Mary Davis for the years 1990 through 1994.
5. The fee schedule in effect for the practice.
6. Depreciation schedules for furniture and equipment owned by the practice.
7. Minutes of shareholders and board meetings of Mayville Clinic, Inc., from 1990 through February 1994.
8. Schedules of gross fees charged that were attributable to various payers.
9. A compiled schedule of patients by ZIP code developed by American Health Care Appraisal.
10. Accounts receivable aging report/medical assistant service for Mayville and Mayville Clinics.
11. *Socioeconomic Characteristics of Medical Practices*, AMA 1995.
12. *Estimated Useful Lives of Depreciable Hospital Assets*, 1988 Edition.
13. *The Goodwill Registry*, 1995, The Health Care Group, Plymouth Meeting, PA.
14. Conversations with Affiliated CPAs, Detroit, Michigan, the Mayville Clinic, Inc., corporate accounting firm.

Bruce Krider, AHCA, toured the office and interviewed both physician-owners and the practice manager.

For economic data, we used information from Claritis, Business Information Services (formerly the National Planning Data Corporation), Ithaca, New York.

For industry data, we researched various articles in *Medical Economics* and the American Medical Association's *Socioeconomic Characteristics of Medical Practice*, 1995.

SUMMARY AND CONCLUSION

Based on the analysis completed and discussed in this report, it is our opinion that the current value of the Mayville Clinic is Four Hundred Twenty-Three Thousand, Eight Hundred Ninety-Six Dollars, or $424,000 rounded. The selected method of valuation was the excess earnings on income available to the physician-owners. We also considered the discounted cash flow method, a goodwill factor (times gross patient revenue) plus tangible assets, an income multiplier approach, the standard excess earnings approach, and the use of an adjusted goodwill factor (on gross patient revenue) plus tangible assets.

ECONOMIC PROFILE

Demographics data for 1990 and updated through 1994 have been analyzed and broken down in the demographics data table in the addenda under "Area Demographic Data." The Mayville area is typical of its surrounding communities and the region in terms of population and economic characteristics, those being a much lower than usual nonwhite population mix.

The population of Mayville increased 14.7 percent from 1990 to 1994. The number of households increased 15.08 percent, which would indicate that there is a significant in-migration of people coming from elsewhere as opposed to growth in population by birth. The tremendous growth in the size of the community substantiates the need for increased health care facilities to treat the population.

In terms of the average age, we note that the average age for the population of Mayville decreased slightly from 46.9 in 1990 to 46.3 in 1994. Despite the slight decrease in overall age, this is a slightly older population than the average, and Medicare reimbursement is and will continue to play a major factor in the life of Mayville Clinic.

Neighborhood Area Data

The immediate neighborhood is a developing strip shopping center for the Mayville area. The area's complete facility airport is also located within the corridor.

The neighborhood is just east of the US-27 expressway on M-55, which provides access to the south half of the west side and the south side of Mayville (the body of water). US-27, old US-27, and M-55 all serve the neighborhood. There is 220-volt electric power, natural gas, and sanitary sewers available. The Village of Mayville is the center of a popular summer and winter resort and vacation area noted for boating, snowmobiling, and sport fishing. The peak season runs from Memorial Day through Labor Day, with lesser activity beginning with the first snowfall and safe ice on the lake. The village is also the major shopping and medical care center for the area.

Area Demographic Data

1990/1994 DEMOGRAPHIC REPORT
ZIP Code: 12345 MAYVILLE
MILLSWORTH COUNTY, MICHIGAN

	1990 Census	*1994 Update*
Total Population	5,704	6,543
Total Households	2,505	2,883
Median Age	46.9	46.3
Median Household Income	$ 17,230	$ 18,169

1994 POPULATION BY AGE

0–4	5.9%
5–14	11.8%
15–24	9.6%
25–44	21.5%
45–64	22.5%
65–74	17.5%
75–84	9.0%
85+	2.2%
	100.0%

1990 OCCUPATION

(Employed Persons 16+)	
Mgr/Professional:	
Exec/Manager	12.0%
Professional	9.2%
Tech/Sales/Admin:	
Technical	1.0%
Sales	15.9%
Admin. Support	11.8%
Service:	
Private HH	0.2%
Protective	0.7%
Other	19.9%
Farming/Forestry	2.9%
Craft and Repair	12.6%
Operator/Inspector	4.8%
Transport/Moving	3.4%
Laborer	5.5%
	100.0%
1990 Average Home Value	$ 53,746
1990 Average Rent	$ 244

1994 POPULATION BY RACE

White	99.2%
Black	0.3%
American Indian	0.4%
Asian/Pacific	0.1%
Other Races	0.0%
	100.0%
Hispanic Origins*	0.3%

*1994 HOUSEHOLDS BY INCOME***

< $15,000	38.0%
$15,000–$24,999	27.0%
$25,000–$34,999	15.3%
$35,000–$49,999	9.6%
$50,000–$74,999	7.4%
$75,000–$99,999	1.6%
$100,000–$149,999	0.9%
$150,000+	0.2%
	100.0%

1990 HOUSEHOLDS BY TYPE

Family Households	68.9%
Married Couple	59.4%
Other Family	9.4%
Male Householder	2.8%
Female Householder	6.6%
Nonfamily Households	31.1%
1 Person Households	27.6%
2+ Person Households	3.5%

1990 OCCUPANCY STATUS AND TENURE

(Total Housing Units)	
Occupied	47.4%
Owner	38.1%
Renter	9.3%
Vacant	52.6%

1990 YEAR STRUCTURE BUILT

(Occupied Housing Units)	
1989 to March 1990	0.9%
1985 to 1988	7.0%
1980 to 1984	12.7%
1970 to 1979	26.1%
1960 to 1969	21.2%
1950 to 1959	12.3%
1940 to 1949	12.3%
1939 or Earlier	7.6%
	100.0%

*Persons of Hispanic Origin may be of any race.

**Income amounts are expressed in current dollars for 1990 and 1994.

Area Health Care

Current services in the immediate area are considered good. Based on our review of the data, based on the utilization by diagnosis-related group (DRG) by the actual population as reported by area hospitals, area facilities actually have the capability for serving 96 percent of the needs of the population. Considering the location of the subject and the location of various hospitals in the region, there are only three that are within reasonable driving distance, with a combined bed capacity of 230 licensed acute care beds, 15 psychiatric beds, and 50 bassinets.

Mental health services are provided by the county departments of mental health and independent practitioners.

There are 150 licensed physicians in the county, including approximately 45 family practitioners. Most, however, are located within the largest community in the county, Hancock, some 35 miles away from the subject.

Three managed care organizations have a presence in the county: the Blue Cross HMO (Blue Care), Federated Managed Health (FMH), and "All in the Family" Care (AFC). To date in the county, there is an 18 percent market penetration by managed care carriers. The penetration is growing slowly but steadily. Area employers surveyed indicated that their companies were advocating managed care and their employees were opting for it more and more. We expect that area will continue to follow with not only the rest of the state but will build on its own trends in this direction. Hospitals surveyed indicated that they are seeing a steady decrease in the payer mix of indemnity policies toward managed care.

Medical Practice

Over the past five years, the field of medical practice has seen significant changes in reimbursement, and market dynamics and a change from emphasis on specialty care to primary care. For the first time in decades, the composition of physicians entering primary care and, in particular, family practice has changed dramatically. In short, there is a renewed interest by physicians entering the field in the practice of family or general practice. This is augmented seriously by the market and economic influences of the health care system. Primary care physicians have assumed roles of gatekeepers and the guardian of financial resources for the rest of the health care system.

A review of regional medical schools and residency programs has indicated that typically where 20 percent of the graduating physicians would go into family practice and 80 percent would specialize in other areas, the trend is turning more in favor of the generalists. Indeed, area specialists have begun enrolling in programs to re-enter general practice. This speaks to the pivotal role that our subject and primary care physicians in general (family practice, internal medicine, OB-Gyn, and pediatrics) are beginning to play in the health care arena.

Personal Background

Dr. Dennis Williamson is 50 years old and describes his health as good. He received his bachelor's degree in Biology from Elmira College, Elmira, NY, in 1970. He attended medical school at the University of Minnesota and graduated in 1975. He performed his internship at Ochsner Institute in New Orleans in 1976, and he completed his residency in Family Practice at Cook County Hospital in Chicago in 1980.

Dr. Williamson sees 30 patients per day in his office in addition to those he sees on hospital rounds. He has a broad spectrum of patients by age and payer and spends approximately 10 minutes per patient in the office and 5 minutes per patient in the hospital.

Medicare patients comprise approximately 50 percent of his practice, whereas Medicaid patients comprise 15 percent, 15 percent managed care, 15 percent commercial (indemnity) pay, and the balance (5 percent) private pay.

According to the practice manager, Dr. Williamson spends approximately 10–12 hours per day, five days per week, on clinic patient–related matters. He does hospital rounds and hospital medical records each day of the week for approximately two hours.

Dr. Roger Davis is 54 years old and describes his health as good. He received his bachelor's degree in Biology from Cornell University, Ithaca, NY, in 1966. He attended medical school at the University of Massachusetts and graduated in 1970. He performed his internship at Syracuse Hospital, Syracuse, NY, 1971, and he completed his residency in Family Practice at Johns Hopkins University Hospital in 1975.

Dr. Davis sees 28 patients per day in his office in addition to those he sees on hospital rounds. He has a broad spectrum of patients by age and payer and spends approximately 12 minutes per patient in the office and 7 minutes per patient in the hospital.

Medicare patients comprise approximately 55 percent of his practice, while Medicaid patients comprise 10 percent, 15 percent managed care, 15 percent commercial (indemnity) pay, and the balance (5 percent) private pay.

According to the practice manager, Dr. Davis spends approximately 10 hours per day, five days per week, on clinic patient–related matters. He does hospital rounds and hospital medical records each day of the week for approximately one to two hours.

Subject Background

General

Each physician owns 50 percent of the professional corporation, Mayville Clinic. The main hospital used by the physicians is Gotham City Hospital in Gotham City. The practice itself is in the midst of a commercial shopping area, which has proved very good as a location for the clinic. It is the only clinic in the central commercial district and the only clinic in the community, although from time to time, others have tried for a year or two.

The practice was established 20 years ago in 1975 by Dr. Davis. Dr. Williamson joined him as a full partner two years later. Both have been working exclusively in the clinic since that time. In addition to their patient care duties, both physicians serve as adjunct faculty for the University of Michigan School of Medicine and Cornell University.

Dr. Davis has been the Chief of Staff for three separate terms at Gotham City Hospital and Chief of the Department of Family Practice twice. Dr. Williamson has similarly been the Chief of Family Practice once and serves on the board of trustees at Gotham City Hospital.

Staffing

The Mayville Clinic is a typically managed, reasonably well-functioning rural family medical practice. Although not immediately able to answer some of our questions, the staff was usually able to secure the answer in most cases.

The current employee composition of the Mayville practice operation is

1 Office Manager (Mrs. Barbara Williamson, part-time)
2 Administrative/Recep/Billers
2 Nurse Aides/Techs
2 M.D. General Practitioners

The office makes use of the CivaTech Computerized Billing System.

During our visit to the Mayville practice, the staff appeared to be versed in the basic functions of their jobs. We do think, however, that based on a review of their collections experience, there is some need for assistance. The overall collections rate is approximately 87 percent, but we think that there may be improvements possible in this area. We refer you to the attached accounts receivable exhibits relating to Drs. Williamson and Davis and the Mayville practice.

Collections

Several things that we looked closely at were the amounts of collections by physician and the aging of accounts receivable by physician and by both private pay and third-party payer. Dr. Davis tends to have a much higher amount of receivables in the >180-day third-party category than does Dr. Williamson. Conversely Dr. Williamson has an unusually high amount of receivables in the >180-day private-pay category. In 1992, the number of patients seen by each physician in the Mayville office were as follows: Dr. Davis—215, Dr. Williamson—351. The average patient charge by Dr. Davis was $25.83 and Dr. Williamson $30.75.

Without an in-depth review, outside the scope of this practice valuation, one can only speculate as to the reasons. These visit charges do not include data from the Mayville operation.

The practice appears to enjoy relationships with third-party payers including what appear to be the vast majority of applicable area/regional managed care organizations.

Location

In terms of proximity, the Mayville Clinic is 44 miles from Granger and Buckley Community Hospital, 39 miles from Gotham City, 23 miles from Owosso, and 18 miles from St. Helens. This practice is middle ground for many hospitals in terms of proximity with Owosso, probably being the most remote. In terms of maintaining market share, however, it would be more prudent to review the locations of the patients of the Mayville Clinic in terms of ZIP code.

The bottom line is again that this practice is on the periphery of the hospital's service area and as such will be a contested area from time to time among hospital providers to the extent possible. (It is noteworthy that in the past, the Mayville Clinic has carried a note payable to Hennepin Memorial Hospital in St. Helen, the closest hospital and a competing hospital to the client.)

Certainly, the strongest link to the practice is the long history of support by and relationship with the hospital, and we deem this to be a very strong factor; however, Hennepin Memorial has indicated its, albeit small, but nonetheless, interest in being supportive of this particular practice in the past.

A review of the top 12 ZIP codes for the clinics includes no patients from St. Helen (location of Hennepin Memorial). In fact, in the listing of communities (ZIP codes) with 5–30 patients, St. Helen is not even on the list. The issue, of course, is not patients seen who live in St. Helen but rather all practice patients who would likely change their hospital affiliation were another organization attempting to change the primary hospital relationship.

Also noteworthy in the ZIP code breakdowns, there are no patients from Owosso; 58 do show up from Granger, however.

The clinic office itself is located in the very middle of the downtown area, on the 100 block of (South) Main street.

Income

We have included the actual income and expense tables for the years 1990–1994, and the reallocated version will be included in the appraisal report.

The revenue potentially attributable to physician/owner income is significantly above average for rural family practitioners. The adjusted income available for physicians, based on a historically five-year weighted basis, was $414,215 (for the two physician-owners or $207,000 per physician). Based on the latest data available from AMA's *Socioeconomic Indicators*, which provides earnings data for all types of physicians by location, age, solo vs. group practice, and several other stratifications, income of the average family practitioner in Mayville (rural, east north central region, family practice) adjusted to 1994 (the latest year for which we have data) was $136,490.

There had been a profit-sharing program for the owners of Mayville Clinic, Inc.; however, it was formally dissolved in December 1992. Mayville Clinic, Inc. has consistently generated an operating profit over the past five years reviewed, and each of its two sites has performed at about the same level of profitability.

Implications for Purchasers

The practitioners take home nearly 60 percent of the gross income amount in this practice. This contracts with a more typical range of 50–55 percent.

Based on our review of their operation, we believe that the practice is indeed a three-physician practice in terms of patient volume. In our review of the practice documentation, we noted the long clinic hours and the greater than usual office visits and time spent in hospital rounds.

If the purchaser were to purchase the clinic based on the revenue or even the revenue attributable to the physicians alone, there might be difficulty in achieving the same level of profitability if the physicians became employees and sought a more normal pace. We think that the client should evaluate and consider the purchase of the practice with this information directly in mind.

Competition

The community has apparently seen several other medical clinics come and go over the past 10 years, with only the existing practice by Drs. Williamson and Davis continuing to service the community and viable.

This continued presence while others have come and gone is seen to be a very positive factor in favor of the practice. The community perception must certainly be that it would be foolish to begin seeing physicians with a new clinic because they will likely leave as the others have done, figuring that it ultimately makes the most sense to go with the local clinic for continuity and dependability. We must add, however, in researching the local health care marketplace that we have identified a tremendous amount of interest in the area and discussions of placing satellite clinics close to the subject. As the push toward managed care and physician referral base development heats up, we believe this is an issue the client cannot afford to dismiss.

Billing and Collection Experience, Mayville Clinic

The clinic seems to have a good accounting system for billing; however, there are some eccentricities that we discuss elsewhere in the report regarding collection percentages, which are dubious and cast a questionable light on the overall sense of their collection efforts. Inasmuch, we have some concerns about collections and the perceptions of those involved in the process about their actual performance.

Medical Assistant database can retrieve many very usable types of patient billing information. It was used to pull a great deal of the information used in the appraisal project.

Aged Accounts Receivable Value

We weighted the individual aged groups of receivables by age and individual or insurance payer type. We weighted the various payers and associated accounts with a deflating factor for the accounts. We began reducing the private pay accounts at 30 days, ending with a residual factor of 0.70 percent. Our weighted value for the receivables as of April 4, 1995, was $33,033, approximately $5,700 less than the booked accounts receivable.

As stated elsewhere in the report, the collection experience at the Mayville practice certainly deserves some scrutiny.

Our review weighting of the receivables by age tended to reveal that there is an overall receivable rate of approximately 87.5 percent. On separate "financial summaries" produced by the office's computerized patient accounts system, however, the following figures for collection rates were noted:

	Insurance Account	Pt. Account	Total
WILLIAMSON	74.8	186.3	99.9
DAVIS	67.9	177.3	87.2

Clearly, figures in excess of 100 percent are impossible so we have some difficulty in assigning much credibility to the figures provided. Further, we have difficulty in believing that the clinics and physicians achieve 99.9 or 99.8 percent collection rates with the large amounts of dollars in the >180-day category for both clinics. These figures must have been based on "adjusted" billings and after contractual allowances.

Schedule of Clinic Expenses by Year

Please also note the associated illustrations regarding clinic historical performance.

Mayville Clinic Equipment Schedule

We performed an inventory and valuation of the equipment, fixtures, furnishings, and leasehold improvements. We inventoried by equipment item, model, serial number, and age. We further checked to note the condition of all items.

The "fair market in-use value," which includes the current fair market value of the equipment plus transportation, taxes, and installation, equals $58,000 (rounded).

VALUATION METHODS AND ANALYSES OF THE MEDICAL PRACTICE AND PROFESSIONAL GOODWILL EXCESS EARNINGS METHOD (AS ADAPTED TO MEDICAL PRACTICES)

This method is one of the most widely used methods in existence today, especially for the valuation of physician practices.

In this method, the weighted average of normalized earnings from the practice are compared with the weighted median earnings for the same category of physicians based on a database of socioeconomic characteristics from the AMA *Socioeconomic Characteristics of Medical Practice,* which is an annual publication.

The difference or excess of earnings between the averaged physician income from the existing practice is capitalized according to an appropriate capitalization rate for excess earnings. Because excess earnings are by their nature higher than the average, a higher risk factor is assigned them. For physician practices, this figure tends to be relatively high at or near 30–50 percent. We used 0.35 in this report.

When contrasted to actual historically weighted physician income 1990–1994 in the 1995 AMA database, the Mayville physician income nearly doubles the average. The value of the clinic according to this method is **$423,896.**

The greatest consideration in using this method is that it does not consider the income of the business but rather the income of the physicians. It does not give the subject practice recognition of the separate business income. This is one of the primary reasons that it is good for a professional practice in which there typically is no business income, only owner income.

We will include the value in the range of values with this understanding as we formulate our final reconciliation of values for an estimate of value. In our opinion, and as we have stated earlier, the physicians in this practice work exceedingly long hours. See the chart comparison hours between their activity and the activity of the norm for various comparison groups. If we were to normalize their hours, there would likely be little clinic income, and they would fall into line with the balance of the comparison groups.

Were the clinic to be purchased and the physicians hired as employees to work a traditional workload, the excess income currently being generated would not be present to value. When this is considered, this approach makes sense.

CALCULATION OF GOODWILL USING PHYSICIAN EXCESS EARNINGS METHOD

Calculation of Clinic Physicians	*Year*	*Per Physician Compensation*		*Weighting Factor*	*Weighted Compensation*	
Weighted Average	1990	$181,621	x	1	$181,621	
Normal Compensation (See Schedule of	1991	$190,480	x	2	$380,960	
Owner's Compensation)	1992	$203,194	x	3	$609,582	
	1993	$216,782	x	4	$867,128	
	1994	$231,820	x	5	$1,159,100	
	Total			15	$3,198,391	
		Divided by Sum of Weighting Factors				$213,226

Calculation of Comparative Weighted Average	*Year*	*Individual Physician Compensation*		*Weighting Factor*	*Weighted Compensation*	
Compensation	1990	$111,730	x	1	$111,730	
(Median Physician Net Income after	1991	$117,610	x	2	$235,220	
Expenses before Taxes, Rural, Family	1992	$123,800	x	3	$371,400	
Practice)	1993	$129,990	x	4	$519,960	
	1994	$136,490	x	5	$682,450	
				15	$1,920,760	
Clinic Physician Excess Earnings		Divided by Sum of Weighting Factors				$128,050
Capitalized at 50%					35%	$365,858
Indicated Value of Clinic Physician Goodwill (rounded)						$366,000
Add the Net Tangible Asset Value of the Practice						$57,896
Total Practice Value by This Method						**$423,896**

STANDARD BUSINESS EXCESS EARNINGS METHOD

The traditional form of excess earnings calculations for all businesses may also be applied if there is a larger business with an income after the owners have been paid as opposed to a practice with little or no residual income on the bottom line. Our calculation of the value of excess earnings for this practice (tangible assets included) is $800,000, rounded (see the following table).

This method recognizes the contribution of the practice assets (allows them 10 percent of the income, which is somewhat common and appropriate for health care practices because the service being provided is labor intensive rather than machinery or equipment intensive).

We believe that this application may not be appropriate because it is more oriented to a larger clinic model that generates *significant* income based on normal operating assumptions. As stated earlier, the practitioners have longer office hours, and longer hospital rounds and see many more patients per day than their colleagues and peers.

Excess Earnings	*Unadjusted Balance Sheet Assets*	*Unadjusted Balance Sheet Liabilities*	*ENTER Asset Adjustments*	*ENTER Liabilities Adjustments*	*Adjusted Assets*	*Adjusted Liabilities*	*Net Tangible Asset Value*	
A. Net Tangible Asset Value	$59,235.00	$42,568.00	$44,813.00	$3,584.00	$104,048.00	$46,152.00	**$57,896**	
B. Normalized Earnings That Include All Earnings Available to the Practitioner:								
Practice Net Income	$426,452							
Less Nonrecurring Income	($6,002)							
Less Excessive Expenses (not related to income generation)	($6,235)							
	$414,215							$414,215
Earnings Attributable to Tangible Assets (using standard) 0.10 Cap Rate								$41,422
Excess Earnings (normalized earnings less earnings attributable to tangible assets)								$372,794
Value of Excess Earnings (excess earnings capitalized at standard 50%)								$745,587
(Excess earnings tend to be discounted at a high rate because they are riskier to obtain as "excess" earnings compared with normal earnings.)								
Total Value under the Standard Method ($ NTAV + $ Cap Excess Earnings)								$803,483

DISCOUNTED CASH FLOW OR DISCOUNTED FUTURE EARNINGS

A standard technique for business valuation is the calculation of discounted future earnings. This method is among those available to use in this assignment. In this method, the income approach uses the historical financial performance data. As stated elsewhere, the value of a business is a function of the future anticipated revenue streams. Although there may be other issues involved in the purchase of a business, especially as it relates to hospitals and managed care companies purchasing physician practices, the driving issue is the generation of income.

The following table provides a view of the historical income as well as the projected performance of the clinic using the linear regression method of least squares.

The second component in the discounted cash flow method is the calculation of the present values of both the coming five years of income and the present value of the terminal value (ongoing value in perpetuity).

This form of valuation typically includes payment for tangible assets as opposed to a combination in which one combines some form of income approach with the present "fair market value in-use" of the organization assets. In this approach and in this appraisal, therefore, we are including both goodwill and net tangible assets.

The revenue net to the bottom line (not EBIT or some variation) ranges from $81,939 in the first year of projected income to $121,979 in the fifth year (totaling $285,996). The sixth year, which is what we base the terminal value on, is projected to be $121,737.

In building a discount factor to use in the present-value calculation, we added the following:

Discount Factor Build-Up

Treasury Bond, 30-Year Rate as Risk Free	7.5
Risk Factor for Risk Associated with the Business (SEE THE TABLE BELOW)	8
(Any) Additional Return Required	4
Total Discount Factor To Be Used in PV Calculation	19.5

As can be seen from the present-value model (following the next two tables) when the future anticipated income is reduced to its present value, the collective value of the organization is **$531,932.**

The following is our calculation of the business risk value based (alone) on the variation in the income. This risk is low (approximately 8 percent). We have included this in the above build-up rate.

DEVELOPING A BUSINESS RISK FACTOR

Year	*$ Avail to M.D.s*	*Descriptive Statistics Based on Five-Year Earnings*	
1990	$363,242	Mean	$ 421,138
1991	$380,959	Standard Error	$ 17,778
1992	$406,387	Median	$ 419,976
1993	$433,564	Standard Deviation	35556.78335
1994	$463,641	Sample Variance	1264284842
		Kurtosis	−1.1110887
		Skewness	0.157652153
		Range	$ 82,682
		Minimum	$ 380,959
		Maximum	$ 463,641
		Sum	$ 1,684,551
		Count	4
		Largest (1)	463641
		Smallest (1)	380959
		Confidence Level (95.000%)	34844.95579

Take the	$ 35,556.78	Standard Deviation
Divided by	$ 421,137.75	Mean Income
Equals	**0.084430292**	**Business Risk**

Like the beta used to measure risk in the stock market, we were concerned about quantifying risk in a variable-income stream. We used statistics to analyze the deviation and divide by the mean income.

PROJECTIONS

Med Clinic	*Actual*	*Actual*	*Actual*	*Actual*	*Actual*	*Year 1 Trended*	*Year 2 Trended*	*Year 3 Trended*	*Year 4 Trended*	*Year 5 Trended*	*Year 6 Trended*
INCOME	1990	1991	1992	1993	1994	1995	1996	1997	1998	1999	2000
Gross Patient Revenue	$650,025	$695,527	$744,214	$796,309	$852,050	$899,074	$951,914	$1,004,162	$1,055,374	$1,106,035	$1,158,526
Interest Income	$106	$113	$121	$130	$139	$147	$155	$164	$172	$180	$189
Misc Income	$16,584	$17,745	$18,987	$20,316	$21,738	$22,938	$24,286	$25,619	$26,926	$28,218	$29,557
Total Income	$666,715	$713,385	$763,322	$816,755	$873,927	$922,159	$976,355	$1,029,945	$1,082,472	$1,134,433	$1,188,272
EXPENSE											
Advertising	$598	$628	$659	$692	$741	$769	$807	$845	$882	$916	$955
Donations	$1,000	$1,050	$1,103	$1,158	$1,239	$1,285	$1,349	$1,413	$1,475	$1,532	$1,596
Depreciation	$15,685	$16,469	$17,293	$18,157	$19,428	$20,159	$21,156	$22,157	$23,130	$24,026	$25,038
Employee Benefits	$13,001	$13,651	$14,334	$15,050	$16,104	$16,709	$17,536	$18,366	$19,172	$19,915	$20,753
Utilities	$7,524	$7,900	$8,295	$8,710	$9,320	$9,670	$10,148	$10,629	$11,095	$11,525	$12,011
General Insurance	$2,685	$2,819	$2,960	$3,108	$3,326	$3,451	$3,622	$3,793	$3,959	$4,113	$4,286
Workers' Comp Insurance	$952	$1,000	$1,050	$1,102	$1,179	$1,224	$1,284	$1,345	$1,404	$1,458	$1,520
Malpractice Insurance	$31,654	$33,237	$34,899	$36,643	$39,209	$40,683	$42,695	$44,715	$46,678	$48,487	$50,529
Interest Expense	$4,857	$5,100	$5,355	$5,623	$6,016	$6,242	$6,551	$6,861	$7,162	$7,440	$7,753
Office Salaries	$95,000	$99,750	$106,733	$114,204	$122,198	$128,232	$135,952	$143,204	$150,284	$157,317	$164,748
Miscellaneous	$568	$596	$626	$658	$704	$730	$766	$802	$838	$870	$907
Outside Services	$3,500	$3,675	$3,859	$4,052	$4,335	$4,498	$4,721	$4,944	$5,161	$5,361	$5,587
Accounting and Legal	$7,500	$7,875	$8,269	$8,682	$9,290	$9,639	$10,116	$10,595	$11,060	$11,488	$11,972
Rentals	$13,526	$14,202	$14,912	$15,658	$16,754	$17,384	$18,244	$19,107	$19,946	$20,719	$21,592
Rentals—Equipment	$458	$481	$505	$530	$567	$589	$618	$647	$675	$702	$731
Repairs and Maintenance	$12,005	$12,605	$13,236	$13,897	$14,870	$15,429	$16,192	$16,959	$17,703	$18,389	$19,164
Medical Supplies	$16,500	$17,325	$18,191	$19,101	$20,438	$21,206	$22,255	$23,308	$24,331	$25,275	$26,339
Office Supplies	$5,600	$5,880	$6,174	$6,483	$6,936	$7,197	$7,553	$7,911	$8,258	$8,578	$8,939

Telephone	$10,052	$10,555	$11,082	$11,636	$12,451	$12,919	$13,558	$14,200	$14,823	$15,398	$16,046
Licenses	$502	$527	$553	$581	$622	$645	$677	$709	$740	$769	$801
Taxes— Social Security	$9,875	$10,369	$10,887	$11,432	$12,232	$12,692	$13,319	$13,950	$14,562	$15,126	$15,763
Taxes—Unemployment	$1,065	$1,118	$1,174	$1,233	$1,319	$1,369	$1,436	$1,504	$1,570	$1,631	$1,700
Taxes—Property	$12,654	$13,287	$13,951	$14,649	$15,674	$16,263	$17,068	$17,875	$18,660	$19,383	$20,200
Taxes—Single Business	$5,684	$5,968	$6,267	$6,580	$7,041	$7,305	$7,667	$8,029	$8,382	$8,707	$9,073
Taxes—Other	$25	$26	$28	$29	$31	$32	$34	$35	$37	$38	$40
Total Expenses	$272,470	$286,093	$302,395	$319,648	$342,024	$356,321	$375,324	$393,903	$411,987	$429,163	$448,043
Net Profit (Loss) before Owner Compensation	$394,245	$427,291	$460,990	$497,108	$531,903	$565,838	$601,031	$636,042	$670,485	$705,270	$740,229
Revenue Available to Physicians by Category											
Professional Dues	$2,554	$2,682	$2,816	$2,957	$3,164	$3,283	$3,445	$3,608	$3,766	$3,912	$4,077
Auto Expenses	$15,654	$16,437	$17,259	$18,121	$19,390	$20,119	$21,114	$22,113	$23,084	$23,979	$24,988
Officer Life Insurance	$5,000	$5,000	$5,000	$5,000	$5,350	$5,280	$5,399	$5,529	$5,644	$5,691	$5,829
Officer Salaries	$325,000	$341,250	$365,138	$390,697	$418,046	$438,688	$465,099	$489,907	$514,130	$538,190	$563,613
Medical Education	$3,200	$3,360	$3,528	$3,704	$3,964	$4,113	$4,316	$4,520	$4,719	$4,902	$5,108
Travel and Lodging	$5,689	$5,973	$6,272	$6,586	$7,047	$7,312	$7,673	$8,036	$8,389	$8,714	$9,081
Meals and Entertainment	$2,245	$2,357	$2,475	$2,599	$2,781	$2,885	$3,028	$3,171	$3,311	$3,439	$3,584
Employee Benefits—Disability Policies	$3,900	$3,900	$3,900	$3,900	$3,900	$4,212	$4,212	$4,212	$4,212	$4,212	$4,212
	$363,242	$380,959	$406,388	$433,564	$463,642	$485,892	$514,286	$541,096	$567,255	$593,039	$620,492
Net Income to "Practice"	$31,003	$46,332	$54,602	$63,544	$68,261	$79,946	$86,745	$94,946	$103,230	$112,231	$119,737

PRESENT VALUE

	Year 1	*Year 2*	*Year 3*	*Year 4*	*Year 5*	*Year 6*
Revenue	$79,946	$86,745	$94,946	$103,230	$112,231	$119,737
Enter Risk-Free Rate (Treas. 30 Year Bonds)	7.50%	7.50%	7.50%	7.50%	7.50%	
Enter the Risk Discount Factor	5.00%	5.00%	5.00%	5.00%	5.00%	
Enter the Investment Return You Desire	7.00%	7.00%	7.00%	7.00%	7.00%	
Total Discount Factor	19.50%	19.50%	19.50%	19.50%	19.50%	
Present Value	$66,900	$60,745	$55,638	$50,621	$46,055	
			Five Year Total		$279,959	

Calculation of Terminal Value		*Sum of Present Values*	
Future Income	$119,737	$279,959	Present Value of Five-Year Total
Divided by Total Discount Factor of	19.50%	$251,973	Present Value of Terminal Value
Equals Capitalized Terminal Value	$614,036		
Discounted Back to Present Value	**$251,973**	**$531,932**	**Total Value by This Method**

EARNINGS BEFORE INTEREST DEPRECIATION AND TAXES

In this income method, we move from using the adjusted income and expenses to taking the past three years' weighted income to the clinic and applying a multiplier.

By going through the same weighting process we used in the excess earnings approach with income to the physician income, we are now going to do the same with the organizational income (*after owner compensation but before interest, taxes, and depreciation*).

	Year 1	*Year 2*	*Year 3*	*Total*
Yr's Income	$111,488	$123,238	$131,999	
Weight	1	2	3	6
Weighted Income	$111,488	$246,475	$395,997	$753,960
		3 Yr. Historical Wtd EBIDT Income		$125,660

In this historically weighted EBIDT income average for the past three years, we note that the resulting income is $125,660. If we agree that this is a reasonably mature and secure practice based on its length and dominance in the market and use a multiplier of 4, we obtain a value of **$502,640.**

We chose a multiplier of "4" for several reasons. We typically assign a factor of "5" to well-established businesses, especially those that are showing consistent growth and profitability. A factor of "3," according to our methodology and that of many professional health care business analysts, tends to be used for practices that might have been operating for a time and generating profits and are not as solidly securely established as those entities that rate a "5." By securely established, we mean a practice or clinic in which there is little question that it will be around in the future and the owners or their buyers would continue to be able to count on having a good business.

We also go as low as a multiplier of "1" in this process for practices or clinics that are operating and generating income sufficient to meet their operational needs but have yet to become "established" in a more comfortable sense. Clinics that have been around for several years might be in this category, but they are still very much climbing on the uphill side of the entity's business life cycle and are not assured of a future at all. These could be relatively new practices with a modest income stream.

Returning to the rationale for the "4," although the clinic certainly is well established, we thought that the particular area the practice is located in is a very volatile one, which is a factor that makes us a little uncertain about the future. The physicians are aging, and they are going to be slowing down. In fact, some very recent signs are suggesting this to us.

Additionally, the practice has a high percentage of private-pay, Medicaid, and Medicare patients. Although everyone may soon be under some type of universal health care plan and pay the same, that is not the case now. Although they always pay (as in no bad debts), Medicare and Medicaid pay less and are more subject to the whims and cuts of legislatures. Private pay often means uninsured, and this is not a plus. Health care costs are continually under siege, and we believe that the heavy reliance on these types of payers cannot justify a "5."

Hence, we have a mature practice in which the physicians are working at a high level, generating nearly twice the average for physicians in their comparison groups. The downside is that they will be slowing down (their practice will be moving to the downside slope of its business cycle), the mix of third-party payers is a question and gives us cause for concern, and the local marketplace has shown signs of volatility and increased and aggressive market pressure. These "old school" physicians do not believe in the unprofessionalism of marketing, per their conversations with us, and we believe that this may have significant implications for the future of the clinic.

FAIR MARKET VALUE BY GROSS PATIENT REVENUE MULTIPLIER (FOR GOODWILL) AND NET TANGIBLE ASSET VALUE

Another method considered was a method whereby gross income over the past three years is weighted (very little weight given to most distant earnings and most weight given to current earnings), and this weighted revenue is then factored by a goodwill factor common to family practices based on a database accumulated by The Health Care Group, Plymouth Meeting, PA. These data are a cooperative sharing of goodwill paid to all health care providers by specialty, updated with each sale by data contributing members annually. In the above database, the mean goodwill factor for family practices was approximately 33 percent, the median 30 percent.

We believe that the maturity of the practice and related goodwill goes beyond these averages. Based on our practice evaluation matrix, the goodwill factor of 0.40 was obtained. The (actual) 0.4039 factor is based on practice characteristics as we perceived them. The following evaluation tool was used to determine the subjective (although informed) standing of the practice relative to others. The table following the matrix also depicts the calculation for goodwill adding in the value for tangible assets—**$396,450.**

SUMMARY AND CONCLUSIONS

The Subject

The Mayville Clinic is a two-physician general practice corporation headquartered in Westin, Michigan. The other practice is located in Mayville, Michigan. Both clinics are operated by the same two general practitioners, Dr. Roger Davis and Dr. Dennis Williamson. The subject of this appraisal was the Mayville site.

Financial Statements

We have reviewed in significant detail the financial statements of the clinic and have normalized the balance sheet to develop an accrual-based balance sheet for the Mayville Clinic.

MAYVILLE CLINIC
1-APR-95

	Cash Basis	*Adjustments*	*Adjusted Balance*
Current Assets	3/31/95		
Cash	$254.00	$0.00	$254.00
Short-Term Investments	$0.00	$0.00	$0.00
Inventories	$0.00	$1,650.00	$1,650.00
Checking Account	$3,756.00	$0.00	$3,756.00
Accounts Receivable	$0.00	$51,235.00	$51,235.00
Total Current Assets	$4,010.00	$52,885.00	$56,895.00
Fixed Assets			
Equipment and Furniture	$78,652.00	($20,652.00)	$58,000.00
Other	$70,324.05	$0.00	$70,324.05
Total Fixed Assets	$148,976.05	($20,652.00)	$128,324.05
Other Assets			
Cash Surrender Value—Officers Life Insurance	$54,895.00	$0.00	$54,895.00
Other	$31,985.00	$0.00	$31,985.00
Total Other Assets	$86,880.00	$0.00	$86,880.00
TOTAL ASSETS	$239,866.05	$32,233.00	$272,099.05

	Cash Basis	*Adjustments*	*Adjusted Balance*
LIABILITIES			
Current Liabilities			
Trade Accounts Payable	$0.00	$4,765.00	$4,765.00
Noncurrent Liabilities			
Contract Payable—Eaton Financial	$8,925.45	$0.00	$8,925.45
Note Payable—New England Life	$17,038.23	$0.00	$17,038.23
Note Payable—New England Life	$29,000.00	$0.00	$29,000.00
Note Payable—Comm Natl	$2,036.00	$0.00	$2,036.00
Note Payable—Profit Sharing	$19,985.00	$0.00	$19,985.00
Note Payable—Commercial Bank	$13,324.37	$0.00	$13,324.37
Total Noncurrent Liabilities	$90,309.05	$0.00	$90,309.05
TOTAL LIABILITIES	$90,309.05	$4,765.00	$95,074.05
Stockholders Equity			
Capital Stock—Authorized 50,000 shares par value $1.00 issued 50,000 shares	$50,000.00	$0.00	$50,000.00
Retained Earnings	$57,989.00	$0.00	$57,989.00
Net Income Year to Date	$41,568.00	$27,468.00	$69,036.00
Total Stockholders Equity	$149,557.00	$27,468.00	$177,025.00
Total Liabilities and Stockholder's Equity	$239,866.05	$32,233.00	$272,099.05

ACCOUNTS RECEIVABLE

We reviewed the accounts receivable data and have made our recommendations earlier in this report. We believe that there may be a significant opportunity to increase clinic profitability by a review of the accounts receivable management practices. We believe that the valuation impact would be an increase in value based on a potential increase in a higher collection rate.

OVERHEAD

When compared with the industry standards, the practice overhead expenses appear to be in line, and we have no recommendations regarding this area and believe that there are no implications from a valuation standpoint.

VALUATION

We were able to use a variety of income and combination methods of valuation.

Excess Earnings Method (as Adapted to Medical Practices)

This method of valuation took into consideration the earnings of the physicians versus the earnings of the corporation. We believe that this was a viable approach and a preferred approach for several reasons. Were the physicians working a more normalized schedule, there would be little if any income on the bottom line of the corporation. Further, if the client employed physicians to operate the practice, it would probably take three physicians working a standard schedule to perform the same work that the two physician-owners now perform. From this standpoint alone, we believe that this physician earnings adaptation to excess earnings is an appropriate method. It provided a value of **$423,896.**

Standard Business Excess Earnings Method

This traditional method of valuation for businesses relies on the income and an allocation of tangible assets and labor to the production of an income stream to determine the value of the organization. It separates out the income that can be attributed to the equipment and leaves the income attributable to management.

We have developed this method but have decided against including it in the range of values because it does not quite fit this clinic operation, which is more profitable than the average physician family practice clinic—which favors this approach, conceptually. It is our opinion that the nature of the clinic is, in fact, the nature of a basic physician practice.

Discounted Cash Flow or Discounted Future Earnings

As with the standard excess earnings approach to valuation, the discounted cash flow approach is also used with larger clinics and businesses. Unlike the vast majority of physician practices, however, there is, on average, more than $100,000 on the bottom line of this practice.

We therefore decided that the income generated, although not on the level of larger more sophisticated businesses or clinics, merited the application of this approach and chose to include it in the range of values.

We projected the income of the clinic five years into the future based on the historical performance of the clinic and used linear regression. We then performed a present-value calculation on the projected next five years of income. We then capitalized the income projected for the sixth year and capitalized that amount for an amount to include as a value of the practice, "in perpetuity." We then discounted the capitalized value basic to the present. We added these two values, and this method produced a value of **$531,932.**

Earnings before Interest Depreciation and Taxes

We modified the historical weighted income stream by not subtracting out the interest, depreciation, and taxes. When this was done, the annualized amount (over three years) was $125,660.

We then multiplied this income figure by "4"; the value result from this method was **$502,640.**

Fair Market Value by Gross Patient Revenue Multiplier (for Goodwill) and Net Tangible Asset Value

This combination income and asset approach uses a national (but regionalized) survey of goodwill payments by specialty and location. It factors the gross patient revenue times the appropriate factor.

We use the published goodwill factor but modified it through the use of our practice evaluation matrix tool. In this case, the resulting modification to the 0.30 goodwill modifier for family practices in this area was slightly greater than 0.10, for a total of 0.4039.

We multiplied the gross income by 0.4039 and added the fair market value of the assets for a value to this method of **$396,450.**

Range of Values

The range of values included for use in this appraisal is as follows:

Method	*Value*
Adjusted Goodwill Factor & NTAV	$396,450
Excess Earnings—Avail to Physicians & NTAV	$423,896
Present Value of Discounted Cash Flow	$531,932
EBIT	$502,640

Based on our research, evaluation of the factors involved, and the data available, we selected the *excess earnings available to physicians and net tangible asset value* as the method of choice. This was admittedly a difficult choice because the practice tended to cross some of the traditional medical practice lines. Its income made it possible to apply some approaches and methods more typical of larger organizations. We had, however, to consider all the issues.

Each method had its own merits, and we were divided on them. The central issues, however were the following:

> The practice was fairly normal except that the physicians have been basically working what we consider to be a three-man practice with two men. This is largely why there is income on the bottom line of the corporation.
>
> Rather than rely on this additional income that would have otherwise been going to a third physician as corporate income, the best way to give appropriate credit for the income being generated and available to the physicians was to use a method that provided credit for both the income and the tangible assets.
>
> It would have been misleading to point to a corporate income stream that would not likely be there if the purpose of the valuation report is for the acquisition of the practice.
>
> The adjusted goodwill factor applied to gross income and net tangible asset value (NTAV) would have also produced a value of nearly $400,000 however, it is seen as an inferior approach because gross revenue only reflects one thing, the gross business done and ignores the operation and the net income of the practice. Although it tends to consider a broad market influence from the Goodwill Registry, it is a ballpark value. Being able to point to a method that considers the actual income available to the physician-owners was deemed the approach with better data.

Earnings before Interest Depreciation and Taxes (times a multiple of "4") was also a good candidate, but we thought that it was less worthy in this case than the method selected. Many believe that by using earnings before several different deductions occur, it is possible to get a better idea of the "true" earning power of an organization. We agree to a large extent, but this method is not particularly refined, using a guesstimate income multiplier. It served us as a basic reality check in our range of values but was not selected because more accurate methods with better data were available.

Present Value of the Discounted Cash Flow (PV-DCF) was performed because we had some good data and there was consistency and maturity in the practice. The discount factors were solidly developed, and the linear regression model was well suited to the problem.

We would have selected the PV-DCF method within the income approach if the appropriate physician manpower was in place. We could have then reasoned that the income on the bottom line was *really* corporate income. Short of that, we could not, and the method was not selected.

VALUATION CONCLUSION

Based on the analysis completed in this report and the conclusions reached, it is our opinion that the value of the Mayville Clinic, including both the goodwill and the tangible assets, is

Four Hundred Twenty-Four Thousand Dollars
($423,896, rounded to $424,000)

CERTIFICATION AND STATEMENT OF LIMITING CONDITIONS

(DELETED FROM SAMPLE APPRAISAL)

CONTINGENT AND LIMITING CONDITIONS

(DELETED FROM SAMPLE APPRAISAL)

QUALIFICATIONS OF THE APPRAISERS

(DELETED FROM SAMPLE APPRAISAL)

Data Documents and Sources

The Center for Healthcare Industry Performance Studies, 1550 Old Henderson Road, Ste. S277, Columbus, OH 43220-9923; Phone: 800-859-2447 (hospital comparative data).

Claritas VNU Business Information Services, 53 Brown Road, Ithaca, NY 14850-1262; Phone: 607-257-5757; Fax: 607-266-0425
(for geographic reports on)
Health Care
Demographic Reports for Health Care
DRG Demand
ICD-9 Demand
Physicians
Hospitals, HMOs, and Nursing Homes

Estimated Useful Lives of Depreciable Hospital Assets, 1988, American Hospital Association, 1 N. Franklin, Chicago, IL, 60606-3401.

The Goodwill Registry, The Health Care Group, Address: Meetinghouse Business Center, 140 W. Germantown Pike, Ste. 200, Plymouth Meeting, PA 19462; Phone: 610-828-3888; Fax: 610-828-3658 (annual publication).

Marshall Valuation Service, Marshall and Swift, 1617 Beverly Boulevard, P.O. Box 26307, Los Angeles, CA 90026-0307; Phone: 213-250-2222 (for cost estimation of commercial buildings).

Socioeconomic Characteristics of Medical Practice, American Medical Association, Center for Health Policy Research, 515 North State Street, Chicago, IL 60610 (annual publication).

RECOMMENDED TEXTS

Ackerson, Charles B., *Capitalization Theory and Techniques,* Appraisal Institute, Chicago, IL, 1984

Desmond, Glenn, M., and Richard E. Kelley, *Business Valuation Handbook*, Valuation Press, Inc., Los Angeles, CA, 1988

Mancuso, Joseph R., and Douglas D. Germann, Sr., *Buying a Business (for Very Little Cash)*, Prentice Hall, Englewood Cliffs, NJ, 1990

Nunes, Morris A., *The Right Price for Your Business,* John Wiley & Sons, New York, NY, 1988

Pratt, Shannon, *Valuing Businesses and Professionals Practices,* Dow Jones - Irwin, Homewood, IL, 1986

Unland, James, J., *Valuation of Hospitals and Medical Centers,* The Health Management Research Institute, Chicago, IL, 1989

Index

About the Author

Bruce Krider has more than 25 years of experience in health care management and consulting. Of this experience, he served as a chief executive officer of hospitals in Michigan for nine years and as a chief operating officer for three years. He has been in health care management consulting since 1987.

During his consulting experience, he has served such multihospital chain clients as National Medical Enterprises, Humana, Health One, Sacred Heart Healthcare Corporation, ScrippsHealth, the University of California, San Diego, and HealthTrust—The Hospital Company. He has also consulted for members of the financial community including The National Bank of Detroit and the Federal Deposit Insurance Corporation.

Mr. Krider developed the rationale, and successfully saw an amendment enacted, for the creation of an additional category of rural referral center under the Consolidated Omnibus Reconciliation Act of 1986. He has also served as a state hospital association chair and served as a witness before the State Legislature and Department of Public Health on Capital Capitation for Hospital Capital Spending and on Certificate of Need Criteria for the Michigan Hospital Association.

As a hospital system chief executive officer, he developed a variety of health care businesses and began a regional consortium of hospitals.

Mr. Krider is a co-founder and principal of **American Health Care Appraisal** in the San Diego area.

He earned his undergraduate degree at Elmira College (New York) in 1972 and his Master of Arts Degree in Healthcare Administration at The George Washington University in Washington, D.C., in 1976. During graduate school, he was one of two individuals selected to develop the methodology for the selection criteria for the National Center for Health Planning Information created under PL 93-641. He also completed a special executive studies program at the Wharton School of Business at the University of Pennsylvania in 1980.

Mr. Krider is a former long-time member of the American College of Healthcare Executives and a current member of the Healthcare Financial Management Association and the San Diego Health Care Executives Association. He is a candidate for the Accredited Senior Appraiser designation with the American Society of Appraisers.

He has published several health care journal articles and is a professor for National University and Chapman University graduate programs in Health Care Administration. He is a speaker at national health care association meetings on health care finançial valuation appraisal and marketing strategy development.

Comments or questions about this publication or health care appraisal or valuation can be directed to Bruce Krider at American Health Care Appraisal, 4130 La Jolla Village Drive, Ste. 1072, La Jolla, CA 92037; Phone 760-751-1450; Fax 760-751-1980; Toll Free 888-MED-VALS; or by e-mail at *bgkrider@ahca.com.*

SELECTED TOOLS AND TEMPLATES FOR VALUATION OF PHYSICIAN PRACTICES AND CLINICS

This disk contains several of the spreadsheets and tools discussed in the text. The flies are not executable programs, but are data files designed to be opened with your spreadsheet application. The files are intended for use on a PC running Microsoft Excel version 7.0 for Windows 95. There are eleven Excel files on this disk, as follows:

1. Adjusted Balance Sheet Model
2. Beta Risk Analysis
3. Cash Flow Model
4. Physician Practice Evaluation Matrix
5. Lease Cost (or Clinic Purchase) Linear Regression Model
6. Medical Excess Earnings Model
7. Projections and Present Value Model
8. Quick Start Model
9. Risk Rate Comparison Table
10. Aging Accounts Receivable
11. Other Goodwill Formulas

To Use the Files on the Disk

1. Start Microsoft Excel.
2. From the "File" menu on the menu bar, select "Open." The "Open" dialog box will appear.
3. From the box labeled "Look in" at the top of the dialog box, select "A:" (where "A" is the letter of the drive where you inserted the disk).
4. Click on the file you wish to use in the list, then click the "Open" button on the right side of the dialog box.
5. If you make changes to the files, you may save them to the disk using the "Save" command on the "File" menu, or save the files to your hard drive using the "Save As . . . " command on the "File" menu.

For more complete descriptions of the files on the disk open the file "descrip.txt" with Windows Notepad or any word processing software.

Technical Support

If you need further information about using this disk, please check Microsoft Excel's "Help" feature or your Excel documentation. If you still have questions, call Aspen's Help Desk at 301-417-7543, where Audrey and her staff will be happy to help you. For questions about billing or your account, please call our Customer Service department at 1-800-234-1660.

9 780834 209626

9 780834 209626

Printed in Dunstable, United Kingdom

88161048R00114